REBELLION
AND
CIVIL WAR,
IN
FRANCE.

The difputes which have for fome time paft nvulfed this neighbouring kingdom, have at agth been brought to a crifis, which no man uld have forefeen or fuppofed. The relation of hat PARIS has been during laft week, fills the ind with horror; and although we have all feen d felt the fad effects of an unlicenfed populace our own country, at the time of that dreadful nflagration in London during the riots in 1780, t even that melancholy event was far fhort of e general diftrefs which not only is felt in Paris, it in the neighbourhood for many leagues a- und it.

We have no period in the hiftory of Europe ace the time of CHARLES the IX. of France, in 572, affording fo ftriking an example of a dif- acted Government, and the bloodfhed of a civil ar, as that which France now exhibits. No erfonal fafety,—no protection of property, and e lives of the firft men in the State in fuch mo- entary danger, as to oblige them to fly their untry, and feek an afylum in this land of erty. Such is the picture of Paris at this in- ant; and rebellion has fo widely fpread, that e one can judge where it will have an end. All blic bufinefs is ftopped, the whole fyftem and ength of Government annihilated, and even the ing and Queen obliged to fhut themfelves up in e palace of Verfailles with a ftrong guard for eir own fecurity.

The faithful relation of the hiftory of this aw- l period, muft be a matter of the ftrongeft cu- ofity. Many falfe rumours will, no doubt, be roulated, for the time is aufpicious to thofe of inventive genius, and erroneous accounts muft neceffiry go abroad, where the REAL tranf- tions cannot be obtained. As a proof of this, e fhould notice the WORLD Newfpaper of Sa- rday, which announces that the UNIVERSITY PARIS was levelled to the ground, that the ing had diffolved the States General, and that e had erected a ftandard for his partizans to flock . We are peculiarly happy in having an

among w
Noblema
30 years.
freed in li
der fenten
in the Pri
meditated defign, as well as great caution.

On attacking the Baftile they fecured the Governor, the MARQUIS DE L'AUNEY, and the Commandant of the Garrifon, whom they conducted to the Place de Grieve, the place of public execution, where they beheaded them, ftuck their heads on tent poles, and carried them in triumph to the Palais Royal, and through the ftreets of Paris. The MARQUIS DE L'AUNEY was particularly odious to the people, from the nature of his employment, and it is therefore no wonder that he fhould be fingled out amongft the firft victims of their refentment.

The Hotel de Ville, or Manfion-houfe, was the place that was next attacked. M. de FLESSIL the Prevot de Marchand, or Lord Mayor, had made himfelf obnoxious by attempting to read publicly fome inftructions he had received from the King. In doing this he was ftabbed in fere- ral places, his head cut off, and carried away. M. de CROSNE, the Lieutenant de Police, fhared the fame fate, only that he was hung up in the public ftreets.

Several other very violent exceffes have been committed. The Duc de LATREMOUILLE, and many other Noblemen the friends of the King, who voted againft the Tiers Etat, the people have confined in prifon. The Duc de LUXEM- BOURG, one of the moft confpicuous of that or- der, got away with fome difficulty, and arrived in London on Saturday night, with all his family. The Duc de CHATELET, Colonel of the King's Guard, very narrowly efcaped affaffination. He was mounted on horfeback, attended by fome Huffars, and the people were about to ftop him, when fome of them called out to let him efcape, adding, *that though he was a rafcal, they would not take away his life.*

The number of armed men in Paris is fuppofed to amount to 300,000 men, and they call them- felves the Militia. The way by which fo many people have procured arms is, that all the public

THE  TIMES

GREAT
EVENTS

A MODERN HISTORY
SPANNING 200 YEARS

EDITED BY

JAMES OWEN

Published by Times Books

An imprint of HarperCollins Publishers
Westerhill Road
Bishopbriggs
Glasgow G64 2QT
www.harpercollins.co.uk
times.books@harpercollins.co.uk

First edition 2020

© This compilation Times Newspapers
Ltd 2020

The Times® is a registered trademark of
Times Newspapers Ltd

The contents of this publication are
believed correct at the time of printing.
Nevertheless the publisher can accept no
responsibility for errors or omissions,
changes in the detail given or for any
expense or loss thereby caused.

A catalogue record for this book is
available from the British Library.

ISBN 978-0-00-840930-2

10 9 8 7 6 5 4 3 2 1

Printed and bound in Great Britain by
CPI Group (UK) Ltd, Croydon, CR0 4YY

Cover image © MSSA / Shutterstock

Our thanks and acknowledgements go to
Lily Cox, Joanne Lovey and Robin Ashton
at News Syndication and, in particular,
at The Times, Ian Brunskill and, at
HarperCollins, Jethro Lennox, Lauren
Murray, Kevin Robbins, Louise Robb and
Lauren Reid.

We'd also like to thank Alan Copps for all
his help and expertise.

CONTENTS

INTRODUCTION

The urge to know what is happening beyond the horizon is as old as humankind. There were printed newssheets circulating in Venice by the sixteenth century, and newspapers well-established in Britain by the early eighteenth. Yet it was *The Times* which, almost from its founding in 1785, redefined what newspapers should report and, accordingly, what news was.

Britain was unusual in having a press not controlled by the state, but its journalism hitherto had often been merely gossipy, or polemical, or interested purely in politics, or just parochial. The approach of *The Times* was more professional, reflecting the growing size of the mercantile class and its need to be informed.

In particular, the paper sought from its earliest years to provide regular news from Europe and, later, became one of the first to employ war correspondents to report from the battlefield. Its willingness to print despatches from closer to home, notably details of the Peterloo massacre, was another sign of its independent thinking.

The early development of *The Times* acknowledged a changing world in which the repeal of taxes on papers hugely increased their circulation and new technology transformed the speed at which news could be gathered; its report in 1840 on the Treaty of Waitangi, which established British governance over New Zealand, took six months to arrive by sea. (Publications that had sat alongside *The Times* in its early days, but did not focus on the events of the day, turned into magazines.)

Thereafter, *The Times* evolved as greater competition in the late-nineteenth century challenged its dominant position. It added other sections – editorial leaders, letters, obituaries – which became similarly renowned and valued by its readers. Yet news remained at its core, and still does, even if these days it is filed and edited ever more remotely.

What newspapers afford journalists, that a lens does not, is the opportunity to combine immediacy with a period of reflection. The camera can convey the drama of the moment – an aircraft flying deliberately into a building – but it cannot judge what it signifies. News in print preserves not only the facts, but also the human dimension to great events.

So, in this cavalcade of almost 250 years of history, *Times* correspondents witness triumph and disaster, but they also bring home their impact on those affected by them. Here is the unsuspecting

Doctor Crippen about to be handcuffed by the policeman who has tracked him down, and there the spectators willing the exhausted Dorando Pietri to reach the finishing line of the marathon in the 1908 Olympics.

Japanese soldiers sweep into Nanking, watched by many who will soon become their victims. The Berlin Wall falls, and the Cold War ends, when a single bureaucrat makes a mistake. Thousands of ordinary people queue to pay their respects to the great figures who helped to shape their lives: Sir Winston Churchill; the Queen Mother; Elvis Presley.

Then there are the scoops. It was *The Times* that broke the news of Everest's conquest, just in time for the Coronation, and it was William Howard Russell's reports from the Crimea that changed the nation's opinion of the war, of soldiers and of their right to be nursed. The government first learned of Russia's proposals for peace from the paper. And while *The Times* may not have stooped to cover the first international football match, it did write up the first cricket Test match, in Australia in 1877.

In other words, even if those caught up in it do not always realise at the time, the history of news is the history of the world as it unfolds. To read it is to see how a society that in the eighteenth century had changed little in millennia became, in short order, the modern age.

But it is to see it from two perspectives, that of the day and with the advantage, too, of hindsight – of knowing how the story ended. Reading it, one appreciates how quickly events move and how rapidly their central figures pass from sight, caught in the backwash of time.

It may feel like the not-too-distant past to some, but few people under 50 can recall the drama that led to the downfall of Margaret Thatcher, let alone remember how the Exchange Rate Mechanism worked. (Indeed, how many know that it was she, improbably, who took Britain *into* the ERM?)

How we consume and discover news is changing faster than ever. More and more, it is becoming individually tailored to readers' own interests, and perhaps via some outlets to their prejudices. Fewer people now have to physically turn the pages of a paper to reach their favourite parts, being exposed to news on the way, whether they are interested or not. Historians of the future will find it harder as well to gauge how a story evolved when the multiple editions of a newspaper have given way to the unrecorded swipe of an app.

What the news in this volume therefore represents is an experience that its readers had in common, a consensus – now fractured, if not yet vanished – about what counted as news. For centuries, that did not change, even if the personalities did. The nature of celebrity evolved, society became less deferential, but history was still made by forces and by human factors that were eternal.

What appetite there will be for news in the information age remains to be seen and, above all, how objectively it will be presented. Yet, one thing is certain: people will always want to know what happened next.

The way that stories were reported in *The Times* changed significantly (if not rapidly) over two centuries, not least in response to technological innovations. This included the introduction, for instance, of photographs, but these were rarely integrated into copy until the 1960s, and not widely until rather later.

Many news reports, therefore, especially in Victorian times, ran at great length – those from the Crimea were several pages long – and accordingly it has been decided to limit the extracts in this anthology to about 500 words each. The selection has been confined to accounts of events, rather than taken from editorial opinion or individual comment on them.

Notwithstanding that many of the articles in this anthology were written at a time when views that might give offence today were tolerated, the original language, style and format of them as they appeared in the newspaper has not been amended. The date on the article is that on which it first appeared in the newspaper, and an index of people, places and events can be found at the end of the book.

In case it might be helpful, I have added some contextual notes as seems necessary to explain the background to the events recounted, outline additional accepted facts, and describe what happened subsequently.

JAMES OWEN

GREAT EVENTS

GEORGIAN TIMES

THE FALL OF THE BASTILLE

20 July 1789

The public are already in possession of M. NECKER'S [the finance minister] dismission yesterday se'nnight [a week] which was followed by a total change in the French Cabinet. It does not appear that M. NECKER'S removal was in consequence of any ill will which the KING [Louis XVI] bore him; on the contrary, his Majesty showed him every mark of respect; and it is even said, advised him to resign. It was, however, this change in Administration, which was the immediate consequence of the present violent commotions.

They began on the Monday morning, and have continued unremittingly ever since. It cannot now be said that the present violences are the effect of a mere unlicensed mob, but they are the acts of the public at large. The concurrent voice of the nation demands a new constitution, nor do we foresee that any power can resist it.

On Monday the people joined in greater numbers than they had hitherto done and seemed determined to be revenged for the insult which they said was offered to them, by removing M. NECKER. Previous thereto, the mob had destroyed several of the toll-gates belonging to Government in the vicinity of Paris, as well as the books belonging to the Excise Officers, by which very large entries of goods passed without paying the revenue, and every part of the metropolis exhibited a scene of riot.

The regular troops held for the protection of Paris were persuaded to join the people; they were encamped in the Champ de Mars, to the number of 5000 men, and marched to the Hotel of Invalids, a building in the out-skirts of the city. The invalids joined the rest, and brought away all the great guns, and other ammunition, belonging to the Hospital. With this reinforcement the people then attacked the

Bastille Prison, which they soon made themselves masters of, and released all the State Prisoners confined there, among whom was Lord MAZARINE, an Irish Nobleman, who has been confined for debt near 30 years. The prisoners in the other goals were freed in like manner, excepting such as were under sentence of death, whom they hung up within the prisons. This seemed to argue a premeditated design, as well as great caution.

On attacking the Bastille they secured the Governor, the MARQUIS DE L'AUNEY [now spelled de Launay], and the Commandant of the Garrison, whom they conducted to the Place de Grieve, the place of public execution, where they beheaded them, stuck their heads on tent poles, and carried them in triumph to the Palais Royal, and through the streets of Paris. The MARQUIS DE L'AUNEY was particularly odious to the people, from the nature of his employment, and it is therefore no wonder that he should be singled out amongst the first victims of their resentment.

The Hotel de Ville, or Mansion-house, was the place that was next attacked. M. de FLESSIL, the Prevot de Marchand, or Lord Mayor, had made himself obnoxious by attempting to read publicly some instructions he had received from the King. In doing this he was stabbed in several places, his head cut off, and carried away. M. de CROSNE, the Lieutenant de Police, shared the same fate, only that he was hung up in the public streets.

◆

For Britons – those property-owners that read *The Times*, at any rate – the French Revolution was the most astonishing and shocking event of their era. The fear (or the hope) that the same might happen in Britain coloured much of the foreign and domestic politics of the next century.

The toppling of the French monarchy had begun as a debate about how to fund the state more fairly, but anger at broader grievances in society spiralled into mob violence. The aim of the crowd in storming the Bastille – built as a fortress during the Hundred Years War – was not, however, to destroy a symbol of despotism, but to find powder and shot for the thousands of muskets they had seized earlier. There were only seven prisoners inside; the Marquis de Sade had been moved to a lunatic asylum the previous week.

News of the attack is said to have prompted Louis XVI to ask if this was a revolt. "No, Sire," replied the Duke de la Rochefoucauld. "It is a revolution."

THE BATTLE OF TRAFALGAR

8 November 1805

We have received, by the *Pickle* schooner, several accounts relative to the late glorious action for the truth of which we can vouch.

Towards the middle of last month Admiral VILLENEUVE received orders, from Paris, to sail at all events from Cadiz before the 21st, to accomplish a particular object which the EMPEROR had in view. VILLENEUVE knew that Admiral LOUIS had been detached with several ships from the fleet off Cadiz and supposed that the force had been, in consequence, reduced to about twenty sail of the line, it not having transpired that reinforcement had arrived shortly after Admiral LOUIS'S departure. Lord NELSON had been apprised of the instructions which VILLENEUVE had received, and of his intention to obey them. His Lordship was, therefore, thoroughly prepared to meet the enemy. On the other hand, the Commanders in Chief of the Combined Fleet having learnt that the Hero of the Nile commanded the blockading squadron, were fully sensible of the kind of reception they would meet should he fall in with them, and therefore, it is presumed, had consulted upon all the means necessary for a vigorous defence. It was not possible that two fleets could meet on more equal terms with respect to preparation.

As soon as Lord NELSON was convinced that he had it in his power to bring the enemy to action, on the 21st, he caused it to be understood on board of every ship, "That England expected every man to do his duty." There was, however, little necessity for the intimation; every man seemed to partake of the ardour of the Commander in Chief, and burned with impatience to commence the action. On no occasion whatever have our brave Tars felt such confidence of success. It was the word throughout the fleet, "That when led on by Lord NELSON, they were sure of victory, whatever might be the disparity of force."

At the commencement of the action our ships contested with each other, as far as was consistent with the preservation of order, the honour to get first engaged. The *Victory* did not fire a shot until she was close along-side the *Santissima Trinidad*, when the Commander in Chief ordered her to be lashed to the enemy. As soon as the men began their work, the Commander of the *Santissima Trinidad* desired his men to assist in lashing his ship to the *Victory*. It was about two o'clock, when the battle was at the hottest, that the gallant NELSON received a musket ball in his breast. What was very remarkable, it absolutely penetrated through the star which he wore.

The *Britannia* and *Prince* having driven from their stations, were prevented from sharing in the action to the extent they could have wished. The *Belleisle* did wonders; she was the first in the action, and one of the last out; and, we are sorry to say, the number of her killed and wounded is very great. The *Victory* also sustained a great loss.

◆

It had taken more than a fortnight for news of the battle to be conveyed to London from the waters near Gibraltar. The Franco-Spanish fleet, commanded by Admiral Villeneuve – a survivor of the Battle of the Nile – had left Cadiz three days prior to the action at Trafalgar on 21 October.

Villeneuve was making for the Channel, where Napoleon intended to assemble an even larger navy to protect his projected invasion of Britain. Historians suspect that the French admiral knew he had lost the Emperor's confidence and sailed in the hope of redeeming his reputation rather than await the arrival of the officer sent to replace him.

When it was intercepted by Nelson, Villeneuve's fleet outnumbered the British by 33 to 27 ships. However, the Englishman's unorthodox tactics – slicing through the enemy line rather than sailing parallel to it – proved decisive. Villeneuve was taken prisoner, attended Nelson's funeral and, after returning to France, was found stabbed to death in 1806. Doubts remain about the official verdict of suicide.

THE ABOLITION OF SLAVERY

24 February 1807

His Lordship [Lord HOWICK] said, that he had seldom found himself under greater embarrassment than in rising to perform the duty imposed upon him on the present evening. So many details were pressing on him, that he should be fearful of trespassing at great length on the time of the House were it not that the subject was so well known, had been so often before the House, and had been so thoroughly investigated in all its points, and in all their bearings, that he hoped it would not be necessary for him to take up much of the time of the House in going into detail. At the same time the question was of such great importance, that he should be unwilling to let a discussion of it proceed, especially in this new Parliament, without stating the arguments, reasons and evidence, which ought to weigh with the House in contemplating this Bill. He was apprehensive of bringing forward too much, and much at a loss to know what parts to select, to save as much as possible the time of the House. The question, however, had recently received some very great disembarrassments; and, indeed, he was not aware at that moment that there was much disposition in any one to contest the necessity and propriety of the measure. He believed it was almost generally allowed that the traffic was fraught with cruelty and injustice, and that the results from it in Africa, were the most frightful miseries to the unhappy natives of that country. It had long been a source of encouragement to kidnapping and robbery, and had created incentives to the most barbarous murders; and, in every sense in which it could be viewed, it was a stain and a disgrace to civilized nations to continue it. From this part of the argument he was, therefore, in a great measure relieved: there was, however, one part of the question which deserved some observation, namely, that of carrying slaves to the West Indies, and it gave him great satisfaction to think, that the House had, on the present occasion, heard nothing from the Learned Counsel at the Bar, of the luxuries of the Middle Passage. These topics had now vanished, and he believed there was not a man in the House, who did not allow that the Middle Passage had been fraught with the most dreadful mischiefs. There had, he believed, been one or two individuals, who had differed from him on this subject; one of whom had even said, he was so well convinced of the propriety and policy of the Slave Trade, that he viewed it as a blessing to the Africans; and if there was no such traffic, he would himself propose to establish it. In another place it had been said, that it was justified by Scripture; but he was of opinion, that it was contrary to every principle of humanity, and every sentiment of the Christian religion. It could therefore, only be fairly said, that it existed in policy and justice, and not in humanity.

◆

The introduction of the Slave Trade Abolition Bill by the government of Lord Grenville in 1807 marked the culmination of two decades of campaigning by reformers, notably William Wilberforce.

In that time, British merchants had trafficked more than 600,000 Africans as slaves. The riches to be made from the trade led to opposition to the Bill in the House of Lords from peers with sugar plantations in the Caribbean.

The debate in the Commons lasted 10 hours, and was led by the Foreign Secretary, Howick; as Earl Grey (of tea fame) he would become Prime Minister in 1830. Wilberforce was cheered when he took his place in the House and the Bill was passed by an unexpectedly large majority of 283 to 16 votes.

The Act prohibited the trading of slaves, but slavery itself was not abolished throughout the Empire until 1833 – after the sugar industry in the West Indies had begun its economic decline.

This report, with its mention of the slave trade being considered a blessing by some, reveals how much attitudes have changed in the centuries since, and the scale of the struggle faced by the abolitionists. The deferential tone of parliamentary reporting has also evolved.

THE ASSASSINATION OF
SPENCER PERCEVAL

12 May 1812

About a quarter past five Mr. PERCEVAL [the Prime Minister] was entering the Lobby of the House of Commons, where a number of persons were standing, when a man, who had a short time previously placed himself in the recess of the door-way within the Lobby, drew out a small pistol, and shot Mr. PERCEVAL in the lower part of the left breast. The ball is supposed to have entered the heart. Mr PERCEVAL moved forwards a few faltering steps, nearly half way up the lobby, and was in the act of falling, when some persons stept forward and caught him. He was immediately carried to the room of the SPEAKER'S Secretary, to the left of the lobby, by Mr. W. SMITH, Mr. BRADSHAW and another gentleman. Mr. LYNN, the Surgeon, in Parliament-street, was immediately sent for; but on examining the wound, he considered the case utterly hopeless. All that escaped Mr. PERCEVAL'S lips previously to falling in the lobby, was "murder," or "murdered." He said no more afterwards. He expired in about ten or twelve minutes after receiving the fatal wound. Several Members of both Houses of Parliament went into the room while he was dying: among others, his brother, Lord ARDEN: all of them appeared greatly agitated. There was very little effusion of blood from the wound, externally. His body was subsequently removed into the SPEAKER'S House. Lord FRANCIS OSBORNE, Lord OSSULTON, and some others, were crossing the lobby at the moment of the assassination, and were very near to Mr. PERCEVAL. The deed was perpetrated so suddenly, that the man who fired the pistol was not instantly recognized by those in the lobby; but a person passing at the moment behind Mr. PERCEVAL, seized the pistol, (which was a very small one) from the hand of the assassin, who retired towards a bench to the left; he surrendered it without any resistance. Mr. GOODIFF an Officer of the House, took hold of him, and asked if he were the villain who shot the Minister. He replied "I am the unhappy man" but appeared quite undisturbed. It is said, that he added something about the want of redress of grievances from Ministers; but if he did say so, it was heard by very few. On searching him, a few pounds were found in his pockets, and some printed papers, copies of which he is said to have previously distributed among Members. He was taken to the bar of the House of Commons, and identified as the assassin. Another pistol, similar to that which he had fired was taken from his pocket in the House. All the doors of the House were then locked, and he was conveyed by the private passages up stairs to one of the apartments called the prison rooms, in the upper story, over the Committee rooms. Here he underwent an examination for some time, which was attended by Aldermen COMBE and CURTIS, and by Mr. READ, Mr. COLQUHOUN, Mr. FIELDING, and other Magistrates; and several Members of the House of Commons, Mr. WHITBREAD, Mr. WYNNE, Mr. STEPHEN, Lord CASTLEREAGH, Mr. Secretary RYDER, &c. After an examination of various witnesses, among whom were Lord OSSULTON and FRANCIS OSBORNE, General GASCOYNE, Mr. H. SUMNER, the Officers of the House, and several strangers, the man was fully committed to Newgate for trial. A hackney-coach was brought to the iron gates in Lower Palace yard; but the crowd, which was at first composed of decent people, had been gradually swelled by a concourse of pick-pockets and the lower orders, who mounted the coach, and were so exceedingly troublesome and even dangerous that it was not deemed advisable to send him to Newgate in the manner intended.

◆

An evangelical Christian and abolitionist, Spencer Perceval came to politics from the law and remains the only Prime Minister to have been Attorney-General – and the only one to have been murdered. Although his reputation faded fast following his untimely demise, he had been regarded as one of the Tories' few stars after the death of Pitt the Younger.

The main achievement of his government, which had been formed in 1809, was to keep the future Duke of Wellington's army in the field in Portugal, a decision Perceval had taken when Chancellor. The cost of this, and of other measures needed for the war against Napoleon, led to his personal unpopularity and popular unrest. This was also stoked by Luddites opposed to the industrialisation of work.

It was first feared that Perceval's murder heralded a revolution. In fact, his assassin John Bellingham had long nursed an obsessive grievance against the state and its representatives. This stemmed from his ruin following imprisonment in Russia for debt. He was hastily tried and executed and, like his victim, just as swiftly forgotten by history.

THE BATTLE OF WATERLOO

23 June 1815

The position which I [the Duke of Wellington] took up in front of Waterloo crossed the high roads from Charleroy and Nivelle, and had its right thrown back to a ravine near Merke Braine, which was occupied; and its left extended to a height above the hamlet Ter la Haye, which was likewise occupied. In front of the right centre and near the Nivelle road, we occupied the house and garden of Hougoumont, which covered the return of that flank; and in front of the left centre, we occupied the farm of La Haye Sainte. By our left we communicated with Marshal Prince Blucher, at Wavre, through Ohaim; and the Marshal had promised me, that in case we should be attacked, he would support me with one or more corps, as might be necessary.

The enemy collected his army, with the exception of the third corps, which had been sent to observe Marshal Blucher, on a range of heights in our front, in the course of the night of the 17th and yesterday morning: and at about ten o'clock he commenced a furious attack upon our post at Hougoumont. I had occupied that post with a detachment from General Byng's brigade of Guards, which was in position in its rear; and it was for some time under the command of Lieutenant-Colonel Macdonel, and afterwards of Colonel Home: and I am happy to add, that it was maintained throughout the day with the utmost gallantry by these brave troops, notwithstanding the repeated efforts of large bodies of the enemy to obtain possession of it.

This attack upon the right of our centre was accompanied by a very heavy cannonade upon our whole line, which was destined to support the repeated attacks of cavalry and infantry occasionally mixed, but sometimes separate, which were made upon it. In one of these the enemy carried the farm house of La Haye Sainte, as the detachment of the light battalion of the legion which occupied it had expended all its ammunition, and the enemy occupied the only communication there was with them.

The enemy repeatedly charged our infantry with his cavalry, but these attacks were uniformly unsuccessful, and they afforded opportunities to our cavalry to charge, in one of which Lord E. Somerset's brigade, consisting of the life guards, royal horse guards, and 1st dragoon guards, highly distinguished themselves, as did that of Major General Sir W. Ponsonby, having taken many prisoners and an eagle.

These attacks were repeated till about seven in the evening, when the enemy made a desperate effort with the cavalry and infantry supported by the fire of artillery, to force our left centre near the farm of La Haye Sainte, which after a severe contest was defeated, and having observed that the troops retired from this attack in great confusion, and that the march of General Bulow's corps by Enschermont upon Planchenorie and La Belle Alliance had begun to take effect, and as I could perceive the fire of his cannon, and as Marshal Prince Blucher had joined in person, with a corps of his army to the left of our line by Ohaim, I determined to attack the enemy, and immediately advanced the whole line of infantry, supported by the cavalry and artillery.

◆

After only nine months in exile, following his defeat and abdication the previous year, Napoleon slipped away from the Italian island of Elba and returned to Paris in triumph on 20 March 1815.

The other European powers began to mobilize once more, and to prevent them from uniting their forces, Napoleon marched rapidly North to give battle to the two that posed the most immediate danger. Quartered in what is now Belgium, these were the Prussians under Marshal Blücher and the Anglo-Allied army commanded by the Duke of Wellington.

Historians attribute the French defeat to a variety of causes, ranging from the rain the previous day that limited movement and favoured Wellington's troops, which occupied defensive positions, to Napoleon's worsening health. He suffered from haemorrhoids, which made it uncomfortable for him to sit for long on his horse and survey the battlefield.

Even so, Wellington admitted his victory, which was only secured as evening fell, had been the 'nearest-run thing you ever saw in your life'. This report is taken from his official dispatch to the War Department, published by *The Times* the day after it reached London.

PETERLOO

18 August 1819

We kept the press open until a late hour this morning, in the hope of receiving minute accounts of the circumstances which attended the reformist meeting held at Manchester on Monday. From the statements brought to us in the course of last night, and which appear to have been collected in the midst of a scene of extraordinary uproar and agitation, we learned that HUNT took the chair, according to advertisement, and harangued that portion of the multitude which more immediately surrounded him; that the mob altogether amounted to more than 40,000 persons – some accounts say 60,000 – collected from all the neighbouring districts; that the Riot Act was read, and the troops called upon by the Magistracy to enforce their orders that the crowd should at once disperse. HUNT himself was taken prisoner – and we add with unfeigned sorrow, that several lives were lost.

The troops that were employed were the Manchester, Macclesfield, and Chester Yeomanry. The 15th Light Dragoons were likewise in the field, but were not called into action. The local troops, it is said, behaved with great alacrity. The consternation and dismay which spread among the immense crowd collected cannot be conceived. The multitude was composed of a large proportion of females. The prancing of cavalry, and the active use of the sabre among them, created a dreadful scene of confusion, and we may add, of carnage. By the accounts received through the mail, no less than 80 or 100 persons are wounded, and 8 killed. The mob is said to have dispersed as quickly as they could. At 7 o'clock in the evening some of the Yeomanry are reported to have fired on a crowd that showed a disregard of the mandate to disperse. At night, and up to 2 o'clock yesterday morning, complete tranquillity prevailed, and the streets were as quiet as on ordinary occasions. The great number of wounded had been carried to the hospital. Hunt, Johnston, and others, who were on the scaffolding, were taken into custody, and lodged in the New Bailey.

No manufactory or private building was destroyed or materially damaged, though many windows were broken. We only notice this circumstance, because we had heard early in the evening, that a factory, which it is now unnecessary to name, had been levelled with the ground.

Such is the brief and general outline of occurrences which the lateness of the hour at which we write enables us to lay before our readers. What actual violence or outrages were perpetrated – what menaces were uttered, or symptoms exhibited, which induced the Magistrates to read the Riot Act, and to disperse the meeting by force of arms, we cannot yet positively state. That a large discretion undoubtedly belongs to persons charged with the preservation of public order, which justifies their interference where they see it directly and distinctly threatened by a multitude, who may, nevertheless, have met for purposes or with professions originally not inimical to the King's peace, we are not disposed to question. But the discretion, though large, is not unlimited.

◆

On 16 August 1819, more than 60,000 people gathered in an open space known as St Peter's Field, now in the centre of Manchester. They were to be addressed by Henry Hunt, known for his stirring oratory and for his radical advocacy of universal suffrage.

The end of the Napoleonic wars marked the start of an economic downturn, the effect of which on the poor was exacerbated by the cost of bread being kept high by the Corn Laws. Many of those in the mercantile and propertied classes feared a revolution and in anticipation of trouble the authorities in Manchester called out regular troops and a local cavalry militia.

An attempt to arrest Hunt led to panic, which became in turn a massacre as the soldiers hacked at the crowd. Eighteen people were killed and several hundred wounded. The event was among the first attended by reporters from national newspapers, which dubbed the bloodshed 'Peterloo', in ironic reference to Waterloo. Hunt was subsequently jailed for two-and-a-half years for sedition, but his legacy was the growth of mass pressure for reform.

AN EARLY RAILWAY ACCIDENT

17 September 1830

From all that I can learn from eye-witnesses, the unfortunate event of which I am now going to give you the details, happened in the following manner: Mr. Huskisson was discoursing with Mr. Joseph Sandars, one of the principal originators and promoters of this rail-road, and was congratulating that gentleman as one of the happiest men in the world, in having seen a work of such importance and magnitude happily brought to a conclusion under his auspices, when he was called away to speak with some other gentlemen, who were anxious to hear his opinion on some of the details of the road. Before he left Mr. Sandars, he said to that gentleman, "Well, I must go and shake hands with the Duke [of Wellington] on this day at any rate." The gentlemen who had called him away detained him some time, and whilst he was standing with them, the Rocket engine, which, like the Phoenix, had to pass the Duke's car, to take up its station at the watering place, came slowly up, and as the engineer had been for some time checking its velocity, so silently that it was almost upon the group before they observed it. In the hurry of the moment all attempted to get out of the way. Mr. Holmes, M.P., who was standing by the side of Mr. Huskisson, desired the gentlemen not to stir, but to cling close by the side of their own car – most excellent advice, had it been followed – for as no engine can move off the rail, any person who stands clear of it, is perfectly safe from danger. Unfortunately, in the hurry and agitation of the moment, Mr. Huskisson did not pursue this advice. He hesitated, staggered a little as if not knowing what to do, then attempted to run forward, found it impossible to get off the road, on account of an excavation of some 14 or 15 feet depth being on that side of it, on which he was, attempted again to get into the

26

car, was hit by a motion of the door as he was mounting a step, and was thrown down directly in the path of the Rocket, as that engine came opposite to the Duke's car. He contrived to move himself a little out of its path before it came in contact with him, otherwise it must have gone directly over his head and breast. As it was, the wheel went over his left thigh, squeezing it almost to a jelly, broke the leg, it is said, in two places, laid the muscles bare from the ankle, nearly to the hip, and tore out a large piece of flesh, as it left him. Mrs. Huskisson, who, along with several other ladies, witnessed the accident, uttered a shriek of agony, which none who heard will ever forget.

◆

The Liverpool and Manchester railway – the first line to join two cities – opened on 15 September 1830. It was inaugurated by the Prime Minister, the Duke of Wellington, and by the running of no less than eight locomotives, among them George Stephenson's *Rocket*.

William Huskisson was an MP for Liverpool who had been Secretary of State for War and Leader of the House of Commons. He had resigned, however, in 1828 from Wellington's Cabinet over a matter of parliamentary reform. It was in the hope of repairing his relationship with the Duke that he went to shake his hand.

Huskisson died later that same evening. He had been a staunch supporter of the expansion of the railways and the reports of the accident indirectly helped to publicize the new form of transport.

THE AGE OF VICTORIA

THE CORONATION OF QUEEN VICTORIA

29 June 1838

Shortly after the procession had passed Apsley-house, the amusements of the fair commenced in good earnest. We say in good earnest, because for the last two or three days business in a partial manner has been going on. The altered appearance presented to the eye yesterday from that we had observed on the preceding day, was almost as surprising as the masses of beef and ham to which we then referred; for then there were not any swings, scarcely any shoes, and apparently but few arrangements made to afford entertainment other than those of a supportive nature, or for the cultivation of the disportation of the human frame in the wily mazes of dance.

The lapse of 12 hours, however, worked marvellous results, and at an early hour it became evident that sleep alone had not been the object of the fair-makers. A number of theatres of a minor class had sprung up, and swings, almost beyond enumeration, had been erected, whilst it had been arranged that donkey races and several other attractive pursuits should be added to the originally proposed objects. Much merriment was afforded in the course of the afternoon by a race between donkeys, one of which was ridden by a sailor. It happened that the sea-farer was astride of the second-best runner, whereupon he took it into his head that it would be but proper for him to endeavour to retard the rapid progress of the foremost animal. No sooner, therefore, did the idea strike upon his mind than he coolly slipped off his own donkey, and, running onward laid hold of the tail of the one in advance, with the manifest intention of retarding his hitherto successful progress, and it was not without very considerable difficulty that "Jack" was made to understand that he had been guilty of an action for which the Jockey Club would have imposed some penalty.

During the day a balloon went up from the Green-park, and another from Vauxhall, as was understood, passed over the same place. In reference to the ascent of the former, it was rumoured that Mrs. Graham had met with an accident by a rapid and unexpected descent.

After a minute inspection of the arrangements in Hyde Park, it may be said that on the entrance thereto the spectator was introduced to an extraordinary scene; at the first glance it appeared as if hostilities and not enjoyments were about to occupy all, for an immense encampment covered the crown of the Park from the margin of the tranquil Serpentine to within a trifling distance of the several main entrance to the usually tranquil scene. Marquees, tents, booths, of every form and construction, lay grouped together with, at first, all the confused appearance of haste and chance; but a closer survey showed that much indeed of military regularity had been observed in setting out the grand line of circumvallation, as well as the almost numberless parallels and intersections of the interior. And although banners and pennons there were of every country, tribe, and hue, the breeze that unfurled them passed over the regions of peace. Pleasure had sent forth her pioneers, and had occupied the ground to some purpose, in the provision of every entertainment the most numerous of her votaries could desire.

◆

Victoria had come to the throne the previous year, aged just 18. Her coronation, organized by the government of Lord Melbourne, was the first to be staged since reforms meant that MPs as well as peers had to witness it.

Melbourne, however, went much further with changes to tradition, lengthening the route of the carriage procession so that it ran, for the first time, from Buckingham Palace to Westminster Abbey. This would enable larger crowds to see it. Carried by the new railways, more than 400,000 people came to London for the occasion, with many visiting the vast fair in Hyde Park.

The five-hour long ceremony itself was marred by the lack of any rehearsal. The Archbishop of Canterbury forced the Queen's ring onto the wrong finger, and she had to be called back after part of the service was skipped by mistake. Later, she watched the fireworks display in Green Park and the next day went herself to the fair. There would not be another coronation for more than 60 years.

THE TREATY OF WAITANGI

7 August 1840

When his Excellency had finished, he invited the chiefs to ask explanations on any point they did not comprehend; 20 or 30 chiefs in consequence addressed the meeting, five or six of whom spoke with so much violence and effect that his Excellency was apprehensive that they had fairly turned the tables on him, but at the crisis the Hokianga chiefs, "under Neni and Potawoni, made their appearance," and nothing, says Captain Hobson, "could have been more reasonable." His Excellency insinuates that underhand influence had been at work, and two chiefs whom he names as being followers of the Catholic bishop, were the principal opposers. One of these orators, "Rovewah" said, "Send the men away: do not sign that paper: if you do, you will be reduced to the condition of slaves, and be obliged to break stones for the roads. Your lands will be taken from you, and your dignity as chiefs destroyed." In this dilemma, and when things appeared to be looking very black for his Excellency, at the first pause "Neni" came forward and eclipsed all rivals. He spoke with so much "natural eloquence" as surprised all the Europeans and turned aside the temporary feeling that had been created by the arguments of the other orators. No wonder, then, that Captain Hobson should speak favourably of his talents. He was to him a friend in need, and seems to have done his part of the business effectually. He pointed out to the New Zealanders how impossible it was for them to govern themselves, and concluded his harangue by strenuously advising the chiefs to place confidence in the promises of the British. He was followed by two other favourable chiefs, and after an adjournment of one day, it having been announced that the chiefs had become impatient to sign the treaty that they might return to their homes, his Excellency gratified their wishes; and having accordingly proceeded to the tents, the treaty was signed in due form by 46 head chiefs, in presence of at least 500 of inferior degree; which, being held to be a full and clear recognition of the sovereign rights of Her Majesty over the northern parts of the island, was announced on the 7th of February last by a salute of 21 guns from Her Majesty's ship Herald. By the first article of the treaty, the chiefs of the confederation of the united tribes of New Zealand, and the separate and independent chiefs expressly gave the powers and rights of sovereignty to Her Majesty over their respective territories; and by the second, Her Majesty confirms and guarantees them in the possession of their lands and estates, forests, fisheries, and other properties, so long as they wish to retain the same; but they yield at the same time to Her Majesty the exclusive right of pre-emption over such lands as they may be disposed to alienate; and the third grants to the natives of New Zealand all the rights and privileges of British subjects.

◆

New Zealand had been discovered by Europeans in the seventeenth century, and claimed by James Cook for Britain in 1769, but by the 1830s it was still not a colony subject to the Crown. Instead, it was viewed as an outpost of the settlement in Australia and visited chiefly by whalers and sealers.

Prompted by reports of land speculation and independent projects to develop the country, the British government sent a naval officer, William Hobson, as lieutenant-governor to New Zealand to establish sovereignty. He invited about 500 chiefs of the Maori people to a meeting at Waitangi, in the North Island, on 5 February 1840 (news of it took six months to reach the London papers) and read out the agreement he had prepared.

The Maori wanted to negotiate a treaty to protect themselves from the French, who had colonial ambitions of their own, and to reduce fighting between their tribes. However, the precise meaning of its terms in English and Maori differed, with the latter willing to accept British rule but not to relinquish sovereignty. These conflicting interpretations would lead to a series of wars in the decades that followed.

REVOLUTION IN VIENNA

22 March 1848

This morning (March 13), on going out about half-past 10 o'clock, I found the town in a state of great excitement, great numbers of people in the streets, and an evident impression abroad that something extraordinary was about to happen. All, however, seemed tolerably peaceable; the people were mostly of the better classes, and no one armed. Going into the Burg Platz, a square surrounded by the buildings belonging to the palace, I saw a company of soldiers drawing up, and a number of persons, apparently attracted chiefly by curiosity. In the Ball Platz adjoining, close to the official residence of Prince Metternich, there were at that time no soldiers, and only a few persons passing and repassing. Thence all was quiet as far as the English Embassy, in the Hintere Schenken Strasse. Going thence into the Herrn Gasse, in which the Landhaus is situated, in which the States of Lower Austria (the mockery of a Parliament) hold their sittings, I found it occupied by a very dense crowd, but for the most part orderly, and evidently consisting of rather the better class. It was understood that a deputation of the States was about to proceed to the Emperor; to inform him of the excitement which prevailed and the necessity for doing something to quiet the general agitation. About half past 11 o'clock I returned home; and then took a walk on the ramparts, when I not only saw a number of ladies and children, but even met the Emperor himself, with a single attendant, evidently showing that no very serious disturbance was at that time apprehended. Passing again through the Burg Platz, about 1 o'clock, I found the crowd considerably increased, and soon afterwards the place was completely cleared by the military. In the Herrn Gasse, and the Michaeli Platz adjoining, there was now an immense concourse of people. I was told that they were waiting for the answer to the deputation, which was promised in an hour's time, but had not yet arrived. About 2 o'clock, going to the Landhaus from the Minoriten Platz, I found the building in complete possession of the populace, who had broken in with cries of "Press Freiheit!" "Keine Polizei!" "Pereat Metternich!" ("Freedom of the Press!" "No Police!" "Down with Metternich!") It is said, that during the sitting of the States some few persons had been admitted, and the door then locked, on which they shouted to the mob from the windows that they were made prisoners. On making their way in they completely destroyed all the furniture and every article on which they could lay their hands. I made my way into the court, when I was told that a Jew had just been addressing the crowd from a boarding over the pump. I did not hear the purport of his speech, but it seemed to have given great satisfaction. The cries became now almost deafening. At this time there was no military on the spot, but about half-past 2 o'clock, or a little sooner, a company was brought up, and cleared the portion of the street abutting on the Landhaus. Being pretty well tired out I went to a reading-room, at the opposite end of the town, and stayed there half an hour. On my leaving it, I was told that the soldiers had just fired on the people, and that several were killed – report said six or eight (amongst the number two students).

———◆———

Despite the restoration of the monarchy in France, the radical hopes unleashed by the Revolution, and the liberal ideas developed during the Age of Enlightenment, led to increased tension in much of Europe, still dominated by conservative rulers.

When violent protests broke out in Paris in 1848, Vienna soon followed suit. For 40 years, Austria's leading statesman, Prince Metternich, had kept intact its empire – which stretched from Milan in Italy to Lviv in the Ukraine – by combining astute diplomacy abroad with repressive measures at home. Students were a particular target, with university fraternities being prohibited.

The scale of the demonstrations in March, stoked further by the force used against them, brought about Metternich's resignation. For a time, he went into exile in England, living by the Thames at Richmond. Under a new Emperor, the young Franz Joseph, the Habsburgs reasserted control and Metternich was able to return. Yet he never regained his standing and his death a decade later went largely unreported by foreign newspapers.

THE GREAT EXHIBITION

2 May 1851

The inauguration of the Temple of the Industry of the World, an edifice as unexampled in its magnitude and materials as for the purposes to which it is applied and the collection it displays, will render yesterday for ever memorable as a great epoch in the progress of civilization. Erected at the exclusive cost and by the spontaneous subscription of the British people, it has been dedicated to the celebration of the triumphs of the useful arts throughout the globe. Its portals have been thrown open, without restriction or limit, to all nations, invited to meet there in amicable rivalry and on equal terms – an invitation which has been responded to in a spirit correspondent with that in which it was given. From the east and from the west, from the north and from the south, from the ardour of the tropics and the rigour of the poles, thousands have come to present their offerings at the common shrine – trophies collected in the victories of mind over matter – rich spoils carried away by man in his conquests over nature. The prisoners who follow the triumphal car of the victor are here the elements themselves, brought into subjection to the indomitable sway of the human will. Nothing in nature is so stubborn or intractable as to resist this power. The lightning dares no longer strike. It glides innocuous along a prescribed path, and is made to pass, as though in mockery of its impotence, over the objects which, being uncontrolled, it would have reduced to ruin. The wind and tide no longer obstruct the vessel which advances triumphantly against their force. Space and time are annihilated, and intelligence flies instantaneously between man and man at any distance, however great. Let those who take pleasure in such reflections, and delight to observe the means by which these and numerous other miracles of art are wrought, accompany us to the Crystal Palace, where they will find in every object a fruitful source of wonder and admiration. It will be our part from day to day to point out what is most worthy of attention, to explain and illustrate what may seem obscure, and to supply those links in the chain of useful and elevating information which may not always be suggested by the objects exhibited.

◆

The Great Exhibition was conceived as a showcase primarily for British industry and design in response to similar events staged by the French. Its chief proponents were Prince Albert and Henry Cole, a civil servant with a keen interest in the arts who is said to have been the first person to have sent out Christmas cards.

Designed by Joseph Paxton, and overseen by Isambard Kingdom Brunel, the Crystal Palace that housed the exhibition was manufactured and erected in just nine months on the Knightsbridge side of Hyde Park, London. It was 1848 feet (563 metres) long and 454 feet (138 metres) wide and the 100,000 exhibits within it included the Koh-i-Noor diamond, Samuel Colt's new Navy revolver and the world's largest penknife, which was 22 inches (55.8 centimetres) thick and had 75 blades.

More than six million people visited the exhibition, some of them spending a penny to use the world's first pay lavatories. Profits from the show were used to build the South Kensington museums, including the Victoria & Albert and the Albert Hall. The Crystal Palace was later moved to the area of south-east London to which it gave its name, only to be destroyed by fire in 1936.

THE CHARGE OF THE LIGHT BRIGADE

14 November 1854

As they passed towards the front, the Russians opened on them from the guns in the redoubt on the right, with volleys of musketry and rifles. They swept proudly past, glittering in the morning sun in all the pride and splendour of war. We could scarcely believe the evidence of our senses! Surely that handful of men are not going to charge an army in position? Alas! it was but too true – their desperate valour knew no bounds, and far indeed was it removed from its so-called better part – discretion. They advanced in two lines, quickening their pace as they closed towards the enemy. A more fearful spectacle was never witnessed than by those who, without the power to aid, beheld their heroic countrymen rushing to the arms of death. At the distance of 1,200 yards the whole line of the enemy belched forth, from 30 iron mouths, a flood of smoke and flame, through which hissed the deadly balls. Their flight was marked by instant gaps in our ranks, by dead men and horses, by steeds flying wounded or riderless across the plain. The first line is broken, it is joined by the second, they never halt or check their speed an instant; with diminished ranks, thinned by those 30 guns, which the Russians had laid with the most deadly accuracy, with a halo of flashing steel above their heads, and with a cheer which was many a noble fellow's death-cry, they flew into the smoke of the batteries, but ere they were lost from view the plain was strewed with their bodies and with the carcasses of horses. They were exposed to an oblique fire from the batteries on the hills on both sides, as well as to a direct fire of musketry. Through the clouds of smoke we could see their sabres flashing as they rode up to the guns and dashed between them, cutting down the gunners as they stood. We saw them riding through the guns, as I have said; to our delight we saw them returning, after breaking through a column of Russian infantry, and scattering them like chaff, when the flank fire of the battery on the hill swept them down, scattered and broken as they were. Wounded men and dismounted troopers flying towards us told the sad tale – demi-gods could not have done what we had failed to do. At the very moment when they were about to retreat an enormous mass of Lancers was hurled on their flank. Colonel Showell, of the 8th Hussars, saw the danger, and rode his few men straight at them, cutting his way through with fearful loss. The other regiments turned and engaged in a desperate encounter. With courage too great almost for credence, they were breaking their way through the columns which enveloped them, when there took place an act of atrocity without parallel in the modern warfare of civilized nations. The Russian gunners, when the storm of cavalry passed, returned to their guns. They saw their own cavalry mingled with the troopers who had just ridden over them, and, to the eternal disgrace of the Russian name, the miscreants poured a murderous volley of grape and canister on the mass of struggling men and horses, mingling friend and foe in one common ruin. It was as much as our Heavy Cavalry Brigade could do to cover the retreat of the miserable remnants of that band of heroes as they returned to the place they had so lately quitted in all the pride of life.

———◆———

Following the outbreak of the Crimean War, in which France and Britain became involved to prevent Russia from expanding its reach by exploiting the decline of the Ottoman Empire, the allied forces besieged Sevastopol, home to the Black Sea fleet. The Russians counterattacked the British lines at the nearby port of Balaklava.

When some captured British guns began to be dragged away, Lord Raglan, the army's commander, wrote an order to Lord Lucan, who led the light cavalry, telling him to avert this. From where he was, Lucan could not see the guns and the vague gestures of the officer who delivered the message, Captain Nolan, led him to presume Raglan meant him to attack the artillery positions in front of him, suicidal though this was.

About 670 cavalrymen set off along the mile of what Tennyson's celebrated poem would commemorate as the 'Valley of Death'. More than 300 were killed, wounded or taken prisoner in the charge.

It was witnessed by war correspondent William Howard Russell, whose reports for *The Times* detailing the conditions endured by soldiers suffering from cholera led to Florence Nightingale's nursing mission, and eventually the resignation of the Prime Minister, the Earl of Aberdeen.

THE OUTBREAK OF THE INDIAN MUTINY

29 June 1857

At the two great stations of Meerut and Delhi the whole of the native troops have broken out into mutiny and murder. From the former place they have fled or been expelled. The latter (where no European troops were quartered) remained, at the date of the latest accounts, completely in their possession.

I will endeavour to digest into a continuous narrative as much of the fragmentary intelligence that has been day by day rushing down from Agra as has been proved, or may be reasonably conjectured to be true.

At the commencement of this month the native force at Meerut consisted of the 3rd Light Cavalry and the 11th and 20th Regiments of Native Infantry. Among the men of the cavalry corps the question of the greased cartridges, which had previously been mooted at Barrackpore and other stations, was freely agitated. The result of the movement was that 85 men of the regiment refusing to handle the cartridges found themselves in the early days of the month tried by court-martial, and sentenced to various terms of imprisonment with hard labour. On the 9th their sentences were read out on parade, and the offenders marched off to gaol. Up to this time disaffection had shown itself only through incendiary fires in the lines, hardly a night passing without one or more conflagrations. But on the 10th it appeared at once in all its unsuspected strength. Towards the evening of that day, while many of the Europeans were at church – for it was Sunday – the men of the two native infantry regiments, the 11th and 20th, as if by previous concert, assembled together in armed and tumultuous bodies upon the parade ground. Several officers hurried from their quarters to endeavour to pacify them. Colonel Finnis, of the 11th, was one of the first to arrive, and was the first victim of the outbreak. He was shot down while addressing a party of the 20th, which is said to have been the foremost regiment in the mutiny. Other officers fell with the Colonel or in the terrible moments that ensued, for the troopers of the 3rd Cavalry poured out of their quarters to join the insurgent infantry, and the whole body, now thoroughly committed to the wildest excesses, rushed through the native lines of the cantonment, slaying, burning, and destroying. Every house was fired, and every English man, woman, or child, that fell in the way of the mutineers was pitilessly massacred. Happily, however, many of the officers and their families – the great majority, I hope and believe had already escaped to the European lines, where they took refuge in the Artillery School of Instruction. Mr. Greathed, the Commissioner, and his wife were saved, it is said, by the fidelity of their servants, who assured the assassins that their master and mistress had left their house, though they were at the time concealed in it. The mutineers set fire to the bungalow and passed on. The names of the victims I am unable as yet to give with certainty or completeness.

◆

In the 1850s, the increasingly large portion of India that lay under the sway of Britain was still ruled on its behalf, and anomalously, by the East India Company. Its hundreds of thousands of sepoys – the native soldiers of its army – had, however, grown increasingly resentful of reductions in their status and privileges.

They were also alarmed by rumours that the grease on cartridges of powder with which they had been issued was derived from beef and pork. For Hindus and Muslims, respectively, contact with these fats as they tore open the packets with their teeth was deeply offensive to their religious beliefs.

There had already been several incidents of mutiny elsewhere in the weeks before violence erupted at Meerut, which held one of the largest concentrations of troops in India. From there it spread to Delhi and to many other northern and central parts of the country. The rebellion, marked by acts of cruelty on both sides, was largely suppressed by the middle of the following year. Thereafter, the Company's rule was replaced by that of the Crown.

BIG BEN NEARS COMPLETION

23 April 1859

Our readers, we are sure, will be glad to learn that the great clock at Westminster is at least progressing towards completion. In saying this we by no means intend to convey the impression that the clock will soon be going, or that a considerable interval may not yet elapse before it is completed, or even that it will ever be completed at all. In speaking of a subject which has given rise to such endless disputes as this clock, we must guard ourselves, we suppose, against expressing any opinion at all. We only, therefore, announce the fact that Mr. Dent's workmen have at last begun to do that which should have been done long ago, and that the mechanism of the clock is being put together very slowly in the clock chamber behind the dials. Unquestionably, for a clock whose history now extends over 15 years, and which has been going for nearly three years in Mr. Dent's factory, it is no great matter to say that after all this time it is at length in course of being sent to the very place for which it was constructed. But, little as this may be in the way of progress, it, at all events, is progress, which is more than we have been able to say of the whole affair any time these two years past. Before the clock will be really in going and striking order, many little difficulties, we believe, have yet to be overcome. One is a contrivance which shall catch the hammer of the great bell the instant it has struck, in order to prevent the rebound again dropping it upon the bell, and lift it clear from the side, that the vibration may not be interfered with. This is, of course, a difficulty which can be overcome, though devising and perfecting the means will require time, especially with a clock of such accurate construction that its striking is guaranteed to be true to a single second. Another difficulty is connected with the arrangements for its being regularly wound. To wind it by hand labour is almost out of the question. This monstrous clock will require winding once in three days, and take 11,500 revolutions of the handle to wind it completely. Supposing two men to be able at such labour to work continuously, and make 800 revolutions of the handle per hour, it would require 14 ½ hours of such exertion every third day. If to this is added the delay caused by the men having to make up the difference caused by the descent of the weights when the clock struck (in striking 12 they descend six feet), it is not too much to estimate the labour at nearly 18 hours, instead of 14 ½; or, to speak generally, about four months of every year would be spent in winding it up. Of course, Mr. Denison will devise some contrivance which will obviate this difficulty, and he can scarcely find a better one than has already been worked out by Mr. James and the indefatigable clerk of the works at the New Houses, Mr. Quarm. By the plan of these gentlemen the clock is made self-winding.

———◆———

Like many another prestige project, the rebuilding of the Houses of Parliament after they had burned down in 1834 became a long, drawn-out national drama, one reported in ever more exasperated tones by the press.

The clock tower was the last design of Augustus Pugin before his final descent into madness. It took seven years to complete – six fewer than those needed to decide on, and then to construct, the clock it would house.

The accuracy of this was ensured by a revolutionary mechanism, the Grimthorpe Escapement. The clock became known, however, by the catchier name given to the largest of its five bells – Big Ben. This was probably a nod to the government's First Commissioner of Works, Sir Benjamin Hall.

The clock was started in May 1859 and the first chimes were heard in July. Yet even then, further adjustments were needed. Lighter copper hands were substituted for cast-iron ones to enable the clock to keep time. A lighter clapper had to be made, too, when the original caused the bell to crack. The building has officially been known as the Elizabeth Tower since the Queen's Jubilee in 2012. (See Decimal Day, page 276.)

THE DEATH OF PRINCE ALBERT

16 December 1861

The news of the serious illness of the late Prince Consort alarmed and amazed all England on Saturday. To the attentive readers of the *Court Circular* it was only known his Royal Highness was slightly indisposed, and the bulletin which on Saturday announced that his illness had taken an unfavourable turn spread dismay and astonishment throughout the country. Then, all at once, the fearful affliction which threatened Her Majesty was seen, and on every side information as to the state of his Royal Highness's health was sought for with the most intense eagerness. The announcement which we published in our third edition of Saturday, that a change, slightly for the better, had taken place in the illustrious patient's condition, was welcomed as almost a relief from the state of feverish anxiety under which all had waited for news. Unhappily, this slight improvement, which raised such ardent hopes wherever it was known, proved to be but a precursor of the fatal issue. During Saturday morning – at least in the early part – his Royal Highness undoubtedly seemed better, and, notwithstanding that his condition was in the highest degree precarious, the change, though sudden, was marked, and almost justified the strong hopes which were then entertained that he would recover. This change was but for a short time, and, in fact, but one of those expiring efforts of nature which give delusive hopes to the mourners round so many death-beds. Soon afterwards his Royal Highness again relapsed, and before the evening it became evident that it was only a question of an hour more or less. The Prince sank with alarming rapidity. At 4 the physicians issued a bulletin stating that their patient was then in "a most critical condition," which was indeed a sad truth, for at that time almost every hope of recovery had passed away. Her Majesty, and the Prince of Wales (who had travelled through the previous night from Cambridge), the Princesses Alice and Helena, and the Prince and Princess of Leiningen, were with their illustrious relative during all this mournful and most trying period. The approach of death from exhaustion was so rapid that all stimulants failed to check the progressive increase of weakness, and the fatal termination was so clearly foreseen that even before 9 o'clock on Saturday evening a telegram was forwarded from Windsor to the city, stating that the Prince Consort was then dying fast. Quietly and without suffering he continued slowly to sink, so slowly that the wrists were pulseless long before the last moment had arrived, when at a few minutes before 11 he ceased to breathe, and all was over. An hour after and the solemn tones of the great bell of St. Paul's – a bell of evil omen – told all citizens how irreparable has been the loss of their beloved Queen, how great the loss to the country.

———◆———

Prince Albert was only 42 when he died. He had been married to Queen Victoria for 21 years and they had rarely been apart, with the Prince coming to play an ever more important role in affairs of state as well as supervising the upbringing of their nine children.

These responsibilities began, however, to take a toll on his health. It had never been strong, and illness, perhaps exacerbated by stress, especially affected his stomach. Historians have speculated that he may have suffered from cancer or Crohn's disease, and he had been perturbed by the recent deaths of three relations in the Portuguese royal family.

At the end of November 1861, he got drenched after going to Cambridge to reprimand the Prince of Wales for taking up with a 'low, common woman' – an Irish actress, Nellie Clifden. When Albert fell ill, he was treated principally by Edward Jenner, the pioneer of vaccination, whose own diagnosis of the symptoms was typhoid. The Prince's death shocked the nation and led the Queen to seclude herself from public life for years to come.

THE UNDERGROUND RAILWAY

12 January 1863

On Saturday the Metropolitan (underground) Railway was opened to the public, and many thousands were enabled to indulge their curiosity in reference to this mode of travelling under the streets of the metropolis. The trains commenced running as early as 6 o'clock in the morning from the Paddington (Bishop's-road) station and the Farringdon-street terminus, in order to accommodate workmen, and there was a goodly muster of that class of the public, who availed themselves of the advantages of the line in reaching their respective places of employment. At 8 o'clock the desire to travel underground in the direction of the city began to manifest itself at the various stations along the line, and by 9 it became equally evident to the authorities that neither the locomotive power nor the rolling-stock at their disposal was at all in proportion to the requirements of the opening day. From this time, and throughout the morning, every station became crowded with anxious travellers, who were admitted in sections; but poor were the chances of a place to those who ventured to take their tickets at any point below Baker-street, the occupants being, with but very rare exceptions, "long distance," or terminus, passengers. This circumstance tended to increase the numbers at every station every minute, until there became sufficient to fill any train of empties which might be sent to overflow; and we believe we are correct in stating that ultimately a number of the Great Western narrow-gauge carriages, as well as engines, were brought into requisition, and by this means the temporary wants of the public were accommodated. Possibly the greatest point of attraction, if the collection of numbers may be taken as any criterion, was King's-cross, which is certainly the finest station on the line, throwing even the termini into the shade.

At this point during the morning the crowds were immense, and the constant cry as the trains arrived of "No room" appeared to have a very depressing effect upon those assembled. Between 11 and 12 at this station, and, continuously, for the space of an hour and a-half, the money takers refused to take money for passengers between King's-cross and Farringdon-street, but they issued tickets between that station and Paddington, and many whose destination was city-wise, determined to ride on the railway on its first day of opening, took tickets for the opposite direction in order to secure places for the return journey. At 12 o'clock the clerks informed the public, who were certainly then assembled to the number of some 500 or 600 at King's-cross, that there were enough people at Paddington to fill four trains in succession; and that, therefore, their instructions were to issue no Farringdon-street tickets for an hour. This announcement had the effect of getting rid of very large numbers. While, however, all the tendency of the traffic was towards the Farringdon-street terminus during the morning, the public were enabled to proceed westward with but little inconvenience. Towards afternoon, however, the tide set in the other way, and the approaches to the trains at Victoria-street can be compared to no other than the crush at the doors of a theatre on the first night of a pantomime.

◆

The growth of London created more congestion in the streets as well as giving rise to the first commuters. By the middle of the century, more than 200,000 people each day came in to work in the capital's commercial heart, the City.

The Metropolitan Railway was given the contract to construct the world's first underground railway. Built in less than three years, at a cost of £1 million, this carried passengers in steam-drawn wooden carriages almost four miles beneath London from Paddington Station to Farringdon Street, on the edge of the City.

More than 38,000 people queued up excitedly to use it on opening day. The Times noted approvingly the gas lighting in the compartments. This would reassure ladies when the train entered a tunnel and would allow gentlemen to read their newspapers – if there was not too much wind.

GETTYSBURG

16 July 1863

The field of battle is due north of Washington, at Gettysburg, little more than fifty miles from the seat of the Federal Government. To the north and west of this locality the bulk of the Confederate army appears to have been found at last. Roughly speaking, both armies have described a circle from the Rappahannock, General LEE moving on the larger curve to his present position, and General MEADE on a smaller one, keeping closer to Washington itself as his centre. The battle, or the series of battles, commenced on the 1st of July. A corps of the Federal army, entering Gettysburg on the eastern side of the town, passed through, and encountered a part of the Confederate force, under General HILL, to the west of it. The Confederates were coming from the direction of Chambersburg, a town a few miles to the west of the spot where the armies came upon each other. The engagement commenced immediately, and for two hours the Federal General REYNOLDS held his ground. He was then reinforced by General HOWARD, but both were evidently outnumbered. They had met a portion of the Confederate troops superior to their own. They were outflanked on the right, and were contending with this difficulty when General EWELL came up with a force which was an army in itself, as it is estimated at no less than 25,000 men. The Confederates opened a cross fire of artillery which is described by the Federal reports as "destructive", turned both flanks, and, REYNOLDS'S corps giving way, HOWARD could not hold his ground, and both fell back to a position south of Gettysburg – that is, retreated. General REYNOLDS was killed, General PAUL also fell, and the Federal loss in this engagement they state to have been 4,500 men, with an "immense number of officers."

The battle was renewed in the afternoon of the 2nd, south of Gettysburg, the two corps repulsed on the previous day having fallen back on the main body of the Federal force. Of the second day's engagement the Government have published portions of General MEADE'S report. He states that the Confederates, "after one of the most severe conflicts of the war, were repulsed at all points." It seems to have been principally an engagement of artillery, the hostile batteries firing, on one point, at the distance of two miles. The day of the 2nd was not decisive. The fighting was stopped by the close of night, and each army occupied nearly the same ground as when the battle commenced. General MEADE thought he perceived indications that LEE was retiring, but a reconnaissance discovered that he was still "in force" on the field. There is no report, official or other, later than the night of the 3rd. The whole result, therefore, appears to be that the Federals in the second engagement did not recover the ground they had lost in the first. But the conflict must have been, as General MEADE describes it, severe.

◆

Following the election of Abraham Lincoln as President of the United States in 1860, on a platform to abolish slavery, seven states in the South – the economy of which depended largely on slave labour – seceded from the Union. By the time that the Civil War began in 1861, the Confederates commanded support in 11 states.

General Robert E. Lee invaded Pennsylvania in the summer of 1863 to shift the focus of the war to the North. He encountered the Union forces under the newly appointed General George Meade at Gettysburg on 1 July. The climax of three days of fighting came with the repulse of Pickett's Charge against the centre of the Union line atop Cemetery Ridge.

Both sides suffered about 20,000 casualties in what proved to be the bloodiest, and the decisive, battle of the conflict. Lee was forced to retreat southwards and the Confederacy was eventually defeated two years later.

THE ROAD HILL HOUSE MURDER

26 April 1865

Yesterday afternoon Sir Thomas Henry, the chief magistrate of Bow-street, received information that Miss Constance Kent, formerly of Road-hill-house, near Frome, had arrived in London from Brighton for the purpose of surrendering herself to the officers of justice as the perpetrator of the above memorable crime.

The circumstances of this mysterious murder have never been forgotten, – how, nearly five years ago, the body of a male child, which had been missed from its cot, was found in a privy outside the house, and how, suspicion having been directed towards Miss Kent, the eldest daughter of Mr. Kent by a former wife, she was examined before the local magistrates, at the instigation of Inspectors Whicher and Williamson, of the London Detective Police, and acquitted of the charge. It is hardly a secret that nearly a year afterwards, in consequence of an alleged confession of the crime by Miss Kent to one of her relatives; another attempt to investigate the matter was made by the detective officers, who had incurred the censure of a large proportion of the press and the public for their proceedings in the case. They found it unadvisable, however, to act upon the fresh information which had reached them, and it subsequently transpired that Miss Kent had been sent to a convent in France. Nothing more of a reliable character was heard of the case until yesterday, when the startling intimation was conveyed to the chief magistrate that Miss Kent was in custody upon her own confession upon the terrible charge, having been accompanied to London by the Rev. Mr. Wagner, of St. Paul's, Brighton, to whom she had revealed her guilt.

Shortly before 4 o'clock Mr. Superintendent Durkin and Mr. Williamson, chief inspector of the Detective force, conducted their prisoner to the private room of Sir Thomas Henry. Miss Kent was attired in deep mourning, and wore a thick fall, which almost screened her face from view. She is slender, and much taller than she appeared to be when before in the custody of the officers. She spoke firmly, though sadly, and occupied a seat during the inquiry. She was attended by the Lady Superior of St. Mary's Hospital, Brighton, in which establishment she had been a visitor during the last two years, and she appeared about 21 years of age.

◆

In 1860, Britain had been transfixed by the investigation of the murder of three-year-old Saville Kent, whose body had been found with his throat cut in the outdoor privy of his well-to-do family's house in Wiltshire.

The suspicions of the detective in charge of the case, Jack Whicher, had centred on the child's half-sister, Constance, who was 16 and thought to be angry that her father had remarried. The public, however, and indeed newspapers such as *The Times*, thought that the police's ideas were driven by class prejudice. Scotland Yard was forced to call off the inquiry and Whicher's reputation never recovered. The events inspired books by Charles Dickens and Wilkie Collins.

Constance Kent was sent to France, but in 1865 she told a clergyman, Arthur Wagner, that she had committed the crime. Although many had doubts about the validity of her confession, she was sentenced to death, but this was commuted to life imprisonment. After her release in 1885, she emigrated to Australia, where she died aged 100 in 1944.

THE ASSASSINATION OF ABRAHAM LINCOLN

27 April 1865

The following official telegram from Mr. Secretary Stanton has been received by the United States' Legation in London:-

(Via Greencastle, per Nova Scotian.)

"Sir, – It has become my distressing duty to announce to you that last night his Excellency Abraham Lincoln, President of the United States, was assassinated, about the hour of half-past 10 o'clock, in his private box at Ford's Theatre, in the city. The President about 8 o'clock accompanied Mrs. Lincoln to the theatre. Another lady and gentleman were with them in the box. About half-past 10, during a pause in the performance, the assassin entered the box, the door of which was unguarded, hastily approached the President from behind, and discharged a pistol at his head. The bullet entered the back of his head and penetrated nearly through. The assassin then leaped from the box upon the stage brandishing a large knife or dagger, and exclaiming 'Sic semper tyrannis!' and escaped in the rear of the theatre. Immediately upon the discharge the President fell to the floor insensible, and continued in that state until 20 minutes past [7] o'clock this morning, when he breathed his last. About the same time the murder was being committed at the theatre another assassin presented himself at the door of Mr. [William] Seward's residence, gained admission by representing he had a prescription from Mr. Seward's physician which he was directed to see administered, and hurried up to the third story chamber, where Mr. Seward was lying. He here discovered Mr. Frederick Seward, struck him over the head, inflicting several wounds, and fracturing the skull in two places, inflicting, it is feared, mortal wounds. He then rushed into the room where Mr. Seward was in bed, attended by a young daughter and male nurse. The male attendant was stabbed through the lungs, and it is believed he will die. The assassin then struck Mr. Seward with a knife or dagger twice in the throat and twice in the face, inflicting terrible wounds. By this time Major Seward, eldest son of the Secretary, and another attendant reached the room, and rushed to the rescue of the Secretary; they were also wounded in the conflict, and the assassin escaped."

———◆———

Lincoln was assassinated on 14 April 1865, as the American Civil War was nearing its end. His murder was part of a conspiracy aimed at the leading members of the government of the North, including Secretary of State William Seward.

Its leader was John Wilkes Booth – a relation of the radical British politician – who came from a theatrical family in Maryland and was increasingly well-regarded in his own right as a brilliant actor with striking good looks. Then aged 26, he had supported the Confederate cause and, with a group of half-a-dozen accomplices, had already made at least one prior attempt to kidnap the President.

The Latin tag that Booth shouted as he jumped onto the stage – 'Ever thus to tyrants' – was the motto of Virginia. Twelve days after his escape, he was tracked down to a farm there and killed by Union soldiers. Seward survived his wounds, while the third target, Andrew Johnson, succeeded Lincoln when the intended assassin got drunk instead of carrying out his attack.

THE OPENING OF THE SUEZ CANAL

19 November 1869

The estimates of the cost of the undertaking which he [Ferdinand de Lesseps] himself had put forward had been doubled, and on every occasion when it became apparent that the money which had been provided was insufficient, the burden had been cast upon him of persuading the capitalists of the world to have faith in his promise, and to throw their gold into the sands where so much had been lost. All this he had gone through in the strength of his belief. Even at last, when the moment of realization seemed imminent, there arose a rumour of a new difficulty. The most careful watch that had been possible had been insufficient for the Arab and Egyptian workmen, and it was announced that a rock had been discovered in the Canal between Ismailia and Suez which would be a fatal impediment to navigation until its removal was effected. But on Wednesday the thing was done. The morning arose big with the promise of the coming event, yet, if we judge the character of M. DE LESSEPS aright, it found him undisturbed. He had been too long possessed of the certainty of faith to be tremulous on the day of fulfilment. The visitors were doubtless moved by different feelings. Some of them were not impossibly anxious for their own safety; others were flurried and nervous about the success of the scheme; all must have scanned narrowly the banks and sidings as they performed the fifty miles from Port Said to Ismailia. There is no country in the world which has seen stranger processions than the Desert between Suez and the Mediterranean, yet this most ancient of lands saw something totally unlike all that it had ever seen before in the procession of Wednesday. Forty steamers followed one another in single file along the narrow water-way. The breadth is not sufficient for craft such as were there to pass one another with safety, except at the basin stations, occurring every seven or eight miles. One after another, therefore, they came, and for the first half of the journey from Port Said to Ismailia the Canal or Channel they followed ran through the shallow waters of Lake Menzaleh. We can well imagine the watchful looks that were cast right and left as the procession passed on, and when it crossed the track from Syria to Egypt and the travellers saw nothing but sand on each side, the occupants of the hindermost of the fleet must have become more than ever interested in observing the effect of the wash the vessels before them made on the sand-banks bounding the water-way. After eight hours' careful journey, however, the fifty miles to Ismailia were accomplished, the fleet drew up in the anchorage of Lake Timsah, where the vessels from Suez awaited them, and a great feeling of relief and thankfulness arose in the minds of all, except in the mind of M. DE LESSEPS, whose previous assurance of success excluded exultation.

———————◆———————

In 1854, Ferdinand de Lesseps, a French diplomat who had served in Cairo, used his good standing with Egypt's ruler, the Khedive Ismail Pasha, to obtain the right to build a canal through the isthmus of Suez to link the Mediterranean with the Red Sea.

Despite scepticism about its viability, not least from British politicians and investors, the 120-mile (193-kilometre) long canal was constructed within a decade. Its opening was marked by ceremonies including fireworks and a banquet attended by the Empress Eugénie of France, although Verdi did not (as often believed) write his opera *Aida* for the occasion but for the inauguration of Cairo's Opera House. De Lesseps himself, then 64, celebrated by marrying his second wife, who was 21. He subsequently tried but failed to build a Panama Canal.

With shipping no longer forced to sail around Africa and to brave the Atlantic, journey times between, for instance, Britain and India were greatly reduced. The strategic and economic importance of the Canal led Britain and France to invade Egypt in 1882 to restore the power of the Khedive following a rebellion by nationalists. (See Suez, page 233.)

THE FIRST TEST CRICKET SERIES

14 May 1877

You know the result of our great cricket match. Australians will "blow," to use Mr. Trollope's word, about it for some time to come. It was played on the ground of the Melbourne Club, between Lillywhite's eleven and a combined eleven of New South Wales and Victoria. We are told that it is the first match in which an English professional eleven has been beaten out of England. Each side was under a certain disadvantage. Pooley, the English wicket keeper, had been left in New Zealand, and Allan, the best Victorian bowler, upon whose services the colonial eleven almost entirely depended in his department, suddenly retired, and a substitute had to be found at the last moment. The betting was all together in favour of the Englishmen before the match began, but the splendid play of Bannerman, from New South Wales, soon altered the odds. He made 165 runs before he retired, not out, with his finger badly cut. The Englishmen declared that they had never seen a finer display of batting, not even by the great Grace. The other Australians brought up the score in the first innings to 245. The Englishmen then went in and made 196. The Australians followed and, with Bannerman disabled, made 104, leaving the Englishmen 155 to make to win, and a most interesting game was brought to a close with the fall of their last wicket for 108 runs, leaving our men the winners by 45 runs. This victory is certainly creditable to Australia. The scores were made against presumably the best English bowlers, among whom were Shaw, Emmett, Ullyet, and Southerton, the fielding of the team was excellent, and, although it is considered relatively weak in batsmen, Jupp, Charlwood, Greenwood, and Selby are said to be strong enough to give, at least, an average efficiency. As may be supposed, the game was watched with intense excitement by enthusiastic crowds, and those who could not get to the ground clustered round the newspaper offices to see the last despatches from the seat of war placarded on the door posts. It began and ended in good temper, and Lillywhite's pecuniary success must have consoled him for his defeat.

———◆———

The Times had ignored the staging of the first international football match, between England and Scotland, in 1872, but the gentleman's favoured game of cricket was another matter.

English teams had toured abroad for many years – a trip to France in 1789 had to be abandoned when the Revolution broke out – but the matches played in Australia by James Lillywhite's side in March and April 1877 are retrospectively regarded as the first Tests.

A rival tour organized by W. G. Grace's brother had been cancelled at short notice and Lillywhite's team of professionals featured few of the leading English players, such as Grace. The wicket keeper, Ted Pooley, had been left behind in New Zealand after being accused of an assault arising from his betting on a game he had been umpiring.

The Australian side similarly lacked their finest bowler of the era, Fred Spofforth, while most of their players had been born in England. Nonetheless, 12,000 spectators at the Melbourne Cricket Ground, among them this Australian correspondent, were delighted by Charles Bannerman's feat of compiling what is still the highest percentage of a team's runs in a Test innings. The sporting rivalry instituted between the two nations gave rise to The Ashes five years later.

THE RELIEF OF KHARTOUM

9 February 1885

Sir C. Wilson, with a detachment of the Sussex Regiment and Soudanese, and accompanied by Lieutenant Stuart-Wortley and Captain Trafford, left Metammeh in two steamers on the morning of the 24th ultimo. At Gandabe they stopped for a supply of wood. Here the Sheikh of the Shageya sent them word that his tribe was ready to join the English when their power was established. Our victories had produced a great effect, the enemy saying that their total loss was 3,000 men. They have heard of another English army advancing up the Nile. Next day a few shots were fired from the west bank. One of the steamers ran on a rock.

On the 26th the steamer cleared the rock, and the men landed in order to pass the rapid, but the steamer grounded again and was delayed all day. The party stopped for the night on an island. Two Shageyas who came aboard reported that General Gordon had been fighting for 15 days. The advance of the English was greatly feared, and they repeated that they were only awaiting the turn of events to join us.

On the 27th they passed the Shabluka cataract, where the passage is 30 yards wide between the rocks. On the south side of the east bank at the village of Nefida, an Arab stated that some camelmen had passed that day from Omdurman reporting the fall of Khartoum and the death of General Gordon, but the rumour was generally disbelieved. Shots were fired from the west bank all day.

They started at dawn on the 28th. A man of the Shageya tribe stated that Khartoum had fallen two days before. At noon Lieutenant Stuart-Wortley saw Khartoum through his telescope, but no flag was flying on the Government House. The houses seemed wrecked.

Soon after the guns from Halfiyeh opened on the steamers, together with heavy musketry. The steamers answered with guns and volleys. The firing ceased until the steamers were abreast of Tuti Island, which they expected to find occupied by General Gordon's troops, but a heavy fire was opened at 160 yards, and two guns shelled them from Khartoum. Presently musketry and four guns opened from Omdurman, and the enemy showed in large numbers in Khartoum. The steamers being protected by armour suffered little loss, only one killed and five wounded.

Sir Charles Wilson, seeing Khartoum occupied, ordered the steamers to go at full speed down the river, and they were soon out of range. They stopped at an island some miles down, and sent to collect news. The man soon returned, saying Khartoum had fallen on the night of the 26th by the treachery of Farag Pasha, who opened the gates for the Mahdi's troops, and General Gordon was killed with all his men.

◆

Britain's involvement in Egypt's affairs presented it with an unwelcome problem when an Islamist revolt broke out in the Sudan, which was administered by Cairo. General George Gordon, who had made his reputation fighting for China's emperor during the Taiping Rebellion, was sent to Khartoum early in 1884 to organize its evacuation.

Gordon, who had strong religious convictions and no lack of self-belief, decided instead to prepare the city for a siege, with the eventual aim of defeating the army of the rebel leader, the Mahdi. The British Government initially left Khartoum to its fate but was forced by public opinion later in the year to mount an expedition to relieve Gordon.

Commanded by Garnet Wolseley, this made slow progress up the Nile by boat. Wolseley divided his force, sending part across the desert in the hope of reaching Khartoum more quickly. Using steamers, a group from this force reached the city on 28 January 1885 – two days after it had fallen to the Mahdi.

Gordon had been among the 10,000 inhabitants massacred and his death became an abiding image of the imperial era. Sudan was abandoned to the Mahdi and only reconquered in 1898 with victory at Omdurman.

THE MURDER OF MARY JANE KELLY

10 November 1888

During the early hours of yesterday morning another murder of a most revolting and fiendish character took place in Spitalfields. This is the seventh which has occurred in this immediate neighbourhood, and the character of the mutilations leaves very little doubt that the murderer in this instance is the same person who has committed the previous ones, with which the public are fully acquainted.

The scene of this last crime is at No: 26, Dorset-street, Spitalfields, which is about 200 yards distant from 35, Hanbury-street, where the unfortunate woman, Mary Ann Nicholls, was so foully murdered. Although the victim, whose name is Mary Ann (or Mary Jane) Kelly, resides at the above number, the entrance to the room she occupied is up a narrow court, in which are some half-a-dozen houses, and which is known as Miller's-court; it is entirely separated from the other portion of the house, and has an entrance leading into the court. The room is known by the title of No. 13. The house is rented by John M'Carthy, who keeps a small general shop at No. 27, Dorset-street, and the whole of the rooms are let out to tenants of a very poor class. As an instance of the poverty of the neighbourhood, it may be mentioned that nearly the whole of the houses in this street are common lodging-houses, and the one opposite where this murder was enacted has accommodation for some 300 men, and is fully occupied every night. About 12 months ago Kelly, who was about 24 years of age, and who was considered a good-looking young woman, of fair and fresh-coloured complexion, came to Mr. M'Carthy with a man named Joseph Kelly, who she stated was her husband and who was a porter employed at the Spitalfields Market. They rented a room on the ground floor, the same in which the poor woman was murdered, at a rental of 4s.

a week. It had been noticed that the deceased woman was somewhat addicted to drink, but Mr. M'Carthy denied having any knowledge that she had been leading a loose or immoral life. That this was so, however, there can be no doubt, for about a fortnight ago she had a quarrel with Kelly, and, after blows had been exchanged, the man left the house, or rather room, and did not return. It has since been ascertained that he went to live at Buller's common lodging-house in Bishopsgate-street. Since then the woman has supported herself as best she could, and the police have ascertained that she has been walking the streets. None of those living in the court or at 26, Dorset-street saw anything of the unfortunate creature after about 8 o'clock on Thursday evening, but she was seen in Commercial-street shortly before the closing of the publichouse, and then had the appearance of being the worse for drink. About 1 o'clock yesterday morning a person living in the court opposite to the room occupied by the murdered woman heard her singing the song, "Sweet violets," but this person is unable to say whether anyone else was with her at that time. Nothing more was seen or heard of her until her dead body was found.

◆

During the autumn of 1888, a series of murders of women in the poverty-ridden East End of London became ascribed by the police and the public alike to a single killer. He was known, from a letter claiming responsibility for the crimes, as Jack the Ripper.

Mary Jane Kelly was the fifth and last of those thought most likely, from the brutal nature of their deaths, to have died at the same hand. Despite their customary characterisation, she was also the only one of the women to have worked regularly as a prostitute. Little else, including her true name, is known for certain about her life, the details of which she may have embroidered to evade a gang that had trafficked her to Paris.

The Ripper murders are usually held to have stopped after Kelly's death and were never solved. They lived on, however, in popular culture, in voyeuristic tourism and in an abundant literature about the killings, notable for dwelling more on the possible identity of the murderer than on the fate of the victims.

THE DEDICATION OF THE
EIFFEL TOWER

1 April 1889

The Eiffel tower has now attained its full height – 300 metres (984 feet). When the proposal was made, two years ago, to erect the structure, artists and literary men signed a protest against the scheme, declaring that it would disgrace and disfigure Paris, and would destroy the effect of the great monuments of the city, such as Notre Dame and the Louvre. It must be admitted that the effect produced by the drawings was unfavourable. The form suggested the ugliest parts of a suspension bridge, and it was predicted that the deformity would be increased with the increase of size. The result has not been what was predicted. Even some of those who protested most loudly against the proposal now admit that the effect of the structure is not what they anticipated. They acknowledge that it has a light and graceful appearance, in spite of its gigantic size, and that it is an imposing monument, not unworthy of Paris.

At half-past 2 o'clock to-day the ceremony of hoisting the first flag from the summit was celebrated, in presence of a crowd of spectators. M. Eiffel, with about a dozen persons, ascended the tower to the last small platform, and from that point the flag was hoisted by pulling a rope. The appearance of the flag was saluted by a salvo of 20 guns, followed by the cheers of the crowd. The flag is seven metres and a half long by four metres and a half wide. It bears the letters "R. F." The engineer, M. Condamin, addressed those present on the platform. He said he saluted the flag of 1789, which their fathers had borne so proudly, which had won so many victories, and which had witnessed so much progress in science and humanity. They had endeavoured to erect a monument worthy of the great date '89, and it was for that reason that colossal dimensions were required. To M. Eiffel, who had conceived this idea, and to the fellow-workmen who had enabled him to carry out his work, they were glad to do honour. M. Berger then proposed the health of M. Eiffel, the workmen, and the Municipal Council, which was drunk in champagne, amid cries of "Vive la France! Vive Paris! Vive la Republique!"

The descent from the platform was found to be as trying as the ascent had been, and lasted 40 minutes.

Tables had been arranged for an entertainment to be given to the guests and about 200 workmen. The party were joined by M. Tirard, the Premier, and M. Alphand, city surveyor, and when the repast had ended M. Eiffel delivered a speech, in which he said that it was a great satisfaction to him to have that day hoisted a flag on the highest monument man had ever constructed. After thanking his fellow workmen for the assistance they had given, he said France had shown that she was still capable of great things, and of succeeding where other nations failed.

◆

The Eiffel Tower was the winner of a competition held by the French government to design a fitting gateway for the great exhibition planned for the centenary of the Revolution in 1889. It was created by several engineers working for the construction company owned by the architect Gustave Eiffel, whose previous commissions included devising the interior framework for the Statue of Liberty.

Intended to demonstrate French technological prowess, the wrought-iron structure, planned with extraordinary precision for the times, was erected in just two years. It was then the tallest edifice in the world and the first to top 300 metres. When it was inaugurated, however, the lifts were not completed, and Eiffel's party took more than an hour to climb the 1,710 steps to the summit.

It has since attracted 250 million visitors and become perhaps the best-known symbol of France. Not everyone, however, became reconciled to its charm. The writer Guy de Maupassant was said to have lunched in one of its four restaurants (French, Flemish, Russian and Anglo-American) every day because only there could he not see the Tower.

THE TRIALS OF OSCAR WILDE

27 May 1895

The question which the jury had to decide was whether [Oscar] Wilde was guilty of the charge made against him. His Lordship reviewed the evidence which had been given in the case, and pointed out to the jury the questions for their consideration. There was only evidence as to one of the counts in reference to St James's-place.

The jury retired to consider their verdict at half-past 3 o'clock, and at 26 minutes past 5 o'clock they returned and asked a question in reference to the evidence as to St. James's-place.

MR. JUSTICE WILLS read his note of the evidence of a witness on the subject, and the jury retired again, but returned into Court about five minutes afterwards and said they found Wilde Guilty on all the counts except that which charged him in respect to Edward Shelley, upon which they found him Not guilty. That count, it will be remembered, was withdrawn from the jury by Mr. Justice Wills on Thursday.

The announcement of the verdict was greeted with a cry of "Shame" in a portion of the Court reserved for the public.

The defendant Taylor was then placed in the dock.

SIR EDWARD CLARKE asked Mr. Justice Wills not to pass sentence until next sessions, as there was a demurrer [objection] to be argued in reference to the indictment.

Mr. J. P. GRAIN, who appeared for the defendant Taylor, said that the argument of the demurrer would affect Taylor equally, and he therefore made the same application as Sir Edward Clarke.

The SOLICITOR-GENERAL opposed the application. The passing of sentence now would not interfere with the argument of the demurrer.

MR. JUSTICE WILLS. – There was a verdict of "not guilty".

SIR EDWARD CLARKE. – That does not affect it.

MR. JUSTICE WILLS. – What is the objection?

SIR EDWARD CLARKE. – That the indictment is bad?

MR. JUSTICE WILLS. – What is the point?

SIR EDWARID CLARKE. – The point is the joining of two sets of counts on one set of which the defendants could be called as witnesses and on the other could not.

MR. JUSTICE WILLS said that, as the passing of sentence now would not affect the argument of the demurrer, he thought it his duty to complete the proceedings here.

MR. JUSTICE WILLS, addressing Wilde and Taylor, said that it had never been his lot to try a case of this kind so bad. One had to put stern constraint upon oneself to prevent oneself from describing in language which he would rather not use the sentiments which must rise in the breast of every man who had any spark of decent feeling in him and who had heard the details of these two terrible trials. He could not do anything except pass the severest sentence which the law allowed, and in his judgment it, was totally inadequate to such a case as this. The sentence was that each of them be imprisoned and kept to hard labour for two years.

On the sentence being pronounced there were cries of "Shame" and hisses in Court.

◆

In 1895, Oscar Wilde was at the peak of his fame as a writer and playwright; *The Importance of Being Earnest* opened in London in February that year. He was almost as well-known for his aesthetic ideas and willingness to flout convention. This extended to his private life, for although he was married, Wilde was also homosexual and at the time (and until 1967) sexual acts between men were treated as crimes.

When the Marquess of Queensberry, the father of Wilde's lover Lord Alfred Douglas, accused him publicly of sodomy, Wilde prosecuted him for libel. Since there was ample evidence that the Marquess's allegation was true, this proved disastrous for Wilde, who in April 1895 lost the case and was bankrupted by having to pay his adversary's costs.

He was then arrested a few days later on charges of gross indecency. The jury at a first trial could not reach a verdict, but at a second Wilde and his friend Alfred Taylor were convicted. After his release from Reading Gaol in 1897, Wilde sailed to France, where he died three years later, aged 46.

THE DIAMOND JUBILEE

23 June 1897

By this time all those who intended to witness the procession had taken their places. Every stand in the Strand was packed, and though many window seats were still to be let in the morning, they appeared all to be occupied now. At last the vast good-tempered multitude in the Strand was rewarded for its hours of patient watching. At 10.20 the head of the colonial procession reached Temple Bar. Lord Roberts, the Indian and colonial mounted troops and infantry, and the colonial Premiers were received with a roar of cheering, and it is difficult to say who were the favourites of the populace, so hearty was the welcome extended to all. It was a little after half-past 10 when the last colonials had trooped by the Griffin. The Royal procession followed close on them; but after the Life Guards, Dragoon Guards, and two batteries of horse artillery had passed there was a long check until 11.15, when the bugles sounded to mount, the bands struck up, and the procession proceeded. It was a strong-lunged crowd, and it had evidently carefully studied the programme of the procession, for most of our own generals and our distinguished guests were recognized, called to by name, and cheered individually. The enthusiasm was intense, and, at any rate on the portion of the route, international jealousies were forgotten for the time, and everyone who had come over to honour our Queen by taking part in this procession was cheered with a will.

Just before midday a loud roar of cheering announced the approach of the Queen, and soon the State carriage drew up by the Griffin, where the Lord Mayor and his deputation, on foot, bareheaded, were awaiting her Majesty. The interesting ceremony of the presentation of the sword did not occupy a minute. This handsome sword in its pearl-covered scabbard, which has been presented by successive Lord Mayors at this very spot to many sovereigns, from Queen Elizabeth's time to the present day, was handed to the Lord Mayor by the City Sword-bearer, with a low obeisance. Sir George Faudel-Phillips held the hilt towards her Majesty, who merely touched it, and ordered him to lead the way into the City. The Lord Mayor with considerable alacrity hurried to the spot south of the Griffin where he had left his horse, mounted it and rode off eastward bareheaded holding the sword aloft. The spirited steed caracoled away at a great pace, to the great amusement of the crowd, and it was noticed that the Queen, the Princess of Wales, and the Princess Christian joined in the merriment. But the present Lord Mayor is an expert horseman, and sat his animal well.

The night before in Fleet-street the people passed to and fro, and the noise of the ceaseless traffic mingled with shouts and songs produced one continuous roar. The night was cloudy, but the moon peeped out at times through the driving clouds. When the blue dawn crept imperceptibly above the houses the street presented a curious and unwonted sight. The yellow gas lamps were still blazing, but in the light of the coming day the faces of the people looked wan. Down the street a stream of wagons, omnibuses, brakes, and hansoms, full of sightseers, made their way along the line of route, retarding the progress of the newspaper carts as they rattled along to catch the mails. Every now and then bands of youths or men trooped by singing "God Save the Queen" to a cacophonous accompaniment; many of these carried flags, while others bore youngsters on their shoulders. Factory girls, arm in arm, danced upon the pavements; women seated upon hand-barrows were wheeled along in triumph by men; youths with pasteboard noses and painted faces played pranks in the roadway. These were the harmless saturnalia which took place as the dawn was breaking. Before 3 o'clock a row of people had taken their seats on the projecting stones of the Law Courts branch of the Bank of England, many also were resting on the kerbstones, and by the obelisks at Ludgate-circus men and boys were lying at full length taking a few hours' sleep. The people, as usual, fraternized with the police. While the night lasted the question most frequently asked was, "Where can we get lodgings?" Shortly afterwards the universal question was, "Where can we get breakfast?" and outside the coffee shops the people gathered in little groups until the doors should be opened. Many cyclists threaded their way slowly through the streets, among them some ladies who received from the bystanders equivocal cheers. Before 4 o'clock some people had already taken their seats in the windows of the houses and offices, prepared with Anglo-Saxon patience to sit there for eight or ten hours. In Fleet-street and Ludgate-hill the predominating colours of the decorations were purple and gold. Square columns, surmounted by tripods bearing flowers, were erected at short intervals on either side of the street, and garlands of flowers were stretched from column to column. The obelisks in Ludgate-circus were draped in purple and gold cloth, with embossed shields and palms. In Ludgate-hill the columns were surmounted by relief banners of elephants, through whose trunks the line of garlands passed. These elephants, which were a striking feature of the decorations, were decked with purple and gold trappings, and were mounted on a base of Oriental design. The Griffin at Temple Bar was surrounded with flowers and evergreens, and the pedestal was adorned with palms, flags, and medallions. The newspaper offices in Fleet-street had made as brave a show of the decorative art as could be found anywhere upon the line of route.

◆

In 1896, Queen Victoria became the longest-reigning British monarch but, mindful of the vast sums lavished on her Golden Jubilee celebrations, asked that any commemoration wait until the 60th anniversary of her accession the following year.

By then, the Empire was at its zenith and the Diamond Jubilee festivities became a celebration of this. The six-mile long circuit of the procession through London was lined by soldiers from all the colonies and dominions in their striking dress uniforms.

Seventeen carriages carried the Royal Family and other dignitaries, with that of the Queen pulled by eight white horses. Hundreds of thousands of people watched the parade as the best vantage points were rented out for enormous amounts. A first-floor room with five windows on Fleet Street was let for 300 guineas (about £30,000 now).

The crowd broke spontaneously into renditions of 'God Save the Queen' as she passed, with the throng remaining in good voice well into the night; the pubs stayed open until half past two in the morning. It was, the Queen recorded in her diary, 'a never to be forgotten day'.

THE FUNERAL OF QUEEN VICTORIA

4 February 1901

Nothing could surpass in splendour the pageants which had been witnessed during the progress of the dead Queen from Osborne to Windsor. But it is here, where her life was mainly passed, and where her funeral scene has been performed, that the pathos of the stately ceremonial has been most keenly realized. There is no exaggeration in saying this; nor any underrating of the deep grief which is felt by all the subjects of the venerated lady who has been taken from those who revered her as mother, wife, and Queen. But Windsor seemed in some especial way to belong to Queen Victoria and she to it. It is but a few short weeks since she left the Castle on her customary visit to Osborne. Saturday saw her home-coming not to resume her sway in the ancient home of the English Sovereigns, but wept and mourned by innumerable multitudes. To-day her lifeless body will be laid beside that of her devoted husband, and the place that knew her shall know her no more. The personal affection which the Queen's beautiful character created in the hearts of all her people was intensified in the case of the inhabitants of the royal borough by the fact that she lived among them, was seen month after month and year after year as she took her daily drives, and was known by the countless acts of benevolence and kindness dictated by her generous and sympathetic nature.

The morning of Saturday broke chill and damp, and rain fell during the early hours, causing many an anxious moment to those who had counted on a continuance of the glorious weather which has been experienced throughout the greater part of the week. At Windsor, fortunately, the suspense was not of long duration. As the people flocked into the town the sun pierced through the clouds; and although at no time was the sky serene, the proceedings of the day passed off without excessive discomfort to the public and with complete success from the spectacular point of view. The later hours of Friday saw every hotel in the town crowded with visitors, and on Saturday morning the early trains brought thousands of people from London and all the neighbouring towns, so that by 9 o'clock the streets were congested to such an extent as to render vehicular traffic impossible. All along the line of route to be pursued by the procession the town presented an appearance which none who saw it are likely to forget. The signs of mourning were universal. The houses were shrouded in purple hangings. The people were clad in the profoundest black. The demeanour of the crowds was markedly subdued and respectful, and everything betokened the heartfelt sorrow which is felt by all classes of society.

◆

At the age of 81, Queen Victoria died on 22 January 1901 at Osborne House, her residence on the Isle of Wight. She had been ailing for some time, but her death nevertheless shocked the nation and threw the Court into confusion.

The Queen had not only presided since 1837 over a transformation of Britain's way of life and a vast expansion of its empire, she had also outlived everyone who could remember how to bury a sovereign. Moreover, she had decreed that she wanted no black worn at her funeral and that the ceremony be appropriate to a 'soldier's daughter'.

After much indecision and squabbling, her body was taken first to London and then to Windsor. The Queen was dressed in white and her staff laid keepsakes in her coffin, including those of Prince Albert and of John Brown, the ghillie who had become close to her.

The funeral, attended by the Kaiser and many other European relations, took the form of a military procession. It did not pass off without a hitch, notably when at Windsor the horses pulling the gun carriage became flustered and had to be replaced by sailors, but its solemnity and grandeur were fitting accompaniments to the end of a reign, and of an age.

THE EDWARDIAN ERA

THE GENERAL ELECTION OF 1906

10 February 1906

But it is about the future rather than the present that misgiving prevails; the flood-gates seem to many to have opened, and Heaven knows what water they may let through. The Labour members, and especially the Socialistic element, may increase until they swamp everything. They may; but, if the foregoing diagnosis of the election be at all correct, it provides some reasons for doubting that this will happen. The Labour party will continue, and probably increase, but not at an alarming rate. The special circumstances of the present occasion will not be repeated, and great changes are much more often followed by reaction than by still greater changes in the same direction. The Labour party will now be on trial itself and subject to the pendulum. Behind organized labour stand the far larger ranks of unorganized labour, which everybody seems to forget; and they do not care two straws for trade union leaders or Socialists. On the contrary, being strongly conservative and individualist, they dislike both. Let the Labour members support an ignominious surrender to a foreign foe, or fail to maintain British interests, or attack any cherished institution, and they will meet the same condemnation as any other members. As for the Socialist element, it cannot be denied that a good many members profess some measure of Socialism. Besides those who directly represent the Independent Labour party several trade union members are avowed Socialists. But what is Socialism? No term is more elastic; it may mean an economic theory, a political movement, a class warfare, a revolution by force, a pious aspiration, a sentimental impulse, or a form of hysteria. The Social Democratic formula, "Nationalization of all the means of production, distribution, and exchange," which is borrowed from Germany, may be adopted by trade union leaders as a pious aspiration, but it has no real hold on the rank and file. If realized it would destroy trade unions and co-operative societies alike; both are based on the principle of self-help, of which Socialism is the negation, as the earlier German Social Democrats clearly saw. They only turned to make use of the unions because they were afraid of them; and the alliance now is of the flimsiest, even with the so-called Social Democratic unions, while the other ones are in direct opposition. The Labour party here, consisting of labour men supported by labour money, is entirely different from the Social Democratic party in Germany, which consists of ordinary politicians.

It cannot be too clearly understood that the present election is a triumph of trade-unionism, not of Socialism. No Socialists unconnected with trade union organization got in; only those succeeded who joined hands through the Labour Representation Committee; but nineteen trade-unionists were elected apart from Socialism. Social democrats may be delighted with these results, but they are sanguine and emotional persons, or they would not be Socialists. They look forward to overrunning the country with carpet-baggers next general election, but their failure at the present most exceptional opportunity hardly augurs great success at the next. Labour, meaning the mass of the industrial population, cares nothing for Socialism. It wants what everybody wants, and that is as much as it can get; it wants a larger share of what is going, and will get it, no doubt, by degrees; but the economic and social revolution sounds nonsense in its ears.

◆

From 1895, Britain had a coalition government composed of the Conservatives and a breakaway faction of the Liberals, but its conduct of the Boer War and wrangling over trade tariffs made it increasingly unpopular. It was no surprise when the Liberal Party won a landslide victory in the 1906 election.

Yet, of more significance in the long term were the 29 seats won by – as it was named a few days later – The Labour Party. It had been founded six years before but this was the first General Election that it had contested properly. Keir Hardie was elected the leader of its MPs.

Perhaps surprisingly, *The Times* broadly welcomed their presence in the Commons, downplaying readers' fears of revolution. "They are serious men," it opined, "and intend to take their Parliamentary responsibilities seriously."

THE END OF THE DREYFUS AFFAIR

10 July 1906

Pending the definite verdict of the Court of Cassation, the highest tribunal in France, on the charge of treason brought against Captain Dreyfus, public opinion is expressing a sense of relief that this famous case is shortly to be placed beyond all reach of party strife and to be made a matter of history, where it is to be classed with such great historical trials as those of the diamond necklace or of Calas. General Mercier, is making, however, one last desperate effort. In a second letter published in to-day's papers he calls upon the Court to continue its inquiry by confronting him with the ex-President, M. Casimir-Perier, the ex-Prime Minister, M. Charles Dupuy, and M. Revoil, all of whom were present at the Elysée on the famous night when Count Munster was expected every moment bringing the result of his telegraphic negotiations with his Imperial master, upon which, according to General Mercier, depended the question of peace or war. General Mercier declares that it is of paramount importance to fix the date of this event. This pretension of General Mercier to dictate to the Court of Cassation, implying as it does his profound indifference to the results of that tribunal's inquiry in spite of the demonstration by that Court of Dreyfus's absolute innocence, has called forth the protests of a large number of Republican organs. On the sole point which interests the public – namely, whether the Court is to quash with reference back to a military tribunal or not, M. Cornely, writing in to-day's *Siecle*, repeats what the *Temps* said yesterday – that it is impossible to suppose the Court capable of sending Dreyfus before new Judges. The Court, he says, can rid France of a shame and a remorse.

"If it can, it is bound to do so. If it is bound to do so it will do so."

A duel with pistols, occasioned by the letter of Colonel Picquart impugning the value of General Gonse's word, was "fought" to-day by those two officers. The latter fired but missed his man. Colonel Picquart reserved his fire altogether.

———◆———

The Dreyfus affair, which was to scandalize and divide France for a decade, began in 1894 with the discovery by a French spy in the German embassy of a letter offering to betray military secrets. Suspicion fell on Alfred Dreyfus, an artillery officer, who was convicted of treason, publicly humiliated and imprisoned on Devil's Island, off the coast of South America. He maintained his sanity by teaching himself to read Shakespeare in English.

Two years later, the head of France's counter-espionage bureau, Georges Picquart, discovered that the traitor was in fact Major Ferdinand Esterhazy. Many in the French Establishment already had doubts about Dreyfus's guilt – his stockbroker had recognized Esterhazy's handwriting when the letter to the Germans had been printed by a newspaper – but the case exposed fault lines in society.

The Army had become a symbol of the nation and some thought it more important to protect the Army's standing than to admit it had erred. In addition, Dreyfus was Jewish and many of his detractors ardent Catholics. Esterhazy was acquitted at trial and, having been found guilty again at a second court-martial, and then pardoned, Dreyfus was only fully exonerated in 1906.

THE OLYMPIC MARATHON

25 July 1908

And at last he comes. A tired man, dazed, bewildered, hardly conscious, in red shorts and white vest, his hair white with dust, staggers on to the track. It is Dorando, the Italian. He looks about him, hardly knowing where he is. Just the knowledge that somehow, by some desperate resolve of determination, he must get round that 200 yards to the tape of the finish keeps him on his feet. Fifty yards, and it cannot even do that. He falls on the track, gets up, staggers on a few yards and falls again, and yet again; and then he reaches the last turn. The goal is in sight, though his closed eyes cannot see it. He is surrounded by officials almost, if not quite, supporting him, urging and cheering him on. If they were not there he would fall. He cannot run straight. And yet 50 yards from the end he suddenly bursts into a pathetic, almost a horrible, parody of a spurt, drops again ten yards from the tape, rises, staggers forward over those last terrible few yards, and has reached the goal.

But not with much to spare. Hayes, of the United States, follows him into the Stadium, a long way behind him in time, but comparatively a fresh and strong man, who can actually run, and is fast catching him up. Not quite, however, though he has run a magnificent race. So have several of the Americans. They come in, one after the other, Americans, Indians, Canadians, none of them happily, in the same dreadful state as Dorando, the Italian, but with a bewildered look on their faces, drawn and pale with exhaustion, as though wondering what they are doing. It seems as if the first Englishman will never come. And all the time the cheering goes on, every few minutes swelling round the course into a louder roar, as one by one they come. For if only one man can win, it is something even to finish in this Marathon race. Dorando was very ill after leaving the track, but it was afterwards announced that he was out of danger.

The Americans protested against Dorando's win on the ground that he received assistance, and the protest was finally sustained by the council. So that, after all, the unfortunate man had his agonized struggles to no purpose. Altogether the finish of the race was far from satisfactory. The rule about attendants not being allowed on the course was flagrantly broken. The position of those in authority was undoubtedly difficult. It seemed inhuman to leave Dorando to struggle on unaided, and inhuman to urge him to continue. It did not seem right that thousands of people should witness a man suffering as he did. It seemed hard that he should lose the victory after having reached the Stadium so long before anyone else. And yet, after all, the race was not to the Stadium entrance, but to the finish in front of the Royal box, and it is extremely doubtful whether, by his own unaided exertions, Dorando could ever have got so far. And the Americans, who enjoyed the signal honour of providing three out of the first five men home, are justly entitled to the special glory of claiming the actual winner.

———————◆———————

The Olympic Games of 1908 were held in London from April until October. The Marathon – the first run over what became the official distance of 26 miles 385 yards (42.2 kilometres) – was staged on an unusually hot day in July.

The field set off from Windsor Castle. By the time it neared the Olympic stadium at White City, in west London, the diminutive Italian Dorando Pietri had overtaken the favourites to open a substantial lead. However, exhausted and dehydrated, he first ran the wrong way around the track before falling to the ground.

Implored by the 75,000 spectators, officials helped him to his feet four times as he struggled to reach the finish line, eventually staggering across it 10 minutes later, a little ahead of the American, Johnny Hayes.

Pietri had allegedly been given a reviving injection of strychnine by his trainer during the race and after it lay near death in hospital for several hours; the newspapers recalled the fate of the first runner from Marathon, Pheidippides.

However, Pietri became a popular hero and was presented with a commemorative cup by Queen Alexandra. Pietri retired at 26 and invested the vast sum he had made from appearance money in a hotel, only for it to fail.

THE MESSINA EARTHQUAKE

30 December 1908

The panic of the inhabitants in Calabria is indescribable, but quite justifiable, Palmi and Bagnara being practically destroyed, while in the region around Monteleone, which is most affected, the dead may be counted by thousands. People abandoned their homes by thousands and remained in the torrential rain, half-naked, not daring to return into their tottering dwellings, and filling the air with their lamentations, prayers, and, in many cases, imprecations. At some places the people had the courage to enter the half-wrecked churches and take the statues of the Saints, which they carried in procession, to the open country, in a downpour of rain, invoking the mercy of God. In the mountainous regions of the interior, the population have taken refuge in grottoes, caves, and subterranean cavities, which are safe against earthquake, and are there living in common, peasants, priests, soldiers, and gentlefolk, all sleeping together, on the ground, with a fire in the centre for heat.

Refugees from Messina who are arriving at Catania and Palermo say that yesterday morning, before the sun had risen, the town was almost uprooted, and those who were not killed, descended to find the streets blocked by fallen houses. Everywhere were streams of injured people, half-mad with excitement and fear, most of them in scanty night attire, shivering in the torrential rain, while the lower portion of the town was inundated by a huge wave, the water reaching the hips of the fugitives.

A CAPTAIN'S NARRATIVE.
PALERMO, DEC. 29.*

The captain of the Italian steamer Washington, which went to Messina yesterday morning, says that at 20 minutes past 5, when near the Straits, the ship quivered as though she had lost her screw. The captain thought that his ship had run aground. At the same time a thick fog enveloped the vessel, blotting out the Messina lighthouse and the Calabrian coast. Between 5.25 and 6.45 five separate shocks were felt. At a quarter past 8 a barque approached the steamer and the men shouted out that disaster had overwhelmed the town and appealed for help. At the entrance of the Straits the water was strewn with wreckage, broken furniture, and debris of all descriptions. Everywhere there were appalling scenes of destruction. The steamer was met by sailing vessels all along the coast appealing for help. Near Ganzirri a delegate of the Mayor put out and stated that at that place there were 1,000 killed and 500 injured.

Railway communication between Catania and Messina has been re-established. A train bringing refugees and injured from Messina to Catania has arrived. The refugees, who are almost mad with terror, assert that the Hotel Trinacria with its staff and 90 visitors has been destroyed, as well as the Town-hall, the Bourse, the post and telegraph office, and the barracks. The report of terrible damage having been done by the movement of the sea is confirmed. A gigantic wave overwhelmed Messina.

Troops are leaving here for Messina with doctors and medical appliances. The doctors here have formed a relief committee which will take upon itself the task of organizing a hospital ship to succour the victims.

Heartrending scenes took place on the departure of the steamer Regina Margherita for Messina this morning. The vessel is crowded with weeping men and women going to Messina to search for relatives and friends.

◆

The earthquake at Messina was the most devastating natural disaster to have occurred in Europe, rivalled only by that at Lisbon in 1755. It struck in the early morning of 28 December 1908, while most people were still in their beds, and largely destroyed the Sicilian port of Messina. At least

75,000 people, half of its population, were killed by falling masonry as they slept or tried to flee. Thousands of others lay trapped in the debris.

Ten minutes later, the city of Reggio Calabria on the other side of the strait was submerged by 40-feet (12-metre) high waves from a tsunami. As many as 25,000 victims perished there and in towns along the neighbouring coastline, including 1,800 prisoners in Reggio's gaol.

The catastrophe swept away railway tracks and telegraph lines, hampering efforts at rescue and the government was forced to impose martial law to prevent looting. Britain, which sent four warships to help, was among the countries which took part in the relief effort. Both cities were eventually rebuilt in modern materials.

LOUIS BLÉRIOT FLIES
THE CHANNEL

26 July 1909

M. Bleriot, still forced to use crutches, limped slowly behind his tiny bird-like craft until it was well out in the open, when he took his seat, and at 4.10 a.m. gave instructions for the engine to be started. The propeller in front of the aviator revolved with a deep moaning sound, the firing seemed to be excellent, and at 4.15 the order was given to let go the chassis and rear plane, by which five men were holding the machine down to the ground. After running perhaps 150 yards the two front wheels of the chassis left the earth, followed in a moment by the rear wheel, and then a trial began which convinced all who witnessed it of the aviator's skill, the crowd of villagers who had assembled by the hundred rushing to and fro, shouting excitedly and clapping their hands.

M. Bleriot flew first towards Sangatte in a westerly direction parallel to the coast. He then circled inland, and passing near the old Castle completed a circuit of about 1½ miles. Continuing, he made a larger sweep the second time, which must have been nearly 2 miles in length, and on the completion of this he brought the machine gently to the ground, without the slightest shock or bump, approximately 250 yards from the spot where he had started. The duration of this flight was exactly six minutes, and I judged his average height to be 40 feet above the ground. He then declared his intention of starting in a few moments in a westerly direction as before, circling to the right, and making the best of his way for the English coast, hoping to land anywhere round about Dover, without tying himself to any definite spot. The lightest breeze imaginable could now be felt from the south-west, the course to Dover being north-west by west.

At 4.41 (French time) the engine was again started. The monoplane rose almost immediately, flew half a mile towards Sangatte, then turned to the right and, passing over the sand-hills, crossed the coast line exactly at 4.42, just a hundred yards from where I had taken up the highest position obtainable. The destroyer Escopette (which with two torpedo-boats had been lying off Baraques for an hour or more) was signalled to by a sailor standing beside me, and shaped a course for Dover, but the aeroplane had passed her and had gone rather to the left before the war vessel could gather speed. Through my telescope I was able to watch the tiny craft long after she passed from the view of those around me, and after five minutes I noticed that she made a sudden turn to the left, and seemed to proceed for nearly a mile on a south-west course; after this she again headed for Dover, the height above the sea being, I imagine, 250 feet at most. For 11 minutes I kept her in view, till at last she faded away in the distant misty atmosphere. The destroyer meanwhile was vomiting forth a black column of smoke some three miles to the northward, apparently with no likelihood of overtaking the aviator if he could proceed without mishap to the English shore.

A general stampede was now made for motor-cars, cabs, and bicycles waiting in the road, in order to hurry to the Channel Tunnel works beyond Sangatte, where the wireless telegraphy apparatus was sure to be the first medium for news from England as to the aviator's progress.

At 5.50 the first wireless message from Dover was received, but it was merely a rumour to the effect that an aeroplane had been sighted. Ten minutes later, however, a second message arrived, stating officially that M. Bleriot had descended in a meadow near Dover Castle, and the announcement was greeted with enthusiastic cheers.

———◆———

The Frenchman Louis Blériot, then 37, had invested the money he had made from designing the first headlamps for cars into his passion for aviation. This was still in its earliest years and it was Blériot who built the first monoplane and devised the use of a joystick and pedals to control the flight of an aircraft.

The Daily Mail had offered a £1,000 prize to the first pilot to cross the Channel, but most people – including the Wright Brothers – considered the venture impossible or too risky. Nevertheless, a crowd of 10,000 gathered to watch Blériot take off near the workings of the late-nineteenth century project to dig a Channel Tunnel.

Blériot, limping from burns suffered on a previous flight, took 36 minutes to fly the 22 miles (35 kilometres) to Dover at an average speed of 45 mph. He briefly lost sight of the Kent coast when the visibility dipped but otherwise the journey was uneventful.

Subsequently, he set up a business manufacturing aircraft, including during the First World War. In 1927, Blériot greeted Charles Lindbergh when the American touched down on French soil after becoming the first person to fly solo across the Atlantic. (See Lindbergh, page 138.)

THE ARREST OF DR CRIPPEN

1 August 1910

I have just returned from the steamship Montrose and witnessed the drama that was enacted on her deck.

Inspector Dew, of Scotland Yard, with Chief Constable McCarthy and ex-Chief Constable Denis, of the Canadian Provincial Police – all three disguised as pilots with blue suits and white caps – went off to the Montrose at 8.30 a.m. in a lifeboat rowed by four sailors. "Dr." Crippen was smoking and promenading the deck with Miss Le Neve and Dr. Stuart, the ship's surgeon. He asked the doctor why so many pilots should come, to which Dr. Stuart replied – "They are probably returning to their homes, being out of turn." The supposed pilots went on board and walked along until they passed the spot where Crippen and Miss Le Neve were standing with Dr. Stuart. Then as Inspector Dew got a good, quick look at Crippen and the girl, he gave the preconcerted signal, and the constables made the arrest and took the couple down to separate state-rooms, where they are now confined.

Only 15 minutes elapsed from the time the constables went on board until the arrests were effected. Crippen turned the colour of death, and his voice gurgled some unintelligible sound as he was hurried below. Miss Le Neve became hysterical and fainted.

The signal agreed upon was then blown by the Montrose's whistle for the pilot steam tender Eureka to come alongside to permit the Press representatives and Press photographers to board the Montrose and proceed in her to Quebec, where she will arrive about 9 o'clock to-night. This had been arranged between Inspector Dew and the Press for fear that the appearance of a large number of people might alarm the fugitives and that Crippen might defeat the law by committing suicide. The Eureka stayed only a few minutes alongside the Montrose, and then returned to Father Point wharf with this despatch.

———◆———

The discovery of human remains beneath the basement of the London home of the homeopath Dr Hawley Crippen triggered a manhunt that mesmerized newspaper readers in July 1910, even as the object of the search remained oblivious to the net closing on him.

Crippen's wife Cora had vanished in January, but his explanations apparently satisfied the police. He panicked, however, and with his mistress Ethel Le Neve disguised as a boy took ship for Canada. The captain recognized the fugitive and, in a decisive use of new technology, transmitted a message by wireless telegraphy alerting the authorities in Britain.

His progress tracked by journalists, Chief Inspector Walter Dew boarded a faster liner and was waiting when Crippen's ship entered the St Lawrence River. Crippen's arrest seemed to signal that criminals could no longer flee beyond the reach of the police. He was brought back to London, tried at the Old Bailey and hanged for his wife's murder.

THE LAST EMPEROR OF CHINA

8 February 1912

The terms for the treatment of the Manchus after abdication, agreed to in Peking by the Empress-Dowager and Princes and the Cabinet, and telegraphed to Nanking for the approval of the Republican Cabinet, have been returned with certain modifications, and were to-day communicated to the Palace for final approval. The modifications are so reasonable and the terms so liberal that agreement on this question is now assured.

The terms, as modified, provide specially for the insertion of the words "after his abdication" wherever reference is made in the articles to the Emperor, who is to be known as the Manchu Emperor. The Emperor is to reside first in the Forbidden City and eventually in the Summer Palace, and is to be accorded honours such as are given to a foreign Sovereign visiting China – that is, the Chinese, after his abdication, not being his subjects, will show him due courtesy, not fealty and obedience.

After his abdication, the Manchu Emperor will receive an annual grant of $4,000,000, not taels [Chinese currency]. The explanation ingeniously given is that taels will be abolished when the currency is reformed, while special expenses for ceremonial occasions will be granted by a vote of Parliament. Imperial bodyguards will be allowed, but must be provided and selected by the Republic. Ancestral sacrifices shall continue as for the Ming Emperors. The Republic shall bear the expense of completing the mausoleum of the Emperor Kwang Hsu. The present Palace staffs shall be retained, and all private property shall be respected, whether belonging to the Emperor or to the Princes – Manchu, Tibetan, or Mongol.

Princes and hereditary nobles shall continue as before, and the order of succession shall be maintained. The seal of the Manchu Emperor shall continue to be affixed to all Manchu patents of nobility. The Imperial clan shall enjoy identical privileges with the remainder of the population, and shall in future be exempt from compulsory military service. Manchus, Mongols, Mahomedans, and Tibetans shall be treated on an equality with Chinese in all matters, including residence, occupation, religious toleration, and retention of hereditary titles.

Regarding the Manchu pensions, the agreement provides that "arrangements shall be made for devising a livelihood for the Manchu Bannermen, but pending the completion of these arrangements the pensions shall continue as before." This provision is intended to mean that arrangements will be made by the new Parliament.

The foregoing terms are to be communicated by the representatives of both parties to the foreign Legations in Peking.

The agreement contains no reference to the eunuchs.

All the above terms are well understood by all the classes interested. In this respect the delay has been advantageous. Everybody wants peace and an early settlement.

◆

In 1911, a revolution led by Sun-Yat Sen turned China into a republic after two millennia of imperial government, overthrowing the Manchu Qing dynasty that had ruled the majority Han Chinese since 1644. Pu Yi, as the last Emperor became known, was then six.

He had been chosen to succeed his uncle four years earlier and after his enforced abdication was permitted to continue living in the Forbidden City in Beijing with his eunuchs and other servants. Despite the best efforts of his tutor, the Scot Reginald Johnston, he grew up spoiled and erratic, with a taste for Western consumerism.

By the mid-1920s, China was riven by struggles between warlords. Pu Yi fell under the influence of the Japanese and, when they occupied Manchuria, became their puppet emperor. Captured by the Russians at the end of the war, he then spent 10 years in prison in China. He survived the Cultural Revolution, working as a gardener until his death in 1967.

THE TITANIC SINKS

16 April 1912

An ocean disaster, unprecedented in history, has happened in the Atlantic. The White Star liner Titanic on her maiden voyage, carrying nearly 2,400 people, has been lost near Cape Race, and according to the latest messages there is grave reason to fear that less than 700 of the passengers and crew have been saved.

Early yesterday evening the messages gave no indication of a catastrophe of such terrible magnitude, but later they became more and more serious.

As will be seen below, there is much that is conflicting in them, but the news of brighter import – of the possibility of more lives being saved by the vessels which hurried to the rescue – becomes more slender with each succeeding message.

The White Star liner Titanic (46,382 tons), which left Southampton on Wednesday on her maiden voyage to New York, came into collision with an iceberg at a point about 41.46 North and 50.14 West off the North American coast at 10.25 on Sunday night (American time). The vessel was badly damaged and wireless messages were sent out for help. A number of other liners in the neighbourhood hastened to her assistance, but she sank yesterday morning. The number on board the Titanic when she left Queenstown on her voyage, including the Cherbourg passengers, was:–

First Class	350
Second Class..................	305
Steerage......................	800
Crew...........................	903
Total	2,358

She had also on board 3,418 sacks of mails. The passengers included Colonel and Mrs. J.J. Astor, Major A.W. Butt, President Taft's aide-de-camp, Mr. B. Guggenheim, of the well-known banking firm, Mr. C.M. Hays, President of the Grand Trunk Railway, Mr. Bruce Ismay, chairman of the White Star Line, Lady Rothes, Mr. W.T. Stead, Mr. Clarence Moore, Mr. Isidor Straus, Mr. George D. Widener, Mr. Thomas Andrews, jun., of Belfast, one of the managing directors of Messrs. Harland and Wolff, the builders of the Titanic, and Mr. Christopher Head, a former Mayor of Chelsea, director of Henry Head and Co. (Limited), insurance brokers and underwriters.

NEW YORK, APRIL 15.
The Titanic sank at 2.20 this morning. No lives were lost. – Reuter.

NEW YORK, April 15, 8.15 p.m.
It was stated officially at the White Star offices this evening that probably a number of lives had been lost in the Titanic disaster, but that no definite estimate could be made until it was known positively whether the Parisian and Virginian had any rescued passengers on board. – Reuter.

NEW YORK, APRIL 15, 8.20 P.M
The following statement has been given out by the White Star officials: "Captain Haddock, of the Olympic, sends a wireless message that the Titanic sank at 2.20 a.m. on Monday after all the passengers and crew had been lowered into lifeboats and transferred to the Virginian. The steamer Carpathia, with several hundred passengers from the Titanic, is now on her way to New York." – Reuter.

NEW YORK, APRIL 15, 8.40 P.M
The White Star officials now admit that many lives have been lost. – Reuter.

NEW YORK, APRIL 15, 8.45 P.M.
The following despatch has been received here from Cape Race: "The steamer Olympic reports that the steamer Carpathia reached the Titanic's position at daybreak, but found boats and wreckage only. She reported that the Titanic foundered about 2.20 a.m. in lat. 41deg. 16min., long. 50deg. 14min."

The message adds: "All the Titanic's boats are accounted for. About 675 souls have been saved of the crew and passengers. The latter are nearly all women and children."

———◆———

'The disaster that has overtaken the *Titanic*,' observed *The Times* in the wake of her sinking, 'is a forcible reminder of the existence of natural forces which from time to time upset all our calculations and baffle our precautions'.

Titanic was the embodiment of Britain at the peak of its industrial might. Exactly 200 years before, the first steam engine had been built in the Black Country. In the year that she sank, British textile factories reached their maximum output of 8 billion yards of cloth.

No ship afloat was heavier or, at 882 feet (269 metres), longer. Nor did any have such concern not just for luxury but also for safety. Her new Marconi radio-telegraph equipment allowed *Titanic* to send distress calls by Morse code after striking the iceberg, while the number of lifeboats she carried – though only sufficient for half those aboard – was significantly greater than that specified by law.

Even so, more than 1,500 people perished because no-one wanted to believe that *Titanic* might sink. Observers, wrote her historian Walter Lord, mistook the appearance of safety for safety itself. To some of them at least, *Titanic*'s fate must have seemed a portent for Britain as well.

DISASTER AT THE SOUTH POLE

11 February 1913

News reached London last night that Captain Scott and four of his comrades in the expedition which set out for the Antarctic on board the Terra Nova in 1910 have lost their lives. The circumstances in which disaster has befallen the little party of British explorers will serve to intensify the national concern; for the same telegram from Christchurch, New Zealand, which tells of their fate announces also that they had reached the South Pole on January 18 of last year and were returning in triumph to the base. According to the message which we print in another column, signed by Commander Evans, who was second in command of the expedition, the members of the party were but 155 miles from the base in March when they were overtaken by a blizzard, and Captain Scott, Dr. E.A. Wilson, the surgeon, and Lieutenant Bowers died from exposure. Captain Oates had met a similar fate on March 17 – twelve days before the others perished – and Petty Officer Evans had died exactly a month earlier.

The search party who discovered the bodies found also a message from the leader of the expedition in which he gives the causes of the disaster and says:

I do not regret this journey, which has shown that Englishmen can endure hardship, help one another, and meet death with as great a fortitude as ever in the past. We took risks – we know we took them. Things have come out against us, and therefore we have no cause for complaint, but bow to the will of Providence, determined still to do our best to the last.

CAPTAIN SCOTT'S PROGRAMME.

The British Antarctic Expedition in the Terra Nova reached its base of operations on the edge of the great ice barrier in December, 1910. Operations were at once begun to carry out the programme which Captain Scott had laid down. When the party had been landed at McMurdo Sound the ship went eastwards along the face of the ice barrier for some 400 miles in order to land a party, if possible, on King Edward VII Land; with a view to the exploration of that side of the Antarctic, which is practically unknown. Unfortunately the party were unable to make a landing, and on their return Commander Evans came across the Fram in Balloon Bay, and so ascertained for the first time the presence and position of Captain Amundsen's expedition. The news was taken to Captain Scott, who was naturally affected by the presence of his rival so near his own base of operations. But that did not influence in the least his programme, which he carried out to the letter, to the undoing of himself and the four brave men who accompanied him.

The other work which was included in the comprehensive plan of operation was all started before Captain Scott and his party left for the South. The party which was to have landed at King Edward VII Land proceeded to Cape Adaire, whence exploration was to be carried on along the coast on the sea ice. At the base of the expedition arrangements were made for an extensive scheme of scientific operations, which was carried out with exceptional completeness.

THE START FOR THE POLE.

The party under Captain Scott left Hut Point on November 2, 1911, and on December 10 reached the Beardmore Glacier, one of the most formidable obstacles to the progress of a Polar party on that side of the Great Barrier. The party succeeded in overcoming all obstacles, and on December 21 they were on the plateau, 8,600 feet above sea level. Here they sent back their dogs, and Captain Scott and his companions dragged their own sledges all the way to the Pole. The last supporting party left Captain Scott and his companions in excellent health and spirits on January 4, 1912, in 87.35 South, 150 miles from the Pole. The Pole was reached, according to the information which has been received, in 14 days, which was very good travelling in the circumstances. It was on their return from this brilliant exploit that disaster overtook the party.

———◆———

Captain Robert Scott, a naval officer, had sprung to fame following his first Antarctic expedition of 1901–04, which had discovered the vast plateau that contains the site of the South Pole itself.

When he set off to return in 1910, it was with the aim of reaching the Pole for Britain first, ahead of a Norwegian attempt led by Roald Amundsen. But when Scott gained his goal on 29 January 1912, he found his rival had beaten him by a month.

Scott and the four others with him set off again on foot for their base, 862 miles (1387 kilometres) away. Dogs failed to meet them as he had ordered, and two of the team had died by the time that the remaining three, including Scott, perished in their tent during a blizzard at the end of March 1912. They were 12 miles from the next food depot.

Their bodies were not retrieved until November. As with the *Titanic*, Scott's death seemed to a generation to presage wider disaster and comfort was sought in the stoic manner of his sacrifice. His reputation was subsequently savaged by historians writing when new technology had made such journeys seem futile, but more recently his competence has been re-established.

THE GREAT WAR

ARCHDUKE FRANZ FERDINAND ASSASSINATED IN SARAJEVO

29 June 1914

The Austro-Hungarian Heir-Presumptive, the Archduke Francis Ferdinand, and his wife, the Duchess of Hohenberg, were assassinated yesterday morning at Serajevo, the capital of Bosnia. The actual assassin is described as a high school student, who fired bullets at his victims with fatal effect from an automatic pistol as they were returning from a reception at the Town Hall.

The outrage was evidently the fruit of a carefully-laid plot. On their way to the Town Hall, the Archduke and his Consort had narrowly escaped death. An individual, described as a compositor from Trebinje, a garrison town in the extreme south of Herzegovina, had thrown a bomb at their motor-car. Few details of this first outrage have been received. It is stated that the Archduke warded off the bomb with his arm, and that it exploded behind the car, injuring the occupants of the second carriage.

The author of the second outrage is stated to be a native of Grahovo, in Bosnia. No information as to his race or creed is yet forthcoming. It is presumed that he belongs to the Serb or Orthodox section of the Bosnian population.

Both criminals were immediately arrested, and were with difficulty saved from being lynched.

While this tragedy was being enacted in the Bosnian capital, the aged Emperor Francis Joseph was on his way from Vienna to his summer residence at Ischl. He had an enthusiastic send-off from his subjects in Vienna and an even more enthusiastic reception on reaching Ischl.

SCENE OF THE MURDER.
(FROM OUR SPECIAL CORRESPONDENT.)
SERAJEVO, JUNE 28, 9.30 p.M.

To-day at 9.50 a.m. the Imperial train conveying the Archduke Francis Ferdinand and his Consort arrived here from Hidzhe. After inspecting the troops on the Filipovitch parade ground the august visitors drove in a motor-car along the station road and the Appel Quay to the Town Hall.

The first attempt, when the bomb was thrown, took place at 10.15, as the car was driving along the Appel Quay, just before reaching the Chumuria Bridge. An Aide-de-Camp seated in one of the motor-cars which followed the Archduke's car was wounded in the neck by fragments of the bomb and several passers-by also received light injuries.

The perpetrator was arrested. He is a young printer, 20 years of age, Nedjeliko Cabrinovitch by name, and a native of Herzegovina, belonging to the Serb-Orthodox faith.

When the motor-car conveying the Archduke and his Consort reached the Town Hall, his Imperial Highness said to the Mayor:

"What is the good of your speeches? I come to Serajevo on a visit, and I get bombs thrown at me. It is outrageous."

When the procession drove back from the Town Hall the second attempt was made. At 10.40, as the Heir-Apparent's motor-car reached the corner of the Appel Quay and of the Franz-Josefsgasse, another bomb was thrown at the car by Gavrilo Prinzip, a Bosniak High school student, also belonging to the Serb-Orthodox faith. This bomb did not explode.

Thereupon the assassin fired three shots from a pistol. The first shot hit the Archduke in the neck, the second hit him in the leg, and the third hit the Duchess of Hohenberg in the lower part of the body.

General Potiorek, chief of the Administration, who was sitting in the Archduke's motor-car, escaped injury. The perpetrator was seized by the crowd and severely mauled.

The Archduke and the Duchess of Hohenberg were rapidly conveyed to General Potiorek's official residence. Both were past all human aid and received the last Sacrament. The Archduke expired a few minutes after his Consort.

———◆———

Franz Ferdinand, who had sat next to Queen Victoria at dinner on the eve of her Diamond Jubilee, was the nephew and heir of the elderly Emperor Franz Joseph, ruler of Austria-Hungary, whose only son had committed suicide in 1889 at his hunting lodge, Mayerling.

Although Franz Ferdinand had so deeply offended the Emperor by his marriage to an obscure Czech aristocrat, Sophie Chotek, that their children were barred from the throne, he was still being groomed to succeed.

Sarajevo was the couple's last stop on a visit to the former Ottoman territories of Bosnia-Herzegovina, which the Austrians had recently annexed, to the ire of Serbia, which had designs on them. There had been many warnings that the tour should be postponed.

The assassin, Gavrilo Princip, was a 19-year-old student who belonged to a nationalist movement with ties to the Serbian army. He was only presented with the chance to shoot Franz Ferdinand when the car carrying the Archduke and the Duchess took a wrong turning and slowed down. Princip was too young to be executed but died in prison of tuberculosis in 1918. By then, the consequences of his actions had led to the deaths of millions of others.

WAR DECLARED

5 August 1914

The following statement was issued from the Foreign Office at 12.15 this morning:–

Owing to the summary rejection by the German Government of the request made by his Majesty's Government for assurances that the neutrality of Belgium will be respected, his Majesty's Ambassador at Berlin has received his passports and his Majesty's Government have declared to the German Government that a state of war exists between Great Britain and Germany as from 11 p.m. on August 4.

Yesterday morning the British Government dispatched an Ultimatum to Germany.

It required that Germany should give an unequivocal assurance that she would respect the neutral territory of Belgium, guaranteed by her under the Treaty of 1839 – a guarantee endorsed in writing in 1870.

It also intimated that, failing this assurance, Great Britain would declare war on Germany at midnight.

The steps by which the Prime Minister and the Government of Great Britain approached the moment of decision were as dignified as they were inexorable.

Following upon Sir Edward Grey's statement in the House of Commons on Monday, the Government on Tuesday morning telegraphed to the British Ambassador at Berlin, protesting against the violation of Belgian neutrality by Germany and asking for an immediate reply.

The reply came quickly. On the same morning the German Government telegraphed to the German Ambassador in London, instructing him to repeat most positively "the formal assurance that, even in the case of an armed conflict with Belgium, Germany will not under any pretence whatever annex Belgian territory."

The German Ambassador was also instructed to inform Sir Edward Grey that Germany had disregarded Belgian neutrality in order to "prevent what means to her a question of life and death, the French advance through Belgium."

Thereupon followed the British ultimatum.

In the House of Commons yesterday the Prime Minister, with admirable dignity and conciseness, set before the nation the action which the Government had thus found it necessary to take in vindication of British honour.

Then, proceeding to the Bar of the House, he handed to the Speaker a Proclamation by the King, providing for complete mobilization of the Army.

Vice-Admiral Sir John Jellicoe has assumed command of the Home Fleets, with the acting rank of Admiral.

Two British Ministers, Lord Morley and Mr. John Burns, finding themselves unable to approve of the action taken by the Government, have resigned from the Cabinet.

Admiral Mahan, the American naval expert, in an interview published in New York on Monday, expressed the opinion that "Great Britain must at once throw her preponderating Fleet against Germany, for one chief purpose – that of maintaining her own position as a world Power."

German troops have entered Belgian territory. On the German frontier more minor incidents between French and German troops have taken place. Near Belfort, German detachments are making requisition upon the inhabitants of French territory.

The Turkish Government is reported to be mobilizing its forces.

The King has issued a Proclamation to the Dominions, thanking them for their loyalty and their proffered help, and expressing his "confident belief that in this time of trial my Empire will stand united, calm, resolute, trusting in God."

◆

The technical reason for Britain's declaration of war on Germany was the latter's violation of Belgian neutrality, which it had invaded to get around France's defences. Herbert Asquith, the Prime Minister, took the decision reluctantly as his Liberal Party had a strong tradition of pacifism. Yet, in reality, conflict between the great powers of Europe had long been anticipated and was made inevitable by a complex interweaving of international alliances and national ambition.

The assassination of the Archduke gave Austria a pretext to attack Serbia, which lay under the pan-Slavic protection of Russia. Vienna was egged on by its neighbour Berlin, the Germans long having planned to fight Russia and France simultaneously. Those two nations were allied with Britain, whose naval and thus imperial supremacy the Kaiser burned to challenge.

The United States would remain aloof until 1917 but other nations gradually became involved, including Japan and Italy, which joined the Allies, and the Ottoman Empire, which sided with the Central Powers. The war, the outbreak of which had been reported in such an understated fashion, spread around the world through European colonies until it became truly global.

THE EASTER RISING

27 April 1916

The Prime Minister read a telegram from Dublin stating that Liberty Hall and Stephen's Green had been occupied by British troops and that martial law had been proclaimed in the city and the county. Drastic action to suppress the rising and to arrest the culprits was being taken. Only three minor cases of disturbance had been reported outside Dublin. Steps were being taken to give information to our friends abroad as to the full significance of this most recent German campaign. Mr. Asquith added that the associations concerned in the rising were being proclaimed illegal associations. He hoped that English journalists would be allowed to accompany the American journalists who, according to Mr. Ashley, were going to Ireland to-night. It was not true that the rebels had a considerable number of machine-guns. The Lord Lieutenant had been in Dublin throughout the disturbances. Whilst he was speaking Mr. Asquith was handed another telegram, and he stated that it announced the situation in Dublin to be satisfactory and that the Nationalist Volunteers at Drogheda had turned out under arms to assist the Government.

After informing the House that Mr. Long would introduce a new Military Service Bill to-morrow and that the House would afterwards adjourn until Tuesday, Mr. Asquith observed the presence of strangers, and thereupon strangers were ordered to withdraw.

LORD LANSDOWNE'S DETAILS.

At the instance of Lord Midleton, who charged the Irish Government with having tolerated the preparations for rebellion and ignored all kinds of warnings, a similar statement to the Prime Minister's was made in the House of Lords by Lord Lansdowne, with, however, the addition of certain details. He said that on Monday the rebels made a half-hearted attack on Dublin Castle, which was not pressed through; that they "held up" troops on their way from barracks and fired on them from the windows of houses, and that in addition to the Post Office, the City Hall, the Law Courts, Westland-row Station, and, he thought, Broadstone Station were occupied by Sinn Feiners. The Dublin garrison had had reinforcements from Belfast and England and the Sinn Feiners had been driven out of Stephen's Green with a certain number of casualties. On Tuesday morning they were still occupying the buildings mentioned, but by the evening the military had succeeded in protecting the line from King's Bridge Station, via Trinity College, to the Customs House and the North Wall. By midday yesterday it was learned that Liberty Hall, the headquarters of the Citizen Army and formerly of Mr. Larkin, had been wholly or partially destroyed and occupied by the military.

LORD LANSDOWNE added that the latest details showed that there was a cordon of troops round the centre of the town on the north bank of the river, that two more battalions were to arrive in Dublin yesterday afternoon from England, and that there had been a small rising at Ardee, in County Louth, and a rather more serious one at Swords and Lusk, near Dublin. The casualties he put at 19 killed and 27 wounded.

SIR ROGER CASEMENT`S CAPTURE.

Lord Lansdowne volunteered an interesting and quite fresh account of the attempted German landing on the west coast of Ireland. A German vessel disguised as a Dutch trading vessel, and a German submarine, brought the invaders. From the submarine there landed in a collapsible boat three individuals, of whom two (one Sir Roger Casement) were made prisoners. The disguised German ship was stopped by one of his Majesty's ships, and while she was being taken into Queenstown Harbour, no prize crew having been put on board, she exhibited the German flag and sank herself.

◆

Ireland, which had been under English control for centuries, was formally united with Great Britain in 1800 and thereafter governed from Westminster. Opposition to this arrangement grew throughout the nineteenth century, with calls for Home Rule – greater autonomy – leading to this being enacted in 1914, only for it to be suspended for the war's duration.

At Easter 1916, about 1,500 republicans (not in fact members of Sinn Fein, despite British accusations) mounted an uprising in Dublin and seized sites such as the General Post Office. Sir Roger Casement, an Irish-born diplomat honoured for his work investigating abuses of human rights in the Congo, organized a shipment of arms from Germany for the rebels, only for this to be intercepted and he arrested.

The revolt was put down within a week. The city centre had been much damaged and 485 people killed, half of them civilians. The Rising failed to attract wider support until the execution of 15 of its leaders by the British, and the internment of thousands more suspects, radicalized public opinion. Further violence and civil war would lead by 1922 to the partition of Ireland and the establishment of the Irish Free State, precursor of the modern Republic.

THE FIRST DAY OF THE SOMME

3 July 1916

FROM OUR MILITARY CORRESPONDENT.
PARIS, JULY 2.

I returned here from Italy on Saturday at the exact hour when the Allied offensive on the Somme began and had the pleasure of communicating the first news of the Anglo-French success to General Belayeff, Chief of the Russian General Staff, who is here on a short visit, while congratulating him upon the victories of the Russian Armies. He spoke in the highest terms of the British Armies, with whose progress he has been kept well informed by the Russian military missions abroad.

The success of the preliminary attacks of the Allies on both sides of the Somme has caused the liveliest satisfaction here, but every one recognizes that the enemy is strong, and his defences powerful and that his resistance is sure to be desperate. The attack has been impatiently awaited in France, and there is no harm in saying now that we were ready to begin long ago, and that the date selected for the first infantry attack was fixed by General Joffre, who had to take all the circumstances into account. The cooperation of the Anglo-French Allies has been shown to be perfect, while our Belgian friends in the north have played a useful part by taking over more of the line and by hammering the Germans with their guns during the preliminary bombardment.

The theatre selected for the Anglo-French effort is more favourable than that to which Lord French was necessarily restricted last year. It is an agricultural, not a mining, district, and there are none of those extensive villages and agglomerations, such as are grouped round the mining centres further north, which afforded the Germans such useful points of support. In Picardy, on the Somme, the ground is open and only slightly undulating. The villages are small and contain only a few hundred inhabitants in ordinary times, while there is a better field of fire for our guns and more scope for employing superior forces. There is a fair field and no favour, and here we have elected to fight out our quarrel with the Germans and to give them as much battle as they want.

The tactics hitherto followed have been those which I ventured to recommend in an article on the Western Front published in *The Times* on January 20. It is a methodical attack which makes full use of modern artillery and does not impose upon the infantry a number of distant objectives until each position won has been consolidated and secured and the guns made ready to support the next advance. In these tactics the artillery plays a leading role, and the infantry suffers less loss than in the old style attacks, but the task of the infantry is still a heavy one, and we must expect a good many set-backs before we gain our ends.

◆

By July 1916, the fighting on the Western Front had become a grim, largely unavailing slog for territory. In a bid to end the stalemate, the British commander, Sir Douglas Haig, planned a massive offensive with the French, though by the time it began the latter were preoccupied with the German effort to take Verdun.

Conscious of the need to limit losses, artillery pounded the German trenches for a week before the attack. More shells were fired than in the whole of the first year of the war and the reports could be heard in London.

Yet, when on 1 July the infantry – many of them 'Pals' units with no experience of battle – began to advance, they found the barbed wire often uncut and enemy defences intact. In gaining less than a mile of ground, some 20,000 men were killed and twice as many wounded – the worst casualties ever suffered by the British Army in a single day.

For much of the war, strict censorship and willing collusion by the newspapers with the government meant that the public at home had little idea of the true situation in Flanders. Even so, the scale of the toll was becoming evident.

THE RUSSIAN REVOLUTION

16 March 1917

After a brief revolution in Petrograd, born of the united forces of the Duma and of the Army, the Emperor Nicholas II has abdicated. His younger brother, the Grand Duke Michael, second son of the Emperor Alexander III, has been appointed Regent.

The representatives of the nation, headed by M. Rodzianko, President of the Duma, and a Provisional Government of 12 members, have established the new order.

The success of the Revolution was made secure by the cooperation of the Guard Regiments in Petrograd and by the active support given by Moscow.

In announcing the abdication of the Tsar in the House of Commons last night Mr. Bonar Law made it clear that the revolution which had led up to this event was not an effort to secure peace, but an expression of discontent with the Russian Government for not carrying on the war with efficiency and energy.

Our Petrograd Correspondent in a remarkable series of dispatches describes in detail and in chronological order the incidents of these historic days, but we are still without news of the first outbreak.

HISTORY OF THE MOVEMENT.
THE FIRST VOLLEY.
(FROM OUR OWN CORRESPONDENT.)
PETROGRAD.
MONDAY.
11.45 a.m. – The events of Friday were multiplied manifold yesterday. Scores of people were killed and wounded in various parts of the Nevsky Prospect during the afternoon.

The fine weather brought everybody out of doors, and as the bridges and approaches to the great thoroughfare were for some unaccountable reason left open, crowds of all ages and conditions made their way to the Nevsky, till the miles separating the Admiralty from the Nicholas Station were black with people. Warnings not to assemble were disregarded. No Cossacks were visible. Platoons of Guardsmen were drawn up here and there in courtyards and side streets. The crowd was fairly good-humoured, cheering the soldiers, and showing themselves ugly only towards the few visible police. Traffic was impossible, but as the trams were not running and the cabmen had vanished, the obstruction was not serious, except for the unfortunate people who happened to arrive or intended to start at the Nicholas Station.

Shortly after 3 p.m. orders were given to the infantry to clear the street. A company of Guards took up their station near the Sadovaya and fired several volleys in the direction of the Anithkoff Palace.

Something like 100 people were killed or wounded. Motor ambulances arrived shortly afterwards and began removing the victims and conveying them to various hospitals. The Anglo-Russian Hospital, situated in close proximity, received three killed and eight wounded, the Marinsky Hospital over 60 cases, and the Obuksoff Hospital over 100.

On the scene of the shooting hundreds of empty cartridge cases were littered in the snow, which was plentifully sprinkled with blood.

After the volleys the thoroughfare was cleared, but the crowd remained on the sidewalks. No animosity was shown towards the soldiers. The people shouted "We are sorry for you, Pavlovskys! You had to do your duty."

The same company later returned to its barracks situated in the Champ de Mars, near the British Embassy.

I had just called on Sir George Buchanan, who arrived at 4 p.m. from Finland, where he went for a few days' rest, and I was walking through the Summer Gardens when the bullets began to whiz over my head. The Pavlovsky Guards on approaching their barracks on the other side of the Field of Mars found the way blocked by another crowd, who cheered them, but refused to disperse.

The Colonel in command ordered the men to lie down, so as to avoid killing people. After several volleys the crowd gave way, and sending his men forward he himself superintended the removal of the wounded.

Following his men, he then crossed the canal bridge. Two individuals, apparently disguised – one as a student, the other as an officer – barred the way. The student wrested the colonel's sword and slashed him savagely over the arm and head, causing serious but not dangerous wounds. The assailants then disappeared.

This incident gave rise to the wildest rumours of a mutiny in the Guard regiments.

The events of March 1917 (February in the Old Style calendar) were the first of the two revolutions that year in Russia that were to sweep away the rule of the Tsars and transform society. Tensions had simmered for decades but it was the immense losses suffered during the war by the Army – at some six million casualties, the most of any of the combatant nations – that led protests to break out spontaneously in St Petersburg.

The city's population had doubled in 20 years and many of its inhabitants led lives of destitution, made yet worse by food and fuel shortages resulting from the war. The autocratic Nicholas II, who had taken personal command of the war's direction, had ignored advice to implement social reform and had lost the trust of parliament, the nobility and the military. When hundreds of thousands of demonstrators began to seize and set fire to government buildings, he had little choice but to abdicate.

A provisional government instituted liberal measures such as freedom of speech but it also continued Russia's involvement in the war. In November (Old Style: October), it was overthrown by the more extreme, working-class Bolsheviks led by Vladimir Lenin.

THE EXECUTION OF
THE ROMANOVS

22 July 1918

The following news is transmitted through the wireless stations of the Russian Government:

"At the first session of the Central Executive Committee elected by the Fifth Congress of the Councils a message was made public, received by direct wire from the Ural Regional Council, concerning the shooting of the ex-Tsar, Nicholas Romanoff.

"Recently Ekaterinburg, the capital of the Red Ural, was seriously threatened by the approach of the Czecho-Slovak bands. At the same time a counter-revolutionary conspiracy was discovered, having for its object the wresting of the tyrant from the hands of the Council's authority by armed force.

"In view of this fact the Presidium of the Ural Regional Council decided to shoot the ex-Tsar, Nicholas Romanoff. This decision was carried out on July 16.

"The wife and son of Romanoff have been sent to a place of security. Documents concerning the conspiracy which was discovered have been forwarded to Moscow by a special messenger.

"It had been recently decided to bring the ex-Tsar before a tribunal, to be tried for his crimes against the people, and only later occurrences led to delay in adopting this course. The Presidency of the Central Executive Committee, after having discussed the circumstances which compelled the Ural Regional Council to take the decision to shoot Nicholas Romanoff, decided as follows: 'The Russian Central Executive Committee, in the persons of the Presidium, accept the decision of the Ural Regional Council as being regular.'

"The Central Executive Committee has now at its disposal extremely important material and documents concerning the Nicholas

Romanoff affair; his own diaries, which he kept almost to the last days; the diaries of his wife and children; his correspondence, amongst which are letters by Gregory Rasputin to Romanoff and his family. All these materials will be examined and published in the near future."

———◆———

The reports of the Tsar's execution disseminated by the new Russian government proved not to contain the whole truth. After Nicholas II's abdication, he and his family had been placed under house arrest, in conditions of some comfort, but following the Bolshevik takeover they were subjected to more stringent restrictions and moved to Yekaterinburg, east of the Urals.

By the summer of 1918, with civil war raging, it seemed possible to the local Soviet that the city would fall to Czechoslovak soldiers fighting for the 'White' forces opposed to the Bolsheviks. It was decided that the whole imperial family should be killed lest they be liberated.

Early in the morning of 17 July 1918, the Tsar, his wife, their five children and their remaining retainers were murdered in the cellar of the building in which they were imprisoned. Their execution was chaotic, as a dozen guards tried to dispatch them with guns and then bayoneted the survivors.

The bodies were secretly buried in a forest. Continued obfuscation by the Soviet authorities about the family's fate, however, fuelled rumours for years that at least some of the Tsar's children had survived.

THE END OF THE GREAT WAR

11 November 1918

THE WAR: 5ᵀᴴ YEAR: 100ᵀᴴ DAY.

The Kaiser has abdicated, and has taken refuge in Holland. Prince Max of Baden, with the assent of all the Secretaries of State, has handed over the Imperial Chancellorship to Herr Ebert, a Majority Socialist. Herr Ebert has issued a manifesto stating that he intends to form a "People's Government," the endeavour of which will be to bring peace as speedily as possible. The Independent Socialists have been invited to join the Government.

Before Prince Max of Baden left office, he issued a decree announcing the Kaiser's abdication, the renunciation of the Throne by the Crown Prince, and the appointment of Herr Ebert as Imperial Chancellor. The decree also proposed the election by general suffrage of a German National Assembly, which should settle finally the future form of government of the German nation, "and of those peoples which might be desirous of coming within the Empire."

All over Germany the revolution is taking effect. Bavaria, Wurtemburg, Saxony, the Mecklenburgs, Brunswick, Hesse, and other countries are suppressing their Governments. In Bavaria the King has fled from Munich. Soldiers are joining the insurgents. In Berlin the greater part of the garrison and other troops stationed there are supporting the new Government. At most centres a general strike had been declared.

No news has yet come of the return to France of the courier bearing the conditions of armistice to the German Headquarters at Spa. The courier only reached Spa at 10 o'clock yesterday morning, as he was greatly delayed at the lines owing to the intensity of German fire. The time allowed for the consideration of the terms by the

German delegates in France expires at 11 o'clock this morning, but may possibly be extended.

German opposition on the Western front is dying away. Everywhere the British Armies are going forward. In the north the Fifth and Second Armies have crossed the Scheldt on the whole of their front. The Fifth Army has taken Tournai, where 20,000 people were rescued from captivity, and the Second Army has taken Renaix.

Maubeuge was captured by the Guards and the 62nd Division on Friday night, and Mons was reached yesterday morning.

Before the French the German retreat "is becoming more and more hasty." Hirson has been captured, Mézières has been surrounded, and the Meuse has been crossed. Very few German troops are now on French soil, for east of the Meuse American troops are pushing forward towards Montmedy and the Briey basin.

———◆———

At the start of 1918, Germany seemed to be in as strong a position as ever in the war. The new Bolshevik government had taken Russia out of the conflict, freeing up German and Austrian forces for the Western Front, while Italy seemed on the brink of suing for peace after its rout at Caporetto.

Yet, as the months wore on, the Allies slowly gained a decisive advantage. The entry of America into the conflict in 1917, and the productivity of British industry, gave them the edge in manpower and munitions, which blunted the final enemy offensives. Weariness set in, both in the German High Command and at home, leading briefly to a more liberal government under Prince Max of Baden, then widespread revolution and the signing of the Armistice.

The reverberations from the war would be felt for decades to come. Not only had the old map of Europe been redrawn, but its remaining Great Powers, notably Britain, were now aware that in the United States they had a mighty new rival. Meanwhile, the harsh terms imposed on Germany would plant the seeds for the conflict to be revived a generation later.

SPANISH INFLUENZA

12 November 1918

The Royal College of Physicians have drawn up the following memorandum, "in view of the alarming and contradictory reports of the present epidemic of influenza that have appeared in the public Press":–

The past few weeks have now afforded sufficient experience to permit some positive statements to be made. Though the epidemic shows signs of abatement in London, it is still severe elsewhere; more over, its after-effects call for intelligent anticipation. The present epidemic is virtually world-wide, irrespective of race, community, or calling. Similar world-wide epidemics occurred in 1803, 1833, 1837, 1847, 1890. The long intermission since the last wide-spread epidemic had already made an early reappearance probable, but the conditions of epidemic prevalence of influenza are too obscure to allow of precise prediction. This outbreak is essentially identical, both in itself and in its complications, including pneumonia, with that of 1890. The disproportionate occurrence of a special symptom, a well-recognized phenomenon in the case of epidemics, as, for example, nose-bleeding in the present epidemic, does not invalidate this statement. The present epidemic has no relation to plague, as some have suggested.

Although there can be no question that the virus of influenza is a living organism, and capable of transference from man to man, yet the nature of the virus is still uncertain. It is possibly beyond the present range of microscopic vision. The bacillus discovered by Pfeiffer, commonly known as the influenza bacillus, has in the past been regarded as the probable cause, though on insufficient evidence. There is doubt as to the primary part it plays in the disease, important though it probably is as a secondary infecting agent. Pfeiffer's bacillus the pneumococcus, and, above all, in this epidemic the streptococcus, seem to be responsible for most of the fatal complications of influenza. Infection is conveyed from the sick to the healthy by the secretions of the respiratory surfaces. In coughing, sneezing, and even in loud talking, these are transmitted through the air for considerable distances in the form of a fine spray. The channels of reception are normally the nose and throat. It is manifest that, the closer the contact, the more readily will this transmission occur; hence the paramount importance of avoiding overcrowding and thronging of every sort, whether in places of public resort, public conveyances, factories, camps, dwelling-rooms, or dormitories. The sum of available evidence favours the belief that the period of incubation is about 48 hours, or even somewhat less.

The dangers of influenza are gravely increased by the complications, and much can be done to avoid or to mitigate these. Such complications may develop insidiously, and without previous signs of severe illness. Carefulness does undoubtedly decrease, and carelessness increase, both morbidity and mortality; it is important, therefore, that the public should have a clear idea of such measures of personal prophylaxis as are available against infection; larger measures of Public Health, administered by Government or local authorities, stand outside the scope of the present memorandum. The individual must be taught to realize and acquiesce in his duty to the community. Well-ventilated, airy rooms promote well-being, and to that extent, at any rate, are inimical to infection; draughts are due to unskilful ventilation, and are harmful; chilling of the body surface should be prevented by wearing warm clothing out of doors. Good nourishing food, and enough of it, is desirable; there is no virtue in more than this. War rations are fully adequate to the maintenance of good health, though they may not afford just the particular articles that each fancy demands. Alcoholic excess invites disaster; within the limits of moderation each person will be wise to maintain unaltered whatever habit experience has proved to be most agreeable to his own health. The throat should be gargled every four to six hours, if possible, or, at least, morning and evening, with a disinfectant gargle, of which one of the most potent is a solution of 20 drops of liquor sodae chlorinatae in a tumbler of warm water. A solution of common table salt, one teaspoonful to the pint of warm water, is suitable for the nasal passage; a little may be poured into the hollowed palm of the hand and snuffed up the nostrils two or three times a day.

———◆———

Forty million people had lost their lives during the four years of the war. Perhaps twice as many then succumbed between 1918 and 1919 to an invisible assailant: Spanish influenza.

Medical scholars remain deeply divided about the causes, progress and human cost of the pandemic. Almost the only certain fact is that it did not begin in Spain; reports of its outbreak there were not suppressed by the press for reasons of morale – as they were in some other countries – as Spain was neutral during the European conflict.

It is estimated that one in three of the world's population was infected, with the virus spread by troop movements, and that up to 100 million people died of it – most during a second wave that began in late 1918. Half were young adults in the prime of life, with the infection proving especially deadly to pregnant women.

The Times initially suggested that the illness lay largely in the mind, 'the general weakness of nerve power known as war-weariness'. The hardships of the Great War may have increased its toll, as did the absence of official strategies to fight it. It faded away as mysteriously as it had appeared, to be largely forgotten for almost a century. (See Coronavirus, page 423.)

WOMEN VOTE FOR THE FIRST TIME

10 December 1918

It is not surprising that women should be the most incalculable element in a peculiarly perplexing election, but it is none the less important to frame some estimate of their influence on the poll.

Women were enfranchised on a much wider scale than was commonly supposed at the time the Reform Act was passed. Lord Cave estimated that 6,000,000 women would be placed on the Parliamentary register. This figure has been largely exceeded, and, although the official statistics are not yet available, it seems probable that between 7,000,000 and 8,000,000 women will be qualified to vote next Saturday. It is even thought that of the voters who are at the moment resident in the constituencies women will be in a slight majority. When the 4,000,000 or so absent voters in the fighting forces and the Mercantile Marine are added in, the balance will again incline to the side of the men, but in any case the women have it in their power to exercise a profound and possibly a decisive influence on the election.

The experience of other countries which have enfranchised women, and especially of Australia and New Zealand, has been that the mass of women are slow to avail themselves of their new privilege. Still the percentage of women's votes recorded steadily increases at every election until a point is reached at which they exercise the franchise in much the same strength as men. An exhaustive poll of the male electors is not to be expected on Saturday. At specially exciting contests in the past between 85 and 90 per cent of the total electorate has actually been polled. Such a figure is quite out of the question now. Accordingly, if the women do not poll up to their full strength, they will be in excellent company.

The experience of candidates and canvassers among the women electors in London seems so far to have been disappointing. It is a mistake, however, in political affairs to pay too much attention to the surface tendencies of London elections. The attitude of women in the better organized Midlands and North is a far surer guide. There they have had a rough sort of political education for more than a generation in industrial and cooperative organizations, and their electoral sense has been largely developed. It is difficult to say how the women workers of Yorkshire and Lancashire will vote, but those who know them best have no doubt that the great majority will go to the poll. The general conviction is that the women's vote will be unequally divided between the Coalition and the Labour Party, and that the Asquith Liberals will make a very poor show. Women instinctively demand something of a positive character, and the old party creeds seem to have little attraction for them. The invariable testimony of candidates is that, when they have once got women interested in politics, they show an extraordinarily keen grasp of the realities of the situation. For them the chief issues are a settlement with Germany, which shall leave nothing to chance and a radical reconstruction at home, which shall remove the worst evils of our social system.

◆

The campaign to give British women the vote began in the mid-nineteenth century but was suspended by leaders of the suffrage movements for the duration of the war. By its end, although women's contribution to victory through their labour was widely recognized, there was more broadly an awareness that former divisions between the classes and sexes could no longer be justified.

It was this that led in 1918 to the franchise being extended to women over 30 who owned property – or whose husbands did – as well as to all men over 21. Until then, just over half of the male population had the vote, a consideration that had caused politicians to hesitate to impose conscription.

Thirty was chosen as the minimum age to prevent women from forming the majority in the electorate because so many men had been killed or were serving overseas. Most women voted in the election for the coalition led back to power by the Prime Minister, David Lloyd George.

In the event, their chief concern seems to have been less the terms of peace with Germany than social reform: making Britain a 'country fit for heroes'. The vote was given to all women over 21 in 1928.

LADY ASTOR TAKES HER SEAT

2 December 1919

The House of Commons is intensely human, and the coming of the first woman member excited more widespread interest than any single event since the present Parliament assembled. It was the ladies' day, and it will long be remembered for the clean sweep which was made of many of the traditions of the most conservative institution in the world. It was nothing less than the capitulation of a fortress which had been exclusively masculine for over 600 years.

The oldest Parliamentary hand could not recall an occasion on which so many women had sought orders of admission to the public galleries. The Central Hall was crowded with women, all eager to see Lady Astor take her seat, and, if that was denied them, at any rate to greet her as she passed into the House. They were disappointed, for Lady Astor entered by the members' entrance, and walked through the Lobby practically unnoticed. Many women, friends whom members had brought in the vain hope of securing orders at the last minute, were in the Lobby at the time, and it was only when Lady Astor stopped short at the entrance to the Chamber to introduce herself to the doorkeepers that they became aware of her presence. It was a strange experience for the doorkeepers to give free access to Lady Astor across the threshold which no woman had passed before during the sittings of the House except at her peril.

When the moment for Lady Astor's introduction came, the House had an unfamiliar appearance. There seemed to be many more women than men in the Strangers' Gallery – another sign of the times, for it was reserved for men until a few months ago. At the other end of the Chamber the Ladies' Gallery, with the hated grille removed for ever, was crowded with a company which included many of Lady Astor's personal friends. One of her children was there with

Mrs. Spender-Clay, and Mrs. Lloyd George was one of the spectators of the Prime Minister's obvious self-consciousness. Lord Astor smiled encouragement to his wife from the Distinguished Strangers' Gallery, where also the American Ambassador and the High Commissioner of Canada were seated. The Peers' Gallery was quite full. These two galleries were the only parts of the House in which the masculine element remained supreme, for two women journalists, greatly daring, sought and secured admission to the Press Gallery for the first time in its history. The invasion was unexpected, but the Serjeant-at-Arms held that, as the House and the public galleries were now open to women, he could not prevent duly accredited women representatives of newspapers having the entree from enjoying a similar privilege.

After the formal introduction. Lady Astor was shown over the precincts. She has many friends in the House, and Captain Spender-Clay is her brother-in-law. She spent some time in the Lobby, with members pressing round her all the time with the offer of cordial congratulations. On re-entering the House during the premium bonds debate, Lady Astor took the corner seat on the second bench below the gangway on the Opposition side among a young Unionist group. She did not make her maiden speech on the night of her introduction: only Irish members do that. But she recorded her first vote, and it was against premium bonds.

◆

Although the vote had been given to women over 30 in February 1918, they were still unable to stand for Parliament until a test case led to that being amended in time for the General Election at the end of the year (by what remains the UK's shortest statute, with just 27 words).

The first woman to be elected was Constance, Countess Markievicz, friend and muse of the poet WB Yeats and a founding member of the republican movement in Ireland. Since Sinn Fein, the party for which she stood in a Dublin constituency, did not recognize British sovereignty, she did not take up her seat at Westminster.

Accordingly, the first woman to do so was the American-born Nancy Astor, who in 1919 won the by-election at Plymouth Sutton occasioned when her husband, Waldorf Astor, was obliged to resign as the MP. This was because he had succeeded his father as Viscount Astor and so become a member of the House of Lords. Known for her wit and her outspoken views, Nancy Astor made her maiden speech about the virtues of teetotalism.

THE TWENTIES
AND THIRTIES

PROHIBITION

4 October 1920

During 1919 the average of intoxicating liquor consumed in the United States worked out at nine gallons per head of the population. Even then prohibition was fairly pervasive. A majority of the States had "dry" laws of one sort or another, and there was stringent Federal war-time regulation.

Now, since the Volstead Law put into force the prohibition amendment to the Constitution, the country is supposed to be utterly arid. Nothing with an alcoholic content of more than one half of 1 per cent can be legally offered for sale. Yet this year's average of liquor consumption promises to be pretty high.

A certain amount of liquor is, of course, still consumed in private houses, for, despite the agitation of Mr. Bryan and his friends, people have been allowed to keep and drink their "private stocks." Last winter the Press was full of picturesque tales of smuggling from the Bahamas to the pleasure resorts in Florida. It was as though the blockade-running days of the Civil War had been revived and modernized, with swift motor-boats, and even aeroplanes, in place of the rickety steamers of the sixties. Now it is the Canadian border that delights the gossips. There is much chasing of motorboats on the Lakes and the St. Lawrence, and much watching for smugglers in the wilder parts of the frontier.

Washington is bothered by the suspicion of a much more serious traffic through the bonded warehouses. Every day one reads of raids. Last Sunday $100,000 worth of contraband was confiscated in the hotels and restaurants of Atlantic City by Federal officials under the leadership of a Methodist parson. Now it is the turn of the cafes and cabarets of New York.

The raids have not yet rendered it more difficult for anyone who is "known" to get something with his meals at the "right" places. In some of the biggest night restaurants waiters will produce a bottle of whisky, which parties are supposed discreetly to mix with their ginger-ale or lemon-squash. The authorities are not very severe in dealing with that type of peccadillo. They regard it as symptomatic rather than fundamental.

Their trouble lies in keeping secure the vast stores of spirits in the bonded warehouses, which are supposed to go only to accredited agents, for sale to manufacturers for their processes and to chemists for medicine. As a matter of fact, if papers like the *Philadelphia Public Ledger* are to be believed, much whisky is released to a regular gang of liquor dealers, many of whom are becoming millionaires. These people are said to traffic in crooked ways, often in conjunction with poorly paid agents of the Washington Prohibition Enforcement Office.

Bogus manufacturers, we are told, get permits for the removal of vast amounts of whisky, while 8,000 permits have in New York alone been issued to chemists – often for 50 or 100 barrels each. It is alleged that confiscated whisky sometimes finds its way on to the market again. As for the distribution of all this contraband, it is said that there are in New York, and probably in other cities, sundry well defined routes along which lorries can pass behind the backs of the complacent local representatives of the law. The *Ledger*, indeed, recounts a story of a whole van-load being brought by rail from some place in the West to New York, where it and its contents were "lost."

Certainly there is plenty of whisky about. And it is not a question only of single bottles or even cases. A rich citizen, they say, has little difficulty in arranging for a van to drive up to his house, especially in the country, and unload cases by the dozen.

———◆———

The importance of religion and moral convictions in shaping American history tends to be overlooked. If the abolition of slavery was one goal of those who sought to perfect the nation, so was the prohibition of alcohol.

Driven often by women, who had to live with the family consequences of drink, and aided by prominent supporters such as former Secretary of State William Jennings Bryan, the temperance movement gained sufficient momentum by 1920 for the sale of alcohol to be banned nationwide by the Volstead Act. Industrialists and economists had predicted this would lead to greater productivity and a fall in crime but, particularly in cities, evasion of the law was widespread.

The illegal sale of alcohol enriched gangsters such as Al Capone, corrupted officials and policemen, and deprived federal and state governments of hundreds of millions of dollars in excise revenue. Plea bargaining was created as a way of dealing with the tidal wave of offenders that threatened to swamp the court system.

With America mired in economic depression by the early 1930s, one of the central planks of Franklin Roosevelt's successful campaign for the presidency was the repeal of Prohibition, which was carried through in 1933.

TUTANKHAMUN'S TOMB

30 November 1922

First they saw three magnificent State couches, all gilt, with exquisite carving and heads of Typhon, Hathor, and lion. On these rested beds, beautifully carved, gilt, inlaid with ivory and semi-precious stones, and also innumerable boxes of exquisite workmanship. One of these boxes was inlaid with ebony and ivory, with gilt inscriptions: another contained emblems of the underworld; on a third, which contained Royal robes, handsomely embroidered, precious stones, and golden sandals, were beautifully painted hunting scenes.

There was a stool of ebony inlaid with ivory, with the most delicately carved duck's feet: also a child's stool of fine workmanship. Beneath one of the couches was the State Throne of King Tutankhamen, probably one of the most beautiful objects of art ever discovered. There was also a heavily gilt chair, with portraits of the King and Queen, the whole encrusted with turquoise, cornelian, lapis, and other semi precious stones.

Two life-sized bituminized statues of the King, with gold work holding a golden stick and mace, faced each other, the handsome features, the feet, and the hands delicately carved, with eyes of glass and head-dress richly studded with gems.

There were also four chariots, the sides of which were encrusted with semi-precious stones and rich gold decoration. These were dismantled, with a charioteer's apron of leopard's skin hanging over the seat.

Other noteworthy objects were Royal sticks, one of ebony with the head of an Asiatic as a handle in gold, another of the handsomest filigree work; also a stool for a throne with Asiatics carved on it, denoting that the King had placed his foot on the neck of the Asiatic prisoners taken in war. There were some quaint bronze-gilt musical instruments and a robing dummy for Royal wigs and robes.

There were also some exquisite alabaster vases with very intricate and unknown design, all of one piece, and some handsome blue Egyptian faience, and enormous quantities of provisions for the dead, comprising trussed duck, haunches of venison, &c., all packed in boxes according to the custom of the time. There were some remarkable wreaths, still looking evergreen, and one of the boxes contained rolls of papyri, which are expected to render a mass of information.

A further chamber revealed an indescribable state of confusion. Here furniture, gold beds, exquisite boxes, and alabaster vases similar to those found in the first chamber were piled high one on top of the other, so closely packed that it has been impossible to get inside yet.

◆

The tomb of Tutankhamun had been discovered in the Valley of the Kings, near Luxor (Thebes), by the British Egyptologist Howard Carter after five years of searching. His patron was the Earl of Carnarvon. *The Times* obtained exclusive rights to cover the excavation after the inner burial chamber was opened in 1923, revealing intact the treasures such as his sarcophagus that would become the symbol of the boy pharaoh.

Enthroned aged about nine, Tutankhamun reigned for a decade from circa 1334 BC. His father was Akhenaten, whose most senior wife was Nefertiti, herself the subject of a famous bust now in the Neues Museum, Berlin. They had instituted a religious revolution by replacing worship of the numerous Egyptian deities with that of just one, the sun god Aten, but Tutankhamun restored the old order.

Examination of his remains and the artefacts found revealed that he had suffered prolonged ill health that meant he had to walk with a cane, which may have been caused by genetic abnormalities.

Lord Carnarvon's death several months after the tomb's opening sparked rumours of a curse but these were generated by the press. He had himself been frail for many years following a car accident. The treasures of Tutankhamun were acquired from his heirs by the Egyptian Government.

THE DEATH OF LENIN

24 January 1924

The Soviet Congress was sitting in the Grand Theatre in Moscow when Kalinin announced the death of Lenin. The gathering was deeply moved, many persons wept, and they all sang "Eternal Memory," which is generally sung by Russians at funerals. The people learnt of Lenin's death from notices posted outside the newspaper offices.

A fortnight ago the official Communist leaders, on announcing that Trotsky had obtained sick leave, declared that Lenin was making rapid progress, and spent part of his leisure in hunting. They also said that he desired to go to Moscow to address a few authoritative words to his squabbling disciples, but was dissuaded from doing so. The Communist leaders, however, had long known that his recovery was impossible. For more than a month his condition was becoming worse. Gorky, where Lenin died, is 20 miles from Moscow, and was formerly the estate of the Morosoffs.

At 1 o'clock to-day the body was brought to the Trade Union Hall in Moscow, where it is lying in state.

Kalinin has issued instructions for the formation of a committee, of which Dzherzhinsky, the Chief of the Unified State political department, is chairman, to make all arrangements for the funeral. For the moment party squabbling has ceased, and it is thought that Lenin's death has influenced opinion in favour, at least temporarily, of the ruling clique, since its occurrence just when the All Russian Soviet Congress was sitting, and on the eve of the Congress of the Union of Socialist Soviet Republics, in which a certain number of non-party delegates will take part, is likely to disarm the Opposition. It was known that the Opposition had decided to oppose the ruling clique not only at the Party Conferences but also at the mixed Soviet congresses in which they expected to obtain support from non-Communists. This plan seems to have been abandoned for the present at any rate. Zinovieff, Stalin, and Kameneff, who have the reputation of having been Lenin's nearest counsellors, intend to utilize the occasion of his funeral for a great demonstration which would drown opposition in a flood of eulogy and culminate in the various congresses being invited to swear obedience to Lenin's commandments.

Although the Soviet Legation states that Trotsky is still in Moscow and taking part in the councils of the Government, the order issued to the army and fleet on the occasion of Lenin's death does not bear his signature, but those of the other members of the War Council.

According to the latest reports the formal question of Lenin's successor as the head of the Political Bureau of the Central Committee and the People's Commissars is occupying the attention of the Communists in Moscow. The question was raised after Lenin's relapse a year ago and produced a serious controversy, of which the result was that Lenin remained the nominal head of the Soviet. Kameneff, Tsurupa, and Rykoff were appointed deputies. In the Political Bureau of the Central Committee, Lenin's place was taken by Kameneff, Stalin, and Zinovieff.

Now the Political Bureau has decided to submit to the Congress of the Union of the Soviet Socialist Republic a candidate for the headship of the People's Commissars, but it is uncertain whether they intend to make the appointment of their own motion or proceed by means of election by the present or the next Congress. Neither Trotsky, Kameneff, nor Zinovieff is likely to be appointed because of their Jewish origin. The Georgian, Stalin, has a chance, but a Russian is likely to be preferred.

◆

Vladimir Lenin, who had created the Soviet Union and led it since the Revolution, died on 21 January 1924. He was 53 and had suffered a series of strokes. In the months prior to his death, Lenin had indicated that he favoured Leon Trotsky as his successor, thinking Joseph Stalin too crude. But Stalin proved more able at taking power.

Lenin's body was transported by train to Moscow. There it lay in state for three days while as many as one million mourners filed past the bier. It was then conveyed to Red Square, where tens of thousands more defied sub-zero temperatures to attend their leader's funeral. St Petersburg had already had its name changed to Leningrad to mark his passing.

Yet, even in death, Lenin could aid the cause of revolution. Against the wishes of his widow, his body was embalmed and became the focus of a personality cult that for the next 60 years served as the Party and the country's religion. Despite the collapse of the Communist system, Lenin's body remains on display in its mausoleum to this day.

JOHN LOGIE BAIRD
DEMONSTRATES TELEVISION

28 January 1926

Members of the Royal Institution and other visitors to a laboratory in
an upper room in Frith-street, Soho, on Tuesday saw a demonstration
of apparatus invented by Mr. J.L. Baird, who claims to have solved
the problem of television. They were shown a transmitting machine,
consisting of a large wooden revolving disc containing lenses, behind
which was a revolving shutter and a light sensitive cell. It was explained
that by means of the shutter and lens disc an image of articles or
persons standing in front of the machine could be made to pass over
the light sensitive cell at a high speed. The current in the cell varies
in proportion to the light falling on it, and this varying current is
transmitted to a receiver where it controls a light behind an optical
arrangement similar to that at the sending end. By this means a point
of light is caused to traverse a ground glass screen. The light is dim
at the shadows and bright at the high lights, and crosses the screen so
rapidly that the whole image appears simultaneously to the eye.

For the purposes of the demonstration the head of a ventriloquist's
doll was manipulated as the image to be transmitted, though the
human face was also reproduced. First on a receiver in the same room
as the transmitter and then on a portable receiver in another room,
the visitors were shown recognizable reception of the movements of
the dummy head and of a person speaking. The image as transmitted
was faint and often blurred, but substantiated a claim that through
the "Televisor," as Mr. Baird has named his apparatus, it is possible to
transmit and reproduce instantly the details of movement, and such
things as the play of expression on the face.

It has yet to be seen to what extent further developments will carry
Mr. Baird's system towards practical use. He has overcome, apparently,

earlier failures to construct light sensitive cells which would function at the high speed demanded, and as he is now assured of financial support in his work, he will be able to improve and elaborate his apparatus. Application has been made to the Postmaster-General for an experimental broadcasting licence, and trials with the system may shortly be made from a building in St. Martin's-lane.

◆

Baird was not the first person to develop the process of transmitting recognisable images for broadcast, but he was the first to perfect it. Central to his television was the work of a German scientist, Paul Nipkow, who in the 1880s had used a rotating disk with spirals in it to divide up an object into a linear series of points that could be encoded and relayed.

Baird had given public demonstrations previously of earlier versions of his invention, showing silhouettes, before transmitting the first true television picture in October 1925. It was of the head of the ventriloquist's dummy, known as 'Stooky Bill'. His laboratory in Soho later became the premises of the celebrated Bar Italia.

In 1928, Baird successfully broadcast images internationally for the first time, using telephone lines between London and New York. That same year, he made the first transmission in colour, showing a young girl in a series of hats; Noele Gordon grew up to become the star of the television soap opera, *Crossroads*.

The first television remote control had been invented by 1955.

THE GENERAL STRIKE

5 May 1926

A wide response was made yesterday throughout the country to the call of those Unions which had been ordered by the T.U.C. to bring out their members. Railway workers stopped generally, though at Hull railway clerks are reported to have resumed duty, confining themselves to their ordinary work, and protested against the strike. Commercial road transport was only partially suspended.

In London the tramways and L.G.O.C. [London General Omnibus Company] services were stopped. The printing industry is practically at a standstill, but lithographers have not been withdrawn, and compositors in London have not received instructions to strike. Large numbers of building operatives, other than those working on housing, came out.

The situation in the engineering trades was confused; men in some districts stopped while in others they continued at work. There was no interference with new construction in the ship building yards, but in one or two districts some of the men engaged in the strike with the dockers.

FOOD – Supplies of milk and fish brought into Kings Cross, Euston and Paddington were successfully distributed from the Hyde Park Depot and stations. The Milk & Food Controller expects it will be possible to maintain a satisfactory supply of milk to hospitals, institutions, schools, hotels, restaurants and private consumers. Milk will be 8d. per gallon dearer wholesale and 2d. per quart retail today. Smithfield market has distributed 5,000 tons of meat since Monday.

MAILS – Efforts will be made to forward by means of road transport the mails already shown as due to be dispatched shortly from London. The position is uncertain and the facilities may have to be limited to mail for America, India and Africa.

At Bow Street Mr. Saklatvala, M.P., who was required as a result of his Hyde Park speech on Saturday to give sureties to abstain from making violent and inflammatory speeches, was remanded for two days on bail.

◆

One of the most significant events of the inter-war years, the General Strike was called by the Trades Union Congress (TUC) in a bid to force the government to help the country's 1.2 million miners. The industry had entered a slump after the war and employers had cut wages and imposed longer working hours.

When the miners struck after being locked out, the TUC called out in sympathy almost one in three of all men in work, including dockers, hauliers, railwaymen and lithographers and compositors from the print industry; *The Times* managed to put together an emergency edition using other staff.

The strike lasted from 4 May to 12 May, but the government had had time to prepare and was able to keep many key services running with the help of middle-class volunteers. 'Try living on their wages before you judge them', remarked King George V of the strikers, but they were defeated, and the miners forced to return to work.

Whilst this meant that mass unemployment in the 1930s provoked little unrest of the same kind, the strike nevertheless boosted the standing of the unions and gave organized labour a greater sense of its own power.

LINDBERGH FLIES THE ATLANTIC

23 May 1927

It was not until the latter part of the afternoon that the first telegram, with a Kerry dateline, reported him as crossing the south-west corner of Ireland, flying high and fast. The effect was electrical. The streets suddenly became crowded with people crying. "Vive Lindbergh!" Soon afterwards the news was flashed that the aeroplane had been sighted by the ketch Saint-Marc making for Cherbourg, and next by the lighthouse as crossing the coastline, coming from the west at a great speed and flying very high in the direction of Paris. There could now be no doubt that Lindbergh was coming. He had done it! He would succeed! Paris cheered. Paris was now no more than 34 hours from New York. "Vive Lindbergh!"

Elaborate preparations had been made at Le Bourget to greet the airman. A committee of welcome was hastily formed headed by Mr. Myron T. Herrick, the United States Ambassador, which included M. Fallierès, Minister of Labour (who deputized for M. Bokanowski, Minister of Commerce), and many distinguished French air and military authorities. Five hundred special police and the 34th Aviation Regiment were mobilized to maintain order at the aerodrome. When the first telegrams announcing that Captain Lindbergh's aeroplane had been sighted off Ireland were issued, crowds of people immediately set out for Le Bourget. Tourist agencies hastily organized regular motor-coach services from the Grands Boulevards, and special omnibus and tramway services reinforced the normal means of communication.

Although Captain Lindbergh was not due to arrive before 10.30 large crowds had assembled at Le Bourget in the late afternoon and soon grew to 50,000. The main road from Paris was packed with motor-cars in an apparently unending stream. The *Octroi* [a toll on local transport] was almost unworkable and did its best to complicate matters. The extra handful of police on the Le Bourget main road was unable to cope with the huge mass of motor vehicles and left the road, and incoming tramcars and motor-cars were abandoned. Motor-cars mounted the raised tramway tracks, and then the pavements, driving pedestrians into cafes. Some became inextricably locked with incoming traffic and were abandoned by their occupants, who continued the journey on foot. Pedestrians clambered on to the roofs of the few moving vehicles.

The night was calm and cloudless, with practically no wind. Long before dark the aerial lighthouse at Le Bourget was flashing, and from time to time the white fingers of searchlights swept the sky. At 9 o'clock rockets and storm shells were sent up at intervals of two minutes. An hour later powerful projectors lit up the landing field as with daylight and rockets were fired every minute. At 10.10 the faint drone of an engine was heard and excitement increased. All eyes searched the darkness, but the searchlights were unable to locate the aeroplane. A few minutes later the "Spirit of Saint Louis" was observed flying at about 900ft. Captain Lindbergh announced his arrival by dropping a fuse. He circled the aerodrome three times, and, dipping carefully, made a perfect landing. The machine taxied for 100 yards and came to a standstill at the west-end of the field. The huge crowd, which had viewed this last difficult manoeuvre of a tired man with anxious eyes, gave him a roar of welcome, brushed the strong cordon of police and soldiers easily aside, and surged over the field in a rush for the aeroplane. Barbed-wire fences and flimsy barricades were swept away, iron gates were smashed. Several people were knocked down and trampled on.

Captain Lindbergh was dragged, feet first, from his machine and only the efforts of a few French pilots and soldiers, using their rifle butts, saved him from serious injury at the hands of a mob now completely out of hand. He was probably saved by an amusing diversion. A burly American in the crowd was mistaken for the aviator, hoisted on high, and carried in triumph to the headquarters of the commandant of Le Bourget. This incident enabled the real Captain Lindbergh to be smuggled quietly away to the offices of the French Air Union, where a moving and informal reception took place. The few French pilots on duty repeatedly embraced Captain Lindbergh.

Charles Lindbergh, an unknown pilot working for US Air Mail, had begun his historic flight to France 33½ hours before and some 3,600 miles away on the earthen runway of Roosevelt Field, Long Island. His single-engined aircraft, the Spirit of St Louis, was weighed down by fuel and barely cleared telephone wires as it took off.

The flight itself was perilous, as Lindbergh had only basic navigational skills and faced hazards including fog banks and icing on his wings. His supplies were four sandwiches and two cans of water. He landed to be greeted by a 150,000-strong crowd and to find himself world famous, having made the first solo transatlantic flight and the first between two important cities, heralding a new age in aviation.

On his return home, Lindbergh was greeted with the largest ticker tape parade ever seen in New York. The subsequent kidnap and murder of his infant son, and the attendant press attention, led him to take his family to Europe in the mid-1930s, and his reputation was later sullied by accusations that he sympathized with the Nazis' views about race.

THE WALL STREET CRASH

25 October 1929

A Niagara of liquidation fell upon the American Stock Exchanges to-day. For three hours trading was completely demoralized with blocks of 10,000, 15,000, and 20,000 shares of stock pressing for sale and prices melting away 5 and 10 points at a time. Never before, even at the outbreak of the Great War, was there such a volume of transactions.

On the New York Stock Exchange in the first hour of trading alone more than 1,600,000 shares changed hands – four times as many as in the same hour yesterday – and by 1.30 o'clock the total was over 10,000,000 shares. By then it was reported that the Chicago and Buffalo Stock Exchanges had closed.

The situation was so serious that shortly after 1 o'clock Mr. Charles E. Mitchell, the chairman of the National City Bank; Mr. W. C. Potter, chairman of the Guaranty Trust Company; Mr. Seward Prosser, chairman of the Bankers Trust Company, and Mr. Albert H. Wiggin, chairman of the Chase National Bank, hastily assembled at Messrs. Morgan and Co's offices to confer on measures for relieving public apprehension. Shortly afterwards Mr. Thomas W. Lamont, one of the Morgan partners, in a statement to the Press, attempted to minimize the excitement by saying that there had been "a little distress selling" on the Stock Exchange but that his conferees had found that there were no brokerage houses in difficulty. Reports as to maintenance of margins, he said, were very satisfactory. Asked if the worst had been seen, he replied, "I don't think we tried to analyse that situation." The trouble was "technical rather than fundamental." Mr. Lamont's statement and the banking support lent to the market at that time produced a rapid rally in a number of stocks, although trading continued to be very excited.

The fact that stock tickers were then more than two hours behind dealings on the floor did not lessen the nervousness, for the actual course of share prices could be known to customers in brokerage houses and elsewhere only by brief telephoned reports covering a few securities, and for most of the time telephone facilities were utterly inadequate to deal with the pressure of the demands upon them. The same was reported to be true of telephone facilities throughout the city, as, seemingly, half the population tried to get in touch with Wall Street.

At the outset of the day the United States Steel, one of the market leaders, opened trading with 5,000 shares changing hands at 1½ points above last night's closing prices. A number of other active issues opened likewise with overnight gains, and for a little while it was thought that there had come an end to yesterday's liquidation, which had broken the prices of leading industrials more than 20 points. But the confidence was short-lived. Inside of half-an-hour the pent-up selling burst upon the market again. There were wide, open breaks in such recent speculative favourites as Radio, Montgomery Ward, American and Foreign Power, Columbia Gas, Consolidated Gas, American Can, Steel, and American Telephone and Telegraph, the most widely distributed of all the stocks – a wholesale unloading of accounts in which the margin had been worn thin by a succession of declines. Good stocks fell with the bad. Losses of 10 to 15 and even 20 to 30 points became too numerous to note, and in the very high-priced shares the losses were far greater still. Call money fell from 6 to 5 per cent, but in the panicky state of traders' minds neither easy money nor anything else was of avail to halt the deluge.

———◆———

The 'Roaring Twenties' had been a prosperous decade for America as it built on the sense of destiny generated by its decisive role in the First World War. With the stock market expanding apace, even small investors became caught up in frantic speculation, but by 1929 the economy was entering decline and many companies were over-valued.

On Black Thursday – 29 October – the market crashed as more than 16 million shares were traded in panic and billions of dollars were wiped off balance sheets. Some investors had already got out; reputedly Joseph Kennedy, father of the future President, had sold up after finding that even shoeshine boys were giving him stock tips.

It is often forgotten that the market subsequently rallied. Nor do historians believe that the crash was responsible for the Great Depression which followed, that being caused by banks having over-extended their lending. By 1933, half of the banks in America had failed and a third of the workforce was unemployed, with knock-on effects for the rest of the world. The economy would not recover fully until the Second World War.

GANDHI'S SALT MARCH

13 March 1930

In the early hours of a dark, cold morning Mr. Gandhi, accompanied by a chosen band of 79 volunteers, started from his *Ashram* [seminary] outside Ahmedabad to-day on the first stage of his civil disobedience march.

The Special Correspondent of the *Times of India*, describing the scene, says that at an early hour, peasants were working in the fields in complete disregard of their saviour's imminent march. Yet their indifference was certainly not the fault of the volunteers, who have been scouring the countryside for support, ordering that the villages through which the procession will pass shall be swept clean, and generously distributing Gujarati pamphlets. [Pamphlets apparently produced at Gujarat Vidyapith, Mr. Gandhi's "university."] One pamphlet demands gifts because one "was soon to ascend the Cross like Jesus Christ," and the appeal for money has been not unheeded. The Correspondent discovered Mr. Gandhi in the densest part of the procession looking old and cold, and it was difficult to believe him equal to the strain. Behind him came a motor-lorry carrying a mass of home-spun cloth, and in the rear was a horse, which Mr. Gandhi later intends to ride.

In Bombay the Provincial Congress Committee and the Youth League organized demonstrations, which in their early stages passed off uneventfully, except that the band of the volunteers, unaccustomed to the Congress atmosphere, played "God Save the King," which was immediately stopped. Later a large crowd of schoolboys became disorderly and broke some shop windows and four windows of the *Times of India* offices, but was dispersed after scuffles with the police.

Mr. Gandhi, in to-day's issue of *Young India*, criticizes the Viceroy's reply to his letter.

"On bended knee," he writes, "I asked for bread, but received a stone instead." He says the Viceroy represents a nation that does not easily give in and does not easily repent.

"Entreaty never convinces it. It readily listens to physical force, and can witness with bated breath a boxing match for hours without fatigue; can go mad over a football match in which may be broken bones, and goes into ecstasies over blood-curdling accounts of war. It will listen to mere resistless suffering. It will not part with the millions it annually drains from India in reply to any argument, however convincing.

"The Viceregal reply does not surprise me. But I know the salt tax has to go, and many other things with it, if my letter means what it says. The reply says I contemplate a course of action which is clearly bound to involve a violation of the law and a danger to public peace. In spite of a forest of books containing rules and regulations, the only law the nation knows is the will of the British administrators, and the only public peace the nation knows is the peace of the public prison. India is one vast prison house. I repudiate this law, and regard it as my sacred duty to break the mournful monotony of compulsory peace that is choking the nation's heart for want of a free vent."

◆

Salt for cooking was a necessity in humid India, yet since 1882 the indigenous population had been forbidden from making or acquiring it themselves. Instead, they were obliged to buy imported salt, which was heavily taxed.

When Mohandas Gandhi made the salt laws the focus of his campaign of nonviolent disobedience to colonial rule, it bemused at first other Indian political leaders. Yet, he had appreciated that the tax affected all Indians alike, whatever their religion or income, and was a demonstration of how Britain governed even the most straightforward aspects of the lives of its subjects.

He and his followers marched 240 miles (386 kilometres) to the coastal town of Dandi. The police there had intended to prevent him from gathering salt from the shore by crushing it into the mud, but Gandhi was still able to collect several handfuls.

Although he was not immediately arrested, more than 80,000 others were held in the protests that followed in other parts of India. Widespread resistance to the Raj, led by Gandhi, had been aroused, and his march to the sea proved to be the first steps on the road to Independence.

TELEPHONE LINKS THE WORLD

1 August 1930

The use of long-distance telephony as a means of communication between Great Britain and the Continent, and also with America and Australia, is rapidly increasing. Progress began to be marked in 1927, and in the following year the number of outgoing and incoming calls reached a total of 887,290. Last year there was a further increase to 1,098,981, and the figures for 1930 are expected to be substantially higher. It is stated that communication has now been established with 90 per cent of the telephone-using people of the world.

Before the Great War telephonic links with other countries were very few. A service between London and Paris was opened in 1891, and in 1903 direct conversation was established with Belgium. Another 10 years then passed before facilities for through communication with Switzerland became available. After 1914 progress was interrupted for a long period, as the chaotic conditions which followed the upheaval of more than four years of strife hindered new developments. The present forward movement can be associated with the introduction of the thermionic valve which opened up fresh fields in long-distance telephonic work. An international consultation committee was appointed and the explorations of this body opened the way for the remarkable advances of the last four years.

Before the new era began Great Britain had fewer than 20 circuits over Europe and the number is now 90. A full service between England and Germany was started in 1927, and with the use of repeater stations, country after country has since been brought within the operation of the international system. Direct communication can now be obtained through the British Post Office with Austria, Belgium, Czechoslovakia, Denmark, Finland, France, Germany, Holland, Hungary, Italy, Latvia,

Lithuania, Norway, Poland, Portugal, Spain, Sweden, Switzerland, and, indeed, every important country of the Continent, with the exceptions of Russia, Greece, and Turkey. North Africa is touched at Ceuta.

A world extension of the service has been made possible by the developments in wireless telephony. The Transatlantic service covers the United States, Canada, Mexico, and Cuba, while communication with Brazil, the Argentine, and Uruguay is effected through either Paris or Madrid. As soon as the necessary equipment is provided, it is hoped that direct transmission will be possible between Great Britain and the South American continent. The extensive use made of the Transatlantic service has enabled the authorities to reduce the tariff from an initial charge of £15 for three minutes' conversation to £6 for the same time. Four channels are now available as compared with only one when the system was inaugurated, and calls can be passed from any part of this country to the greater part of the United States. A 24 hours service is provided.

Communication has still to be established with India, South Africa, and New Zealand, but this should not be long delayed.

———◆———

Scientists had attempted to create a telephone from the early part of the nineteenth century, but credit for bringing the idea to fruition in 1876 is customarily given to the Scottish-born Alexander Graham Bell. A teacher of the deaf who had moved to America, his invention was born of his experimental work on the transmission of sounds, initially in an attempt to improve the telegraph so that it could send and receive multiple messages simultaneously.

When he was shown one of the new instruments, Rutherford Hayes, the US President, is said to have asked why anyone would want to use it. Within three years of the first line being installed, 50,000 people were using telephones. The first transatlantic call was made in 1927.

HITLER BECOMES CHANCELLOR OF GERMANY

31 January 1933

The appointment of Herr Hitler as Chancellor of the Reich has aroused the greatest interest in France, in spite of domestic politics, but there is little of the alarm such an event would have provoked a short time ago. Opinion here has been growing steadily more resigned to what appeared to be the inevitable result of successive German crises.

It is recalled that previous attempts at cooperation between President von Hindenburg and Herr Hitler broke down because of the Nazi leader's refusal to accept the President's conditions, and there is sufficient confidence here in the President's consistency to induce the belief that it is certainly not he that has given way. Further confirmation of this belief is seen in the composition of the new Cabinet.

This does not mean that the development of events in Germany will not be watched with a careful and cautious eye. And the last thing expected is any improvement in Franco-German relations. Herr Hitler has spoken too loudly and too often for that. But, added to all the caution which the situation demands, there is the hope that a Hitler in power may prove less dangerous than a Hitler unhampered by responsibility. Moreover, from more than one quarter comes the opinion that, from the point of view of German foreign policy, Herr Hitler may prove less redoubtable than his predecessor, who had already achieved a considerable reputation for the manner in which he got things done where cruder methods had failed.

One inevitable effect of the new situation has been to concentrate public attention on the disarmament problem in general and the latest British suggestions for a programme of work in particular.

Although opinion on the Right has not been slow to hint that the British proposals were intended, in spite of express disclaimers to the contrary, to efface and finally to destroy the French plan, the moderate view gives full credit to the British Government for a serious attempt to grapple with the problem.

On the political side there is a fair measure of agreement with the British idea. That is to say, a solution which will reconcile the conflicting French and German theses would be welcomed here, even at the cost of some concession. But it is once again pointed out that no general reduction of armaments could be accepted by France without some solid guarantee in its place. The suggestion of regional security agreements between the Continental States is hailed as a step, but only a step, in the right direction. They must be rounded off, it is felt, by a clearer definition of the British obligations under Article XVI of the League Covenant, and by the inclusion of the United States in a consultative pact. The hope is expressed that the British omission of these two factors implies no more than a respect for Mr. Roosevelt's peculiar position.

All these things, however, are held to have little more than an academic value for the moment. Everything will depend, it is felt, upon the attitude adopted by the Hitler Government at the Disarmament Conference.

———◆———

As the world tumbled into economic catastrophe, Adolf Hitler and the Nazi Party began to rise to prominence as they tapped into popular discontent in Germany which had its roots in defeat in the First World War.

The power of Hitler's oratory helped the Party to become the largest in the Reichstag in elections held in 1932. Hitler expected to become Chancellor in place of the conservative politician Franz von Papen but the aristocratic President, Paul von Hindenburg, had little respect for the upstart demagogue and refused to make the change.

But when von Papen was sacked at the end of the year, as Hindenburg tried to construct a coalition that could govern, the former Chancellor allied himself with Hitler. Hoping to become Vice-Chancellor, he convinced Hindenburg to appoint Hitler as Chancellor on the basis that between the two of them they could control such an inexperienced leader.

Instead, Hitler used his position, and fears of a Communist takeover, to turn Germany into a one-party state. Rivals were violently eliminated, opponents increasingly monitored by the police, and when Hindenburg died in 1934, Hitler was proclaimed head of state in his place.

BONNIE AND CLYDE

24 May 1934

Clyde Barrow, a desperado of the South-West, and Bonnie Parker, the woman who shared many of his murderous exploits, were killed in an ambush by Louisiana and Texan policemen to-day. The pair had been hunted for months and while often overtaken, had always managed to shoot their way out. This morning, however, the police had time to prepare for them, and as they drove along a road near Black Lake, Louisiana, at high speed, a volley was fired at them from riot-guns. Their car ran into an embankment and was wrecked and both its occupants were found to be riddled with bullets.

The woman had a machine-gun on her lap and Barrow a pistol in one hand. In the back of the car were found three Army rifles, two sawed-off automatic shotguns, a machine-gun, a dozen pistols, and a large quantity of ammunition.

◆

Clyde Barrow and Bonnie Parker had met in Texas in 1930 when he was 21 and she was 19. Her husband was then in prison for murder, while Barrow was shortly to be sent to gaol. He briefly escaped using a pistol that she had smuggled in. Their crime spree began when he was paroled in 1932.

Although their exploits brought them notoriety and subsequently made them symbols of the Depression era, their lives and crimes were rather less glamorous than later made out to be on film and in popular song. Most of their robberies were not of banks but of small stores and petrol stations and they had to sleep rough much of the time to evade capture.

Photographs of Parker smoking a cigar titillated the public, but any sympathy for her evaporated when it was claimed, probably incorrectly, that she had taken part in the fatal shooting of a police officer. In total, the five-strong gang committed 13 murders before she and Barrow were themselves killed in an ambush.

THE FLYING SCOTSMAN

1 December 1934

All authenticated records for a passenger railway train in Great Britain were broken yesterday by the London and North Eastern Railway, when a speed of 97½ miles an hour was obtained near Essendine [Rutland] on a non-stop run from Leeds to London. It is believed that when the records taken by instruments in the dynamometer car on the train are examined it will be found that the speed of the train actually exceeded 100 miles an hour, but at present a speed of 97½ miles an hour is claimed.

This experimental train made the journey from King's Cross to Leeds and back. On the outward journey the average speed from London to Doncaster was 77 miles an hour, which is equal to that of the Flying Hamburger, and though the train had then to face the heavy gradients between Doncaster and Leeds and a speed limit of 45 miles an hour between Wakefield and Leeds, the average for the whole journey was 73.4 miles an hour.

The fastest regular train between King's Cross and Leeds is the Queen of Scots Pullman, which does the journey in 3 hours 13 minutes, so that yesterday's outward run in 2 hours 31 minutes beat the best regular run by 42 minutes.

The experimental run was not a mere speed test designed to show what can be done under abnormal conditions when everything is sacrificed to secure a very fast run for a special train. It was intended rather as a test of the steam locomotive burning coal on a service similar to that now run in foreign countries by oil-fed Diesel locomotives. During the summer the London and North Eastern and London Midland and Scottish Railway companies sent experts to Germany to study the service run by the Flying Hamburger, which covers the distance between Berlin and Hamburg daily at an average speed of 77 miles an hour.

The British railways have been built up on steam locomotion and they consume 14,000,000 tons of coal a year. So much railway capital is locked up in steam rolling stock and so much importance in the national interest is attached to the continued use of coal as locomotive fuel, that there has been no disposition to make any wide-sweeping changes, particularly as it was felt that the potentialities of the steam locomotive for high-speed work had not been explored sufficiently. When it was decided to undertake further high-speed tests, the German railway authorities were consulted and a time schedule was drawn up which represented approximately the times those responsible for the Flying Hamburger service suggested for a train similar to their own in both directions between King's Cross and Leeds. That schedule allowed for a journey of 185.7 miles in two hours and 45 minutes at an average speed of just under 70 miles an hour.

When Mr. V.M. Barrington-Ward, superintendent, Western Division, who travelled on the train, and Mr. H.N. Gresley, chief mechanical engineer, made the arrangements for the run they did not, as might have been expected, select one of the latest and most powerful types of locomotive. Instead the train was drawn by locomotive No. 4472, a Flying Scotsman engine, an old engine in which the whole Empire is interested.

◆

By the 1930s, the railways were increasingly in competition for passengers with motor cars. This led to a new emphasis on speed, with adherents of diesel claiming that it should be used instead of steam to power the fastest trains.

The Flying Scotsman was originally the name of the service between London and Edinburgh, but from 1925 was given to the Pacific steam locomotive, designed by Sir Nigel Gresley, which pulled it. A Great Western Railway locomotive, City of Truro, had been unofficially timed as exceeding 100 mph while running downhill in Somerset 30 years earlier, but The Flying Scotsman's run was recognized as the first to be authenticated.

When the route was first operated, the journey took 10 hours and 30 minutes, including a half-hour halt for lunch in York. By the time The Flying Scotsman was hauling, it had been cut to 7 hours and 20 minutes.

It ceded the world speed record for steam locomotives to *Mallard*, also designed by Gresley, in 1938.

In the *Thomas the Tank Engine* books, written from 1945 by the Reverend Wilbert Awdry, the green locomotive Gordon is depicted as being the brother of *The Flying Scotsman*.

SPAIN

20 July 1936

The fate of the Monarchist insurrection in Spain is still in the balance. This much, but no more, can safely be assumed from the flood of rumour and report now filtering through a network of censorship and suspended communications. In Madrid and Barcelona the Government seem almost certainly to have the situation in hand – for the moment at all events. But there are persistent reports of successful risings elsewhere, including Seville, Saragossa, and Pamplona, while dispatches from Gibraltar announce the landing of insurgent troops from Morocco at Algeçiras and Cadiz. They are credited with the intention of marching on Madrid if they can gather enough reinforcements on the way.

The principal danger spot at the moment is clearly Andalusia, as it is there that the insurgents stand the best chance of uniting their forces. At Malaga a part of the town is in flames and fighting is in progress.

In Madrid there has been no disorder so far, although excitement is said to be intense – the more so because a strict censorship has been imposed. At 10.30 a.m. to-day the following statement was broadcast from the Government station:

"In Barcelona the military invaded the streets and proclaimed martial law. The Shock Police and Civil Guards went into action against the rebels. It can be assumed that the mutineers were beaten, as they did not succeed in taking their objective. Many prisoners were taken, among them senior as well as junior officers. The insurgents suffered heavy losses. The fighting was between Shock Police, Security Police, and Civil Guards on one side, and the Army on the other. In a short time it appears that the rebels, from whom some guns were captured, will have to surrender to the Republican forces of Barcelona."

Accounts of the uprising in Barcelona show that there was some desperate fighting before the Government forces succeeded in mastering the outbreak. The insurgents, furnished with artillery, made a determined attack on the residence of Señor Companys, the Governor-General, and for a time the situation was critical. The help of the Air Force, which remained faithful, appears to have been decisive, though it is not yet explained what form its support took.

Early this evening a Spanish broadcasting station, believed to be that of Seville, announced that General Queipo de Llano was in control of the town, and that "no human force could stay the triumphant movement of insurrection."

The following telegram alleged to have been received from General Franco, the leader of the revolt in Morocco, was then read:

"In taking over the command at Tetuan of the glorious and patriotic Spanish Army I send to all the loyal [to him] garrisons in Morocco and Spain an enthusiastic greeting. Spain is saved. The provinces of Valencia, Valladolid, Burgos, and Aragon, together with the Canaries and the Balearic Islands, with their garrisons and civil forces, have joined us with enthusiasm. Madrid alone stands apart, sending aeroplanes to bombard the defenceless towns and villages, killing women and children. They will be punished. Let those who are from ignorance still not with us, know that they have little time in which to join our cause."

As a news item, the Seville station announced that 14 lorries, loaded with explosives and coming from Rio Tinto, had been captured by the Civil Guard, which had killed 25 men among the drivers and workmen who formed the escort. The broadcast ended with the cry, "Spain is saved. Long live Spain."

◆

Representing a conflict between Fascism and democracy, the Spanish Civil War is often viewed as the harbinger of the Second World War. Its causes, however, were complex, resulting from decades of fiercely felt differences between traditionalists, reformers and the dwindling numbers of those remaining in between.

The election in February 1936 of the Popular Front government was broadly supported by those on the Left, including middle-class intellectuals and urban labourers. Ranged against it were most businessmen, landowners, military commanders and the clergy. The war broke out when a group of generals, of whom Francisco Franco would become leader, declared their opposition to the government and attempted to seize power.

The country was soon bloodily divided between the Republican forces, which held sway particularly in large cities such as Madrid and Barcelona, and those of the Nationalists. Both sides appealed for international support. The Republicans obtained it from the Soviet Union and foreign volunteers, and Franco from Mussolini and Hitler, who used Spain as a training ground for his air force. By 1939, the Republicans had been defeated and Franco ruled Spain until 1975.

THE JARROW MARCH

2 November 1936

In a downpour of rain on Saturday afternoon the Jarrow unemployed marchers made their way into London, still stepping out briskly and cheerfully as they completed the last stage of their 300 miles journey on foot. They were to have halted in Hyde Park for milk and sandwiches, but owing to the bad weather there was a change of plan and the marchers plodded on through Mayfair, across Bond Street, Regent Street, and Charing Cross Road to a soup kitchen in Garrick Street, where they had a belated midday meal.

The men marched in heavy rain all the way from Hendon. It was one of the worst days since they left Jarrow, and they were thankful that they had left themselves only a short stage to complete the journey. One man, who had developed a temperature, was left behind in hospital at Hendon; but others who had fallen out for various reasons had rejoined the party, and of the 200 who started from Jarrow on October 5, 197 marched into London. The men wore mackintosh sheets thrown over their shoulders but no umbrellas were carried and some of them were very wet by the time they sighted Marble Arch. Among the leaders at the head of the column was Miss Ellen Wilkinson, M.P., who has walked about 200 miles with these constituents of hers. The Mayor of Jarrow, Alderman J.W. Thompson, also marched with his townsmen on this last stage of their journey.

Headed by two mounted policemen and accompanied by only a few foot police, the men marched well and quickly. As they passed along Edgware Road they unfurled banners bearing the words "Jarrow Crusade," and hundreds of people stopped to watch them pass. The friendly feelings shown towards the men during the whole of their long march were equally evident in London. In Edgware Road a woman handed to one of the marchers for distribution among his comrades a dozen packets of cigarettes. The men were frequently greeted with shouts of "Good luck!" and – from North Country people who had turned out to meet them – "Good old Tyneside." As they got nearer to the end of their journey the marchers were joined by many relatives and friends living and working in London and there was a good deal of handshaking.

Through the streets of Mayfair the marchers passed quietly with their banners furled again. Later, they marched to the strains of "The Minstrel Boy" and "There's a long, long trail a-winding," played by their mouth-organ band, to the accompaniment of a drum. Everywhere traffic was held up by the police to let them pass, and there was only one short period of waiting during the whole of the long march through busy West End streets. In Garrick Street a welcome hot meal was provided by Mrs. Scott-Dorrien at St. Peter's Kitchens, and the men gave a cheer when they were given the word to fall out. The marchers afterwards went to the Smith Street Institution, Mile End Road, where they are to stay during their few days in London.

There are some grey-haired men among the marchers, but most of them are young and able-bodied. All of them looked well, and they have been greatly cheered by the kindness and hospitality which they have received everywhere. Mr. D.F. Riley, the Jarrow town councillor, who has marched at their head all the way from Jarrow wearing a bowler hat said on this subject: "I never thought there was so much generosity and good nature in the world."

———◆———

In 1930, Palmer's shipyard at Jarrow, on Tyneside, launched the thousandth ship built there since the business had been established 80 years before. But just two years later, with the global economy in deep recession, the yard closed. It had been the town's main employer and almost three-quarters of the population found themselves out of work, in an era when state benefits were scanty indeed.

The failure of all initiatives to improve the situation culminated in Jarrow being told by the President of the Board of Trade, Walter Runciman, that it must find its own salvation. Accordingly, 200 men – they termed themselves 'Crusaders' – set out to walk to London to petition Parliament. At their head was their MP, Ellen Wilkinson.

The month-long march attracted much attention and sympathy but once the petition, which had gathered 11,000 signatures, had been presented, no new proposals were made by the government. The marchers returned to Jarrow – by train – feeling that they had failed. Historians credit their efforts, however, with having convinced many Britons of all classes that social reform, which was to come after the war, was necessary.

THE ABDICATION CRISIS

12 December 1936

At 10 o'clock last night Sir John Reith announced on the wireless:–

"This is Windsor Castle. His Royal Highness Prince Edward."

The former King then broadcast the following message:–

At long last I am able to say a few words of my own. I have never wanted to withhold anything, but until now it has not been constitutionally possible for me to speak.

A few hours ago I discharged my last duty as King and Emperor, and now that I have been succeeded by my brother, the Duke of York, my first words must be to declare my allegiance to him. This I do with all my heart.

You all know the reasons which have impelled me to renounce the Throne. But I want you to understand that in making up my mind I did not forget the country or the Empire which as Prince of Wales, and lately as King, I have for 25 years tried to serve. But you must believe me when I tell you that I have found it impossible to carry the heavy burden of responsibility and to discharge my duties as King as I would wish to do without the help and support of the woman I love.

And I want you to know that the decision I have made has been mine and mine alone. This was a thing I had to judge entirely for myself. The other person more nearly concerned has tried up to the last to persuade me to take a different course. I have made this, the most serious decision of my life, only upon the single thought of what would in the end be best for all.

This decision has been made less difficult to me by the sure knowledge that my brother, with his long training in the public affairs of this country and with his fine qualities, will be able to take my place forthwith, without interruption or injury to the life and progress of the

Empire. And he has one matchless blessing, enjoyed by so many of you and not bestowed on me – a happy home with his wife and children.

During these hard days I have been comforted by her Majesty my mother and by my family. The Ministers of the Crown, and in particular Mr. Baldwin, the Prime Minister, have always treated me with full consideration. There has never been any constitutional difference between me and them and between me and Parliament. Bred in the constitutional tradition by my father, I should never have allowed any such issue to arise.

Ever since I was Prince of Wales, and later on when I occupied the Throne, I have been treated with the greatest kindness by all classes of the people, wherever I have lived or journeyed throughout the Empire. For that I am very grateful.

I now quit altogether public affairs, and I lay down my burden. It may be some time before I return to my native land, but I shall always follow the fortunes of the British race and Empire with profound interest, and if at any time in the future I can be found of service to his Majesty in a private station I shall not fail.

And now we all have a new King. I wish him, and you, his people, happiness and prosperity with all my heart. God bless you all. God Save The King.

◆

The press had been aware for months of the growing constitutional crisis surrounding King Edward VIII's relationship with Wallis Simpson, but the first that most ordinary Britons knew of it was a report in *The Times* just a week before the Abdication.

The pair had become involved in 1934, when he was still heir to the throne and she was still married to her second husband. Yet although the dilemma that ensued when Edward succeeded as King in January 1936 is usually presented as a conflict between love and convention, it was essentially political in nature.

Edward wanted to do as he pleased, but the monarchy had evolved during his father's reign. The British press might yet refrain from reporting the sovereign's foibles – although American readers knew all about the Mediterranean cruise the couple had taken together – but the King's role now was to unite the nation rather than to divide it.

His decision to abdicate may have shocked many but it also produced a sense of relief, especially at Westminster. The Abdication Bill passed Parliament in a morning and by the time that Edward made his broadcast, the words polished by Winston Churchill, he was already a private citizen.

THE HINDENBURG DISASTER

8 May 1937

The great silver shape, 803 feet long with twin swastikas clearly visible on the rudders, seemed in yesterday afternoon's sunshine as solid as the Empire State building which stood in the foreground as the Hindenburg turned her nose southward towards Lakehurst.

After leaving New York the Hindenburg flew slowly over towns along the New Jersey coast, and reached the air base shortly after 4 p.m. Fearing to land in a persistent thunderstorm, the commander, Captain Preuss, hovered round the landing field until 7 o'clock, when he decided to come down. At 7.20 lines were dropped from the airship's nose to the trained ground crew of 200 men who, divided into two parties, were prepared to haul the airship down. Estimates of the Hindenburg's height at this time vary between 300 feet and 75 feet. As she approached the mooring mast she discarded gas steadily, and it seems likely that she was about 100 feet above the ground when the explosion occurred.

As she dropped lower, passengers could be seen lining the observation windows of the centre gondola and waving to the large crowd of friends and sightseers who pressed behind the barriers below. When the lines reached the ground, disaster followed so swiftly that accounts of it vary greatly. According to one witness, the lines were made fast to cars at the base of the mooring mast and the ground crew began to tighten them. Meanwhile the ship had drifted and the taut starboard line swung her nose round so that it passed just over the top of the mast. Captain Preuss from the forward control gondola gave the order "Pay out," which was heard by the driver of one car but not of the other. Accordingly the line on one side only was paid out and the Hindenburg lost equilibrium. Ballast was dropped and the elevators were set to raise the ship, but the manoeuvre had the contrary effect to that intended. Instead of rising the tail dropped, hit the ground, and rebounded and a terrific explosion took place. Other accounts, however, make no mention of this.

Spectators on the ground saw a great sheet of flame from the burning hydrogen and a column of smoke rise from the stern of the airship. This was followed by a series of smaller explosions which shook the ship throughout her length. Passengers who a second before had been waving to those below were shot out of the observation windows by the force of the explosion, while members of the crew could be seen dropping to the ground from the falling hulk, many with their clothing in flames. In the words of a member of the ground crew: "It burned like a paper balloon." By the time the airship reached the ground she was ablaze from stem to stern, and the shrieks of those trapped within could be heard above the roar of the flames as they mingled with the shrieks of spectators.

Such passengers of the Hindenburg as were able to-day to give any account of their experiences agree that the disaster happened in such a short time that it is impossible to describe the scene. Apparently when the first explosion shattered the tail of the airship some passengers forward or amidships at first were unaware of what had happened, but those not lifted out bodily by the explosion were quickly forced to jump by the encroaching flames. Apart from gas there was little inflammable material in the ship. The explosions tore the envelope asunder and the whole blazing mass collapsed.

◆

The *Hindenburg* airship was the pride of Nazi Germany. It had left Frankfurt three days earlier, bound for America with about 100 passengers and crew aboard. At more than 800 feet (244 metres) in length – not much shorter than the *Titanic* – it was the largest aircraft yet built and could reach speeds of 80 mph.

A large crowd had assembled to watch it moor at Lakehurst, New Jersey. Among them were passengers bound, on the return journey, for the coronation of King George VI in London. The Zeppelin burst into flames when about 100 feet (30 metres) above them and within a few seconds was transformed into an inferno. The official cause of the accident was a static spark setting light to the seven million cubic feet of hydrogen that kept the dirigible aloft.

Thirty-six people died but another 62 escaped. The evocative images of the disaster were seen around the world and became fixed in the public memory; more than three decades later, a photograph of the *Hindenburg* ablaze adorned the cover of Led Zeppelin's first album.

THE FALL OF NANKING

18 December 1937

Sunday evening saw the first signs of the Chinese collapse, when a whole division began streaming towards the River Gate. They were fired on and stopped, and later it was learned that a general retreat had been ordered for 9 o'clock. The movement towards the gate leading to the Hsiakwan river-front, the only way of escape, was orderly at first, but it soon became clear that the Chinese defence of the southern gates had broken down, and that the Japanese were making their way northward through the city. The noise reached its climax in the early evening, by which time the southernmost part of the city was burning furiously. The retreat became a rout, the Chinese troops casting away their arms in panic when they found little or no transport to get them across the river. Many frantically re-entered the city and some burst into the safety zone.

While retreating, the Chinese fired the Ministry of Communications, the most ornate building in Nanking, built at a cost of £250,000, and as it was filled with munitions the explosions caused a tremendous racket. The resulting panic caused a traffic jam along the line of retirement and added to the confusion arising from the discovery that the supply of boats was exhausted. The Ministry was gutted, but it was the only important Government building destroyed: all the Embassies were respected.

On Monday morning the Japanese were still gradually moving northward, meeting with no resistance, and a systematic mopping-up had already begun. The foreigners thought that all trouble was over, though groups of Chinese soldiers were still wandering about. Those coming to the safety zone were told to lay down their arms, and thousands discarded their arms and uniforms, which made a huge pile in front of the blazing Ministry of Communications. The huge crowds of Chinese and the handful of foreigners hoped that the arrival of the Japanese would end the confusion, but when the invaders began their intensive mopping-up operations, that hope was dashed. The Chinese fled in terror, and the horror of the scene was accentuated by the wounded who were crawling around imploring aid.

That night the Japanese opened the Chungshan Gate and made a triumphal entry, in which, owing to the dearth of transport, they used oxen, donkeys, wheelbarrows, and even broken down carriages. Later they began working into the safety zone, and anyone caught out of doors without good reason was promptly shot. On Tuesday the Japanese began a systematic searching out of anyone even remotely connected with the Chinese Army. They took suspects from the refugee camps and trapped many soldiers wandering in the streets. Soldiers who would willingly have surrendered were shot down as an example.

No mercy was shown. The hopes of the populace gave place to fear and a reign of terror followed. Japanese searched houses and began a wholesale looting of property along the main streets, breaking into shops and taking watches, clocks, silverware, and everything portable, and impressing coolies to carry their loot. They visited the American University Hospital and robbed the nurses of their wrist watches, fountain pens, flashlights, ransacked the buildings and property, and took the motor-cars, ripping the American flags off them. Foreign houses were invaded and a couple of German shops looted. Any sympathy shown by foreigners towards the disarmed Chinese soldiers merely served to incense the Japanese.

Young men who might have been soldiers and many police constables were assembled in groups for execution, as was proved by the bodies afterwards seen lying in piles. The streets were littered with bodies, including those of harmless old men, but it is a fact that the bodies of no women were seen. At the Hsiakwan gate leading to the river the bodies of men and horses made a frightful mass 4ft deep, over which cars and lorries were passing in and out of the gate.

———————◆———————

Japan had long wished to extend its influence in Asia and this policy culminated in its invasion of China in July 1937, an event seen by some historians as signalling the start of the Second World War.

After capturing Shanghai, the Japanese forces marched rapidly westwards towards Nanking, then the country's capital, believing that its capture would end the campaign. China's leader, Chiang Kai-Shek, ordered that the city be defended but feared to lose what remained of his trained troops. From the start of December, the government abandoned Nanking, leaving it to be held only by auxiliaries.

Anticipating that it would fall, and having heard tales of Japanese atrocities elsewhere, Western missionaries and residents set up an international safety zone to provide shelter for the city's civilians. This proved of little avail, and while the destruction of records has led to a wide variation in estimates, it is thought that the Japanese raped tens of thousands of women in Nanking and killed up to 300,000 of its inhabitants.

China, however, did not surrender and the war lasted until 1945.

THE SECOND
WORLD WAR

WAR DECLARED

4 September 1939

The House of Commons had an anxious – it might easily have become an acrimonious – sitting yesterday afternoon because of suspicions that the Government (who could not help themselves) were being dilatory in fulfilling the British pledge to Poland. It reassembled to-day with confidence fully restored and a resolution that had never abated.

Yesterday the House, expecting a statement at any time from the Prime Minister, applied itself, with a dispatch that dictatorships could not have excelled, to a string of emergency measures, the most important of which made military service compulsory between the ages of 18 and 41. It was nearly 8 o'clock when Mr. Chamberlain entered, to the accompaniment of a rousing cheer.

The PRIME MINISTER told a tense and anxious House that no reply had been received to the warning message which the British Ambassador had been instructed to deliver at Berlin. Possibly the delay was due to a proposal by the Italian Government that hostilities should cease and that a Five-Power Conference should be held. There was a roar of cheers when Mr. Chamberlain declared that Great Britain could not participate in a conference while Poland was invaded. If Germany, he went on, should agree to withdraw her forces from Poland the way would be open for discussion between Germany and Poland on the understanding that the settlement would safeguard the vital interests of the latter and be secured by international guarantee.

The House was obviously disturbed, and when Mr. Greenwood, the Acting Leader of the Opposition, rose, there were cries by some Ministerial members of "Speak for Britain." He admitted that there might be reasons for delay in fulfilling our obligations to Poland and that "we must march with France. But," he said, "I wonder how long we are prepared to vacillate at a time when Britain and all that Britain stands for and civilization are in peril?" The same feeling was expressed by SIR ARCHIBALD SINCLAIR, and the greater part of the House obviously shared it. Mr. CHAMBERLAIN intervened to say that he would be horrified if the House thought that his statement implied any weakening by Great Britain and France.

VANISHED DOUBTS

To-day doubts had vanished. Members, who were crowded in the Chamber, knew how events had moved, and their knowledge must have been shared by the great array of the Diplomatic Corps in the Distinguished Strangers' Gallery.

In a few brief sentences Mr. CHAMBERLAIN informed the House of the presentation of the final note to Germany. The undertaking regarding Poland which the Government asked for had not been received in the time stipulated, and consequently the country was at war with Germany. The French Ambassador in Berlin was at the moment making a similar *démarche* has an acute on the first e, accompanied also by a definite time limit. Mr. CHAMBERLAIN'S closing words, to which the House listened sympathetically and which members cheered warmly, were:–

This is a sad day for all of us, and to none is it sadder than to me. Everything that I have worked for, everything that I have hoped for, everything that I have believed in during my public life has crashed into ruins. There is only one thing left for me to do – that is to devote what strength and powers I have to forwarding the victory of the cause for which we have to sacrifice so much. I cannot tell what part I may be allowed to play myself. I trust I may live to see the day when Hitlerism has been destroyed and a liberated Europe has been re-established.

◆

Following Germany's occupation of Czechoslovakia in March 1939, Britain and France had pledged to support Poland were it to be invaded. When German troops crossed its frontier on 1 September, both countries presented ultimatums and, having received no response to these, declared war.

The agreement with Hitler that Neville Chamberlain had secured the previous year at Munich, which condoned the annexation of the German-speaking part of Czechoslovakia, had been greeted with wild enthusiasm; Chamberlain was sent some 20,000 congratulatory letters and telegrams.

This was largely caused by relief at war having been averted – *The Times* supported the policy of appeasement throughout the 1930s – but when it became clear that the price had been acceding to German aggression, the public mood changed.

There was far greater acceptance that war with Germany was inevitable and necessary, and thereafter preparations for the evacuation of children from London and for protecting civilians from gas and bombing attacks began to be made even before the Wehrmacht entered Prague in March.

THE NORWAY DEBATE

8 May 1940

Mr. AMERY (Birmingham, Sparkbrook, U.) said that the whole conduct of the war up to date called for searching inquiry in a series of private sittings. By whom and on whose authority was the indispensable hammer-blow on Trondheim countermanded? There were risks, but war was not won by shirking risks.

So long as present methods prevailed our valour and our resources would not see us through. We must have soon a supreme war directorate – a handful of men, free from administrative routine, to frame policy. Mr. Lloyd George earned the undying gratitude of the nation for introducing it in the last war, when it was a new experiment. We must have first a right organization of Government. Equally important, the Government must be able to draw on the whole abilities of the nation; it must represent all the elements of real political power in this country. The time had come when members of the Opposition must take their share of responsibility – (hear, hear) – when the T.U.C. must reinforce the strength of the national effort. The time had come for a real National Government. (Hear, hear.) Somehow or other we must get in the Government men who could match our enemies in fighting spirit, daring, resolution, and thirst for victory. Such men could only be found by trial and by ruthlessly discarding all who failed. We were fighting for life, liberty, and all. We could not go on being led as we were. (Hear, hear.) He would quote Cromwell, with great reluctance, because he was speaking of those who were old friends and associates, but the words were applicable to the present situation. Speaking to the Long Parliament, when he thought it no longer fit to conduct the affairs of the nation, Cromwell said:–

You have sat too long here for any good you have been doing. Depart, I say, and let us have done with you. In the name of God, go. (Cheers.)

◆

Germany had invaded Norway on 9 April 1940, ending the so-called 'Phoney War'. Britain responded by dispatching troops and warships, but at the end of the month they were forced to withdraw. This unexpected reverse heaped pressure on the government, obliging it to agree to a debate about the debacle in the House of Commons.

This was to become one of the most celebrated in its history and a turning point. Leo Amery, a leading critic of appeasement, began to speak at about 8 p.m. Many MPs had gone to dinner and there were only about 20 or 30 then in the chamber. As the devastating power of his 40-minute long speech – reported in a compressed version by *The Times* – became evident, the Commons quickly became crowded once more.

Neville Chamberlain had appeared weary and ineffectual when he had spoken earlier, and Amery made direct attacks on his fitness to conduct the war. The following day, the Government won a vote of no confidence, but with a much-reduced majority. Chamberlain's position had been undermined and, after failing to form a national government, he resigned as Prime Minister. He was succeeded by the First Lord of the Admiralty, Winston Churchill.

THE BATTLE OF BRITAIN

11 July 1940

All day long pilots' combat reports came in. Always they told the same story – victory against odds.

During the morning Spitfires over the South-East Coast met a Dornier bomber with an escort of 30 Messerschmitt 109s flying in three layers between 8,000ft and 12,000ft. Two enemy fighters were shot down, and two more were damaged.

About the same time the Spitfires took on 12 Messerschmitt 109 fighters at 10,000ft. One dived straight into the sea. Two more were damaged.

Later, Spitfires met several Dorniers heavily protected by fighters. "It was like a cylinder of circling enemy aircraft," said the pilot. He climbed to the top of the circle, did a spiral dive down the centre, attacked a Messerschmitt 109 and a Dornier bomber, and put them both out.

In one action a Messerschmitt 109 and a Dornier collided in mid air. The Dornier crashed into the sea. "The Messerschmitt 109," said one pilot, "appeared to be disabled."

The following extracts from combat reports:

Got in a short burst at a Dornier, while two Messerschmitt 110s were attacked by – (another pilot). German fighters damaged, disappeared in cloud.

Attacked three Messerschmitt 109s and two Dorniers, unable to say if they were damaged. Saw three airmen descending by parachute.

Sighted waves of Dornier bombers from the French coast. Rear guns of one Dornier silenced. Explosions in the bottom rear turret. When last seen in mid-Channel the aircraft was flying slowly and losing height.

In aerial combat there is no time to watch what happens to the enemy. So accurate figures of enemy losses in such a day's fights will probably never be known – except to the German High Command. They will not publish them. British fighter pilots are quite content for it to be so.

40 RAIDERS DIVE FROM CLOUDS
BOMBS "LIKE A SHOWER OF HAIL"

People who watched from the South-East Coast to-day the biggest aerial battle so far fought near the British shores gave various estimates of the number of German machines engaged. None gave fewer than 70, while others estimated more than 100.

One eye-witness said:

"I saw 10 machines crash into the sea; they included bombers and fighters. The range of the operations was too extensive to see everything, for it was over land and sea. The British fighters were fewer than the Messerschmitts sent to protect the bombers, but the superiority of our airmen and machines was most convincing.

The first indication of the attack was when watchers saw about 20 German bombers with a similar number of support fighters dive out of the clouds. There was a tremendous rain of bombs on a convoy of ships, but they did not hit. Then came another wave of bombers and fighters, but before a second load of bombs was released anti-aircraft guns from war vessels opened fire.

It was then that a flight of Spitfires was seen and they went right into the midst of the formation, their first bursts of fire catching a bomber, which crashed into the sea. The intensity of the attack apparently took the Germans by surprise, for the enemy machines flew in all directions, the formation being completely broken up.

Spitfires and Hurricanes came from various directions, and some got behind the German machines which tried to fly straight back to the French coast."

The master of one of the ships in the attacked convoy said later that a solitary three engined German bomber attacked them some hours before the main raid. Later he saw 21 German bombers fly high over the convoy.

"Hundreds of bombs fell all around," he said. "It was just like a shower of hail. Some of the raiders were shot down in flames. Through my glasses I saw the tails fall off two of them as they crashed into the sea, chopped off by machine-gun bullets from British fighters. More German aeroplanes then flew over us, and they were attacked by Spitfires and Hurricanes. The sky was black with planes."

———◆———

By the summer of 1940, Germany was master of the greater part of Europe. Hitler believed that Britain would treat for peace and had made no plans to invade. Only when it became clear that Churchill intended to fight on was the Luftwaffe ordered to begin attacks on a large scale.

Its objectives at first were principally ports and shipping, the aim being to bring a besieged Britain to the negotiating table. The early engagements between the two sides in July were akin to a pair of fencers crossing swords, and the RAF did not itself become the target until mid-August. Hitler had by then ordered an invasion fleet to be prepared and needed control of the skies if it were not to be bombed from the air or sunk by the Royal Navy.

This delay gave Fighter Command more time to train up pilots and to perfect its system of defences, notably its chain of radar stations. These proved to be crucial to enabling it to counter the numerical advantage that the Luftwaffe had, and ultimately to winning the battle.

THE BLITZ

31 December 1940

As the official announcement points out, a deliberate attempt to fire the City was made. Shortly after dark the raiders came over, and had soon started several big fires. But almost as soon, the fire-fighters were pouring thousands of gallons of water into the flames and they held on grimly even when the raiders were dropping high-explosives on the fires they had caused.

The night in London was spectacular and even awesome. The enemy demonstrated to the full the senseless ferocity of aerial warfare. They flung down bombs indiscriminately. Here they destroyed one of Wren's loveliest churches, St. Bride's, Fleet Street's own church, with its lovely, slender spire; there they made havoc of a few small shops and a cafe; elsewhere hospitals were targets for their recklessly scattered bombs.

From two or three miles away, St. Paul's Cathedral stood out clearly against a glowing sky – a challenge and an inspiration. At one time fires were raging all round the great church, but it escaped almost without harm. Yesterday morning its doors were open, and in the Chapel of St. Dunstan a clergyman led a small congregation in prayer, while outside the narrow streets were filled with pungent smoke, there was a continuous clatter as broken glass was shovelled up, interlaced hoses covered the roadways, the fire engines went on pumping, and here and there buildings still smouldered sombrely. Approaching from the west one had noticed shining out through the smoke which filled Ludgate Hill the fairy lights on the great Christmas tree on the steps of the cathedral. Inside was another lighted tree, with around it gifts for evacuated children and men of the minesweepers.

A PORTER'S BRAVERY

London carried on with admirable calm and fortitude. Firemen, wardens, and other civil defence workers held on grimly, and many died that London might be saved. They were helped by civilian volunteers. A night hall porter in a news agency office next to St. Bride's dashed into the church to help put out two incendiary bombs. A third incendiary bomb lodged near the steeple, where it could not be reached at once. The porter, Mr. Charles McCarthy, climbed to the belfry, but was driven back by the dense smoke. He went back into the church and rescued the altar cloth, bibles, and a reading desk from the altar, and a large brass lectern, which he dragged to safety as embers fell into the smoke-filled church. St. Bride's was burnt out, though yesterday morning the steeple was still standing. Whether it can be saved is doubtful. Firemen were still playing water on it yesterday morning.

Only a shell remains where stood this finely proportioned church. The vicar, Prebendary Arthur Taylor, looked on as the flames destroyed his church. The gallery, organ, and most of the pews, he said, were just a mass of charred woodwork. The windows had gone; one of them, which depicted Christ being taken down from the cross, was valuable, though modern. The vicarage escaped, though surrounded by outbreaks which damaged a publisher's premises and the offices of the London City Mission.

WOMEN'S WORK

But, with death and destruction all around, London went on with the ordinary work of the night. Newspapers were printed and delivered as usual. The Lord Mayor, Sir George Wilkinson, spent the night with the firemen and A.R.P. workers. He toured his city, seeing how the battle against the vandals of the skies was going on, and congratulating men and women of the civil defence army on their efforts. Many women played a noble part as ambulance drivers, messengers, and in aiding the fire service. They came, too, with mobile canteens from which they handed hot drinks to firemen, whose eyes were red and swollen from their gallant work amid the flames and smoke and the dynamiting which was done in parts to prevent fires spreading.

Bravery was common on this astounding night. Civilians as well as firemen could be seen climbing over roofs and leaning perilously out of windows to cope with incendiary bombs before they could start fresh fires. Flames were leaping high into the sky, smoke which made the eyes smart filled the streets, water cascaded upwards in a hundred fountains, and from the skies rained down splinters from A.A. shells and bombs.

———◆———

After the Luftwaffe had failed to destroy the RAF, and following a British air raid on Berlin, Hitler tried to achieve his aim of shattering the nation's morale by bombing its main cities. London was the chief target and from mid-September was attacked on 57 consecutive nights.

More than 40,000 civilians were killed over the next eight months, but the raids did not severely damage Britain's ability to produce war materiel. There were several reasons for this – it can be argued that the Luftwaffe had not been created to fight a strategic bombing campaign – but contemporaries were surprised by the resilience of the population. This confounded the belief, born of the Spanish Civil War, that bombing was an irresistible weapon. By 1941, Hitler had turned his attention to Russia.

The most celebrated image of the 'Blitz spirit', the photograph of St Paul's Cathedral standing firm amidst the fires, was taken on the night of the raid reported here. Some incendiary bombs did land on its lead roof but were extinguished before they could set light to the timber beneath.

PEARL HARBOUR

16 December 1941

Colonel Knox said that the dry docks, oil storage tanks, and other important base facilities escaped damage. The loss of the Arizona was the result of a "lucky hit." She was sunk by explosions, the first of which was in the boiler and the second in the forward magazine, caused by a bomb through the smokestack.

The other ships destroyed besides the Arizona were the old target ship Utah, the destroyers Cassin, Downes, and Shaw, and the minelayer Oglala. Among the damaged vessels was the old battleship Oklahoma. She had capsized, but could be repaired. The other damage varied from ships which had already been repaired or which had gone to sea, to a few ships which may require from a week to several months to repair.

"The entire balance of the Pacific fleet, with its aircraft-carriers, heavy cruisers, light cruisers, destroyers, and submarines, is uninjured," said Colonel Knox, "and is all at sea seeking contact with the enemy." In answer to a question, he said that this fleet included battleships too.

"NOT ON THE ALERT"

Colonel Knox said that the Japanese had failed in their purpose to knock the United States out before war began, but he said flatly: "The United States Services were not on the alert against a surprise air attack." He said that the President would initiate a formal investigation immediately to determine why they were not on guard.

His visit to Hawaii had convinced him, Colonel Knox added, that after the initial attack the defence was conducted by both Services "skilfully and bravely." The naval dawn patrol had gone up on the morning of the attack, but had sighted neither Japanese aeroplanes nor carriers.

Army losses were severe in aircraft and some hangars, but replacements had arrived or were on the way. "I think the most effective fifth column work of the entire war was done in Hawaii, with the possible exception of Norway," he declared.

The Japanese had the "most perfect information" of the military establishment on the island.

RESOURCEFUL HEROES

In a formal statement Colonel Knox said:

"In the Navy's greatest hour of peril, officers and men of the fleet exhibited magnificent courage and resourcefulness. The real story of Pearl Harbour is not one of individual heroism, though there were many such cases. It lies in the splendid manner in which all hands did their job as they were able, not only under fire but while fighting flames afterwards and immediately starting salvage work and reorganization...

The dying captain of a battleship displayed the outstanding individual heroism of the day. As he emerged from the conning tower to the bridge the better to fight his ship, his stomach was laid completely open by a shrapnel burst. He fell to the deck. Refusing to be carried to safety, he continued to direct the action. When the bridge became a blazing inferno two officers attempted to remove him. But he ordered them to abandon him and save themselves. The latter found themselves blocked by flames. Only the heroic efforts of a third officer enabled them to escape. He climbed through the fire to a higher level, from which he passed one line to an adjoining battleship and another to his trapped shipmates. By this frail means they made their escape to safety."

◆

Tensions between America and Japan had been ratcheting up for decades due to the latter's desire to expand its influence in the Pacific region. This was driven in part by a shortage of land and resources as Japan's population grew by 30 per cent in 20 years. Many Americans expected war, but probably for control of the Philippines.

The two countries were in negotiations about Japan's potential withdrawal from China when its Navy launched a surprise attack on the US Pacific Fleet, based at Pearl Harbor, near Honolulu, Hawaii.

At the same time, Japan began attacking the British possessions of Malaya, Singapore and Hong Kong, also without declaring war. Convinced that America would react to these developments with force, it had decided to strike first. More than 350 aircraft, flying from six aircraft carriers, were involved in the raid on Hawaii.

Frank Knox, the Secretary of the Navy, had had to break the news to President Franklin Roosevelt. All eight battleships in the harbour had been damaged, with four sunk. Fortunately, all three of the fleet's carriers were elsewhere. Congress declared war on Japan the next day, and within three more days America was also at war with Italy and Germany.

ALAMEIN

3 November 1942

Germans and Italians – the German 125th Regiment and an Italian crack regiment – are now resisting from three main strong-points. Smaller parties are holding out in a number of other strong-points. It is clear that these will not be prised out without fierce, bloody, close-quarters fighting. Our troops must be very tired now, as it is 6 p.m., and they have been fighting without rest for 20 hours. The only consolation is that the enemy troops must be equally weary.

I have had a grandstand view of the battle to-day from this ridge. It was only possible because, the attack was going on in daylight, in contrast to the bulk of the heavy fighting since General Montgomery sent in the Eighth Army against Rommel, which has been done at night.

On the way we passed a small graveyard beside the track. Here, behind a fence fitted with a low white-painted gate, 40 or so Australians lie beneath white wooden crosses. It was touching evidence that General Morshead's men have not won their unexcelled reputation at Alamein without hard fighting. We drove on for about a mile, and ran the car into a natural bay at the bottom of a ridge. "It ought to be safe there from stray shells or bombs," a private squatting over a small fire, where he was boiling water for tea, told us.

We climbed the gently sloping ridge and looked out over the battlefield. It was quiet for the moment. A column of black smoke was twisting up from one of the positions where the enemy troops were holding out 4,000 to 5,000 yards to the west.

A lieutenant came walking up the ridge and hailed us. "That is where the enemy is caught," he said, pointing. "See that white sandy feature in the middle of the big, browny-green area of camelthorn? There is the enemy. There are more enemy on that white sandy bluff you can see among the dunes beyond. We were shelling them earlier in the morning." The post was hidden from us by intervening high ground. The lieutenant told us that he did not know whether our troops had yet captured it. "Contradictory reports have come in about it," he said. "We will get it sooner or later, but it is a pretty tough and well-defended post."

The lieutenant left us, and we settled down to our watch. There was plenty of evidence of the earlier fighting. Ugly, jagged-edged splinters from bombs and shells lay here and there among the stones. Below us, perhaps 1,000 yards away, were the shattered hulls of three or four enemy tanks.

There had been a Stuka parade above our troops as we had driven forward. We saw it from far off – anti-aircraft fire blotching the sky, then a line of eruptions about a mile long as the Axis bombs blasted the earth below. Now the day was calm and quiet without a sign of the desperate battle which was being fought, but the silence was abruptly broken by a staccato drumming. It was a Spandau machine-gun opening up. Another Spandau joined in. It was almost like a signal in a film studio. British guns behind us began shooting. Their shells went tearing overhead with a swish like deadly birds of prey flying at incredible speed. Guns were ranging on the position. Shells went splashing on to it, lifting great geysers of white sand which hung over it, then drifted lazily away. I felt half sorry for the enemy troops. They must have been feeling sweatily terrified as they crouched in the bottom of their trenches with the shell-torn air about them.

The guns pasted the position for about 10 minutes. Then the gunners lifted the range and sent shells smashing on to the white sandy bluff beyond it. There was no reply from the enemy guns. You could only think that their guns in the area under attack must have been knocked out or had exhausted their ammunition.

So the battle swayed on through the warm sunny afternoon. It is evening now, and in the light of the setting sun R.A.F. fighters have just flown back after a sweep over the enemy lines. One at least has evidently just knocked down an enemy aeroplane. He roared overhead in an exuberant victory roll. We stood up on the ridge and gave him a cheer for luck.

———————◆———————

In North Africa, Erwin Rommel's forces had threatened to reach Cairo and capture the Suez Canal, the main artery of Britain's global empire. By the autumn of 1942, however, they had been halted and he faced a new adversary in Bernard Montgomery.

Anxious to establish Britain as an equal in the alliance with America, which was soon to land its forces in Algeria and Morocco, Churchill pressed Montgomery to attack. However, he waited until he had built up overwhelming strength, having command of the air as well as twice as many tanks and infantry as his opponent.

The desert fighting was to yield some of the finest writing of the war. Montgomery's plan was to compel the Axis troops to come out of their defences and then steadily wear them down, targeting in particular Italian units that were corseted by German ones. The battle lasted a fortnight, with the decisive breakthrough coming in early November.

D-DAY

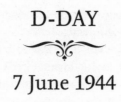

7 June 1944

"E for Easy" weaved its way gently through the not very frightening Flak, and took its place in the queue of Lancasters moving steadily over the target. After the usual directions of "Right, right, steady, steady" from the bomb-aimer lying prone in the nose of the fuselage, the bomber gave a slight lurch as it was relieved of its burden of 1,000-pounders. After what seemed a long interval the bombs exploded among earlier ones which had already ignited ammunition dumps near the guns.

By this time it was light, but although the khaki and green fields, roads, and even houses were clearly visible thousands of feet below, there was no sign of movement; the whole of the inland area seemed to be deserted. Yet along the coast every moment brought increasing evidence of activity. There were several small explosions, one lasting several seconds, and from time to time stabs of flame shot out in the direction of the sea.

As we recrossed the French coast, several miles away from the point of entry, the first fighters were spotted, and they were, no doubt, watched as closely by many other eyes as they were by the gunners of ""E for Easy." They proved to be American, as did others which raced inland a few seconds later.

The cloud was tantalizing. No sooner had one got a glimpse of the sea than everything was blotted out again. A few miles out from the French coast the cloud parted for just long enough to reveal swift-moving objects which reminded one of tadpoles as they wriggled their way landwards. The "tails" were the white streaks left by small ships taking an erratic course, and the "bodies," of course, were the vessels themselves. Another all too brief break in the clouds disclosed three extremely hostile Flak ships guarding the approaches to the same coast, firing furiously through the cloud in the hope of hitting one of the homeward bound Lancasters.

A little farther on there was just time to see the indistinct outlines of several large warships. Flying lower, Flight Sergeant R.J. Armett, of Acton, was able to identify four battleships. From a height of 9,000ft. only a small part of what was obviously one of the main convoys was visible from the cockpit of "E for Easy," but Flight Lieutenant T. Prager, D.F.C., flying some distance below, told me on his return that there were too many to count. "There seemed to be hundreds of them," he said.

◆

The Times's Aeronautical Correspondent had been permitted to witness the start of the Normandy landings from the co-pilot's seat of a Lancaster bomber, probably belonging to 115 Squadron, which was based in Cambridgeshire. The newspaper reported that more than 5,000 tons of bombs had been dropped on 10 coastal batteries as the assault on the German defences began.

It hailed the invasion as 'the greatest operation of its kind in history'. The raid seen by The Times was one of 14,000 sorties flown by Allied air forces on D-Day, while the ships spotted were part of an armada of 7,000 vessels that landed more than 130,000 troops from a dozen nations on the five beaches. And they had been preceded before dawn by 24,000 paratroopers and other airborne units.

By nightfall on 6 June, the Allies were ashore in strength and could begin their advance to Berlin.

THE LIBERATION OF BAYEUX

9 June 1944

Crowds of young and old people stood to-day in the cobbled streets of this town from which allied troops had just driven the Germans. Some of these French people had tears streaming down their faces; all were shouting "Vive l'Angleterre! Vive l'Amérique! Vive la France!" and raising fingers in the victory "V" sign. Over their heads the Tricolor fluttered from nearly every balcony. An old woman, whose face was lined by years and sorrow, told me that their national flags had been hidden away for four years but "Now we are able to bring them out again without fear of Boche reprisals."

Frenchmen, Frenchwomen, and children embraced British soldiers, showered them with flowers, or pressed bottles of wine into their hands.

It was one of the most exciting scenes I have ever seen as I drove into the outskirts of the town early this afternoon. Allied troops were still fighting to consolidate their foothold in the hills beyond the town, and a handful of snipers were still potting away at incautious soldiers inside the town itself; but the inhabitants had swarmed from their homes in their hundreds to greet the liberators.

To reach Bayeux, I drove along a road running through sunny, smiling fields, bearing few marks of the fighting that had swayed over them a few hours earlier. A grey morning had mellowed into a warm clear afternoon and the countryside could hardly have been more peaceful. Poppies are blooming in Normandy and in places they formed a nearly solid crimson carpet across green meadows, or raised vivid heads among standing corn with here and there the white of daffodils and the gold of cowslips.

It was in a poppy-packed field of corn that I saw first evidence of the battle – the corpses of three Germans clad in field-grey uniforms were lying twisted in ugly attitudes. British soldiers, too, had paid with their lives for the ground won. We came on one here, two there as we went on; but the German dead outnumbered them.

An officer, standing by the roadside with a tommy-gun resting on his arm, halted us half a mile from Bayeux and said, "Did you pass through a village a couple of hundred yards back?" We told him yes. He grinned and whistled. "You were lucky. Snipers are still holding out there and we are just sending in a company against them."

We had gone on only about 100 yards when we saw a stalwart British soldier striding along with two Germans marching before him. He told us they had been sniping troops on the road "but me and Matilda," patting his tommy-gun, "soon made them see reason."

I must confess that until to-day I had been uncertain how wholehearted the French reception of the invasion troops was likely to be. After all, they had been exposed to the most unscrupulous pro-Axis propaganda for four years. I shall never doubt their feelings again.

◆

On the morning after D-Day, Bayeux became the first city in France to be liberated. The Germans had moved their forces there out towards the Cotentin Peninsula, and having been told of this by the French Resistance, the Allies did not bomb it. A week later, General de Gaulle made his first speech on French soil in Bayeux.

Although the Allies had a growing preponderance of resources in Normandy, and dominated the air, German resistance there remained strong for many weeks. The sunken lanes and thick hedgerows of the 'bocage' countryside favoured the defenders and often hindered the use of armour.

Caen fell in mid-July, and Normandy was finally secured in late August when most of the remaining German divisions were trapped in the Falaise Pocket. Paris was liberated the following week.

HITLER DEAD

2 May 1945

Hitler died yesterday in Berlin.

The news was announced on the German wireless at 10.20 last night by Grand Admiral Dönitz, who said he had been appointed as his successor.

Dönitz, who described himself as head of the State and commander-in-chief, said he would continue the struggle to save the German people from destruction by the Bolshevists. "As long as the British and Americans hamper us from reaching this end we shall fight and defend ourselves against them as well," he said.

Hitler, it was said, fell at his post in the Reich Chancellery fighting to his last breath against Bolshevism.

DÖNITZ AS HEAD OF STATE
"I TAKE OVER THE LEADERSHIP"

The first indication of the death of Hitler was given at 9.30 p.m. when Hamburg radio announced that "a grave and important announcement to the German people will be made shortly." From then until the announcement solemn music of Wagner and the slow movement of Bruckner's 7th Symphony was played. Then the announcer said:

"It is reported from the Fuhrer's headquarters that our Fuhrer, Adolf Hitler, has fallen this afternoon at his command post in the Reich Chancellery fighting to the last breath against Bolshevism and for Germany.

"On April 30 the Fuhrer appointed Grand Admiral Dönitz as his successor. Our new Fuhrer will speak to the German people."

In his radio talk to the German people Dönitz said:

"German men and women soldiers of the German Wehrmacht! Our Fuhrer, Adolf Hitler, has fallen. The German people bow in deepest mourning and veneration.

"He recognized beforehand the terrible danger of Bolshevism and devoted his life to fighting it. At the end of this, his battle, and his unswerving straight path of life, stands his death as a hero in the capital of the Reich. All his life meant service to the German people. His battle against the Bolshevist flood benefited not only Europe but the whole world."

"THIS FATEFUL HOUR"

"The Fuhrer has appointed me as his successor. Fully conscious of the responsibility, I take over the leadership of the German people at this fateful hour. It is my first task to save the German people from destruction by the Bolshevists and it is only to achieve this that the fight continues.

"As long as the British and Americans hamper us from reaching this end we shall fight and defend ourselves against them as well. The British and Americans do not fight for the interests of their own people, but for the spreading of Bolshevism.

"What the German people have achieved and suffered is unique in history. In the coming times of distress of our people I shall do my utmost to make life bearable for our brave women, men, and children.

"To achieve all this I need your help. Trust me; keep order and discipline in towns and the countryside. Everybody do his duty. Only thus shall we be able to alleviate the sufferings which the future will bring to each of us and avoid collapse. If we do all that is in our power to do, the Lord will not abandon us."

◆

Adolf Hitler killed himself on 30 April 1945 as Berlin fell to the Soviets. Eva Braun, whom he had married the previous day, had taken poison a few moments earlier. Their bodies were then burned using gasoline in the garden of the *Führerbunker*.

Yet despite the announcement of his death the next day by Karl Dönitz, for some months after the end of the war in Europe considerable doubt remained as to Hitler's fate. This was because, although the remains of his body had been found by the Soviets, it suited them not to disclose this and instead claim that Hitler had escaped or was being protected by the British and Americans.

Hitler's name even appeared in the initial list of those charged with crimes by the Nuremberg tribunal. His death was only established to the satisfaction of the British authorities after an investigation in November 1945 by the intelligence officer and historian, Hugh Trevor-Roper.

VICTORY CELEBRATED

8 May 1945

Although by 9 o'clock last night the expectation of a victory declaration by the Prime Minister, which had kept large crowds in Piccadilly and the neighbourhood waiting nearly all day, had been dispelled by official warnings of its postponement, the crowds were even bigger than those which had dispersed two hours earlier.

Tens of thousands of Londoners and others were determined to celebrate the occasion, and there were remarkable scenes at Piccadilly Circus. Civilians and service men and women thronged the road and pavements, carrying flags and wearing paper hats. Cheering demonstrators climbed to the roofs of buses; the only people the crowd would make way for were lines of shouting, singing girls arm-in-arm with service men waving flags and yelling at the top of their voices. Cars trying to press through the crowds emerged with dozens of men and women clinging to the bonnets, the sides, and the back, and others standing on top trying to wave flags and hang on at the same time.

OUTSIDE THE PALACE

A procession about a mile long, including students of the London University carrying a large flag, marched up and down the Strand last night, and then through the Admiralty Arch down the Mall to Buckingham Palace. It was a cosmopolitan crowd, including many representatives of the allied nations, with flags, rattles, and hooters. There were singing and dancing, and outside the Palace several times voices were raised, shouting " We want the King."

Large bonfires ringed London during the night, and most public buildings were floodlit. Tugs, motor-boats, and other small craft raced up and down the Thames, sounding their sirens and blowing their hooters. Now and again an aeroplane flew low over the city, showing its navigation lights. In some places fireworks and rockets were sent up. When cars came to traffic lights which were red they sounded the V sign on their hooters.

Before the daytime crowd in Whitehall dispersed it was able to cheer Mr. Churchill when he left No. 10 Downing Street, after a Cabinet meeting. Mr. Churchill raised his hat and gave the V sign. A dozen police officers tried hard to clear a passage for the car, but it was some minutes before the driver could steer it through the cheering, excited throng.

SHIPS' SIRENS

At Poplar, ships' sirens celebrated the end of the war by hooting for two hours. Large bonfires were lit on bombed sites and in the middle of the streets.

Flags of every allied nation appeared in nearly every district of London yesterday afternoon and were particularly in evidence in the most badly bombed suburbs. In many streets the Coronation flags had been saved and brought out again.

There were food queues in many parts of London yesterday evening, especially outside bakers' shops.

Towards 6 o'clock, as the news of surrender was spreading rapidly, three Lancasters flew low over London dropping red and green lights.

In Edinburgh bonfires were lit by children in many parts of the city, though as Edinburgh has been scheduled a coastal area, bonfires are barred.

◆

Dönitz's government lasted a week. It was not recognized by either the Americans or by the Soviets, and with German commanders beginning to negotiate terms locally, it had little choice but to authorize the signing by the head of the armed forces of an instrument of surrender.

This took place at Reims, in France, early on 7 May. It was the news of this, here reported by *The Times*, which first brought rejoicing Britons out onto the streets. Churchill announced that the following day would be a public holiday and it is the celebrations of 8 May that became known as Victory in Europe (VE) Day.

The Soviets had objected to not being present at the moment of Germany's capitulation. Accordingly, a revised version of the terms was signed in Berlin, also on 8 May. These officially terminated the conflict in Europe at 11 p.m. that night. But, as Churchill reminded the jubilant crowds in London, Japan had yet to be defeated.

HIROSHIMA INFERNO

9 August 1945

Official reconnaissance photographs of Hiroshima show clearly that four and one-tenth square miles of the city, of a total area of almost seven square miles, were completely destroyed by one atomic bomb, and heavy additional damage is shown outside the completely destroyed area. "Destroyed" is the word used officially, but it appears that "obliterated" might be a better word.

Cold figures, however, scarcely give a sufficient idea of what took place. For a more graphic picture one must turn to Japanese broadcasts, which are now beginning to admit the terrible results of this attack. The Japanese state that most of Hiroshima no longer exists, and blasted corpses "too numerous to count" litter the ruined city. "The impact of the bomb was so terrific," say the Japanese, "that practically all living things, human and animal, were literally seared to death by the tremendous heat and pressure engendered by the blast." Buildings were crushed or wiped out. Unofficial American sources on Guam estimate that Japanese dead and wounded in Hiroshima may exceed 100,000.

Tokyo wireless speaks of the "indescribable destructive power" of the bomb, which crushed big buildings as well as small dwellings. The inhabitants of the city were killed by blast, fire, and crumbling buildings, and most bodies are so badly battered that men cannot be distinguished from women.

These broadcasts state the Japanese Cabinet met yesterday to consider the situation.

The official report of the raid from Guam states that a large part of Hiroshima simply dissolved into a vast cloud of dust when the bomb exploded. What had been a city going about its business at a quarter-past 9 on a sunny morning, went up in a mountain of dust-filled smoke, black at the base and towering into a plume of white at 40,000ft. When the bomb exploded the B29 which dropped it was 10 miles away, and so staggering was the sight that the 11 members of the crew exclaimed with awe, and as one man, "My God!"

On Guam this morning the three principal members of the crew, Colonel Paul Tibbets, the pilot, Captain William Parsons, U.S.N., in charge of the bomb, and Major T. W. Ferebee, the bomb-aimer who released it, revealed that they had been specially trained for this work, and had dropped many facsimiles for practice.

———◆———

Nuclear fission had been discovered before the war and thereafter both sides in the conflict had worked on using it to create a bomb. Even the Japanese had had their own project, but it was the Americans who succeeded first, having had significant help from the British.

Much of the heavy water needed for research had been brought to Britain from France by the Earl of Suffolk just as the Germans invaded. Thereafter it was concealed in the safest place that anyone could think of, where the Crown Jewels were kept in Windsor Castle.

The Americans estimated that taking Japan would cost them up to four million casualties, while the Japanese believed that as many as 20 million of their own citizens would die. Although the true toll is unknown, either of those killed by the bomb dropped on Hiroshima or by that on Nagasaki three days later, it is put at a maximum of 250,000 people – probably fewer than those killed by the Japanese in Nanking in 1938. Japan surrendered on 15 August.

FROM
AUSTERITY
TO ASTRONAUTS

INDIA GAINS INDEPENDENCE

16 August 1947

The Dominion of India was ushered in to-day with an elaborate ceremonial worthy of such a momentous occasion and amid scenes of intense popular enthusiasm. When Lord and Lady Mountbatten drove in State this morning to the Council House jubilant crowds broke through the police cordon, swarmed round the carriage, and amid shouting and cheering insisted on shaking them by the hand. Wherever Pandit Nehru and other leaders have made their appearance they have been accorded enthusiastic ovations. Their cars have been mobbed and movement for them has been difficult.

Indians, no less than the British, love dignified pageantry, and all the ceremonies connected with the inauguration of the new State have been most impressive. They have been marked, from the Indian side, by gestures of great admiration for Lord Mountbatten, who has enjoyed a veritable personal triumph, and by expressions of unfeigned good will not only towards Great Britain but also to the West in general. For those who remember past periods of bitterness and hatred it marks a real transformation in the relations between the British and Indian peoples.

Certain themes have run through all the speeches: an awareness of the greatness of the moment; sadness over the fact of partition, combined with good wishes to Pakistan and hopes for eventual reunion; and, most impressive of all, resolution on the part of leaders to dedicate themselves with renewed energy to the service of Indian people.

Although astrologers had declared that August 15 was an inauspicious day, favourable omens have not been lacking. Showers long overdue have come at last and freshened the green of Delhi's tree-lined avenues. The situation in the Punjab continues grave, but from Calcutta come reports of scenes of remarkable intercommunal fraternizing in the streets, with people shouting "Hindu Muslim *ek ho*" (Hindus and Muslims are one), and last night in Old Delhi there were similar demonstrations.

As from midnight last night India has been a fully independent self-governing State within the British Commonwealth. Shortly before midnight there was a meeting of the great Constituent Assembly in one of the great circular halls (formerly the library) of the great Council House designed by Sir Herbert Baker. The flags of the new Dominion hung in the frames which formerly contained the portraits of Viceroys.

The proceedings began with the singing of the first verse of "Vanda Mataram," India's national song, by the wife of the Congress President, accompanied by Indian lutes and zithers. The President of the Assembly, Dr. Rajendra Prasad, spoke first in Hindi, then in English, his address being followed by two minutes' silence with all standing in memory of those who had died in the struggle for freedom in India and elsewhere. Pandit Nehru then moved that at the stroke of midnight all members of the Assembly present should take a solemn pledge of dedication to the service of India and her people.

"Long years ago," he said, "we made a trust with destiny, and now the time comes when we redeem our pledge, not wholly or in full measure, but very substantially. At the stroke of the midnight hour, when the world sleeps, India will awake to life and freedom. A moment comes, which comes but rarely in history, when we step out from the old to the new, when an age ends and when the soul of a nation long suppressed finds utterance."

◆

Weakened by war, Britain had neither the means nor the will to resist India's demands that it finally control its own destiny. Clement Attlee, who had become prime minister, was also a supporter of independence and announced that this would be granted by 1948.

With tensions rising, however, between India's two main political parties, the Congress and the Muslim League, the date was brought forward by the Viceroy, Lord Mountbatten. Furthermore, less than six weeks before the day itself it was announced that India would be divided into two nations, with Pakistan (including what is now Bangladesh) being created as a Muslim homeland.

Jubilation greeted the stroke of midnight on 14 August 1947. However, in the weeks following Partition, as up to 15 million Hindus, Muslims and Sikhs moved countries, fearful of discrimination if they remained, sectarian violence was unleashed and at least a million people died.

THE BERLIN AIRLIFT

29 June 1948

The reinforced air service for the provisioning of blockaded Berlin was brought into operation to-day. For the time being it is a predominantly American effort. In the course of the day more than 100 aircraft arrived at the Tempelhof airport. The R.A.F. flew in 13 aircraft with a total of 40 tons of cargo.

A worse day for the inauguration of the service could hardly be imagined. Pilots flew through pelting rain, and it was not till late evening that the skies cleared. The bad weather did not, however, interrupt the service. By the early afternoon 76 aircraft from the United States zone had landed at Tempelhof; 11 more were then on the way; and 15 others were due before nightfall. They brought food for the American community and the German population. The aircraft which reached the city in the morning had, for example, mostly flour on board for the Germans.

The 13 R.A.F. aircraft brought in supplies for the British community and garrison, but plans are in hand for flying in provisions for the Germans in the western sectors, and these plans, it is hoped, will be put into operation in the near future.

The point must be emphasized that what the Americans and the British are proposing to do cannot be regarded as a solution of the appalling problem, not only of supplying the bare necessities of life but also of maintaining the industrial activity of the western sectors. Coal cannot be flown in, nor can raw materials.

Supplies of coal and petrol are for the moment satisfactory, but the position in six weeks will, without a reopening of land communications, be desperate. Food may be enough for a month. Western Berlin needs to import 50,000 tons a month; and the most that the present emergency service can hope to do is to extend the feeding of the population a little beyond the month which, it is calculated, existing stocks will cover.

RESOLUTE MOOD

If the blockade is maintained, western Berlin must face a cut in rations. With diminishing stocks of raw materials and no prospect of exporting their products, factories will be brought to a standstill. In their present resolute mood the people will be prepared to endure these hardships and difficulties so long as there is the assurance that at the last the western Powers do not march out.

The arrival yesterday of 10 barges consigned from the British zone to the allied Kommandatura here is announced to-night. Nine of the barges carried food – 1,000 tons in all – and one barge 150 tons of general goods. All this is destined for the German population of the western sectors.

The barges left Hamburg between June 21 and 23. Another 23 barges, also carrying freight and food for the western sectors, crossed the British control point into the Soviet zone between June 23 and 26 and are believed to be moving towards Berlin. So far they are not reported as having reached Brandenburg. Inland water traffic was excluded from the Russian restrictions imposed on June 18, but barges from the British zone have been arriving here irregularly and in reduced numbers.

◆

The post-war peace conference had left Berlin, still the capital of a divided Germany, marooned 100 miles (160 kilometres) inside the Soviet-controlled east of the country. Moreover, the city itself was split into four zones, one run by the Russians and the others by the Western Allies.

America, in particular, favoured aiding the economic reconstruction of what became West Germany, so as to create a bulwark against Communism. Central to this was the introduction of a new currency, the Deutsche Mark, which was also to be used in West Berlin. This plan was opposed by the Soviets as it undermined their ability to manipulate the old currency, the Reichsmark, and through it the inhabitants of Berlin.

Accordingly, they imposed a blockade of the city, refusing to allow the West access to its sectors from outside via road, rail or canal. The Allies responded by laying on 200,000 flights in a year, lifting in 4,000 tons of supplies daily to feed the population of West Berlin. Fuel there often ran short but on 12 May 1949 the Soviets ended their siege.

The airlift signalled the determination of the West to stand up to Soviet expansionism, but the Cold War had begun in earnest.

THE OLYMPIC GAMES IN LONDON

30 July 1948

No one present ever fails to remember the ceremonial opening of the Olympic Games. Least of all will anyone in the vast crowd at Wembley Stadium yesterday forget the great spectacle with which the XIV Modern Olympiad was started. The blazing sunshine in which it was carried out alone would surely stir any flagging memory. It really seemed as if the long-disparaged British climate had suddenly turned in its tracks to deal a blow at its detractors. It remains to be seen how long the mood will last.

Waiting for the arrival of the Royal Party, which may be said to have been the first active item on the programme fully to capture the attention, the minds of many veterans must have wandered back to the last time, 40 years ago, that the Games came to Britain. Then, after a morning's rain, one was glad enough of a little sunshine. King Edward VII, accompanied by Queen Alexandra, spoke the opening words which, yesterday, came quietly from the lips of George VI but reached the ears of everybody, thanks to the microphone. Only the members of the International Olympic Committee, lined up on the Wembley turf in their top hats and frock coats, seemed to sustain the rigid etiquette of Edwardian days.

One could have wished that the late Baron de Coubertin could have been among them to see how far the Games themselves and British organization had travelled in 40 years, for all the interruption of two world wars. A thousand or so athletes, representing 18 nations, mostly European – including Bohemia, curiously enough, as well as Austria and Hungary – joined in that march past in 1908. The United Kingdom supplied more than a quarter of the athletes. The United States, with 68, were only a few more than half the Danish and Swedish contingents. Canada, Australasia, as it was called, and South Africa completed the list of entries.

Now, even without Bulgaria, Rumania, and Venezuela, there were 58 teams in the march and 6,000 competitors, drawn from all over the world, some of them members of independent States undreamed of even 10 years ago.

The United Kingdom team of 1908, one recalls, was headed by an Oxford Blue, a Cambridge Blue and a former member of the Eton eight, and in appearance compared only in size with the well turned out team representing Great Britain, but no longer Eire as well, which rounded off yesterday's stupendous cavalcade. Yesterday, in spite of the belated return of foreign tickets, the crowd was fully worthy of the occasion. There one may leave comparisons for the moment, except to add that the opening ceremony of 1908 was followed by some heats of the 1,500 metres.

◆

There had been no Olympics during the war, so these were the first since the Berlin Games of 1936. London became the first city to host the Games twice but with wartime rationing still in force, and with austerity the government's watchword, they were staged on the cheap.

Most events were held at Wembley (then known as the Empire Stadium), made ready for athletics by pouring 900 tons of cinders onto the greyhound track. Competitors were boarded locally to avoid the expense of building an Olympic Village, while equipment and food was donated by other governments. With meat in short supply, the British team got its protein by tucking into slices of whale.

The Soviets did not send a team and Germany and Japan were *non gratae*. Britain, however, only won three gold medals. The star of the Games, who claimed four, was the Dutch sprinter Fanny Blankers-Koen. These Olympics were the first to be televised, and the last to feature events in the arts (among them sculpture and literature), staged at the Victoria and Albert Museum.

THE PEOPLE'S REPUBLIC OF CHINA PROCLAIMED

3 October 1949

In a brief statement read at a mass rally held yesterday before one of the massive gateways to the Forbidden City in Peking, Mao Tse-tung, who on the previous day had been unanimously elected chairman of the central People's Government of the People's Republic of China, formally proclaimed the inauguration of the new regime. It was an epoch-making moment in the history of Asia. Though not all of China is yet in the hands of the Communists, there can be no doubt that, for good or for evil, this is now the Government of nearly 500m people, the largest single homogeneous racial group in the world.

Mao declared: "The people throughout China have been plunged into bitter sufferings and tribulations since the Chiang Kai-shek reactionary Government betrayed the fatherland, conspired with imperialists, and launched a counter-revolutionary war. However, our People's Liberation Army, supported by the people throughout the country, fighting heroically and selflessly to defend the territorial sovereignty of the fatherland, to protect the people's lives and property, to relieve the people of their sufferings, and to struggle for their rights, has eliminated the reactionary troops and overthrown the reactionary rule of the National Government. Now the war of the people's liberation has been fundamentally won and the majority of the people throughout the country have been liberated." The People's Political Consultative Conference, representing the will of the Chinese people, had enacted the organic law of the central People's Government, had elected officers and members of the central People's Government Council, had proclaimed the founding of the People's Republic of China, and had decided that Peking should be the capital of the new republic.

"The central People's Government Council took office to-day in this capital and unanimously made the following decisions: To proclaim the formation of the central People's Government of the People's Republic of China: to adopt the common programme of the Chinese People's Political Consultative Conference as the policy of the Government; to appoint Lin Po-chu from among the members of the Government Council as secretary-general of the council, to appoint Chou En-lai as Premier of State Administration in the Council and concurrently Minister of Foreign Affairs, to appoint Mao Tse-tung as chairman of the People's Revolutionary Military Council, to appoint Chu Teh as commander-in-chief of the People's Liberation Army, to appoint Shen Chun-ju as Chief Justice of the Supreme People's Court, and to appoint Lo Jung-huan as Procurator-General of the People's Procurator-General's Office and to entrust them with the task of the early formation of the various organs of government."

Mao concluded "At the same time the central People's Government Council decided to declare to the Governments of all other countries that this Government is the sole legal Government representing all the people of the People's Republic of China. This Government is willing to establish diplomatic relations with any foreign Government which is willing to observe the principles of equality, mutual benefit and mutual respect of territorial integrity and sovereignty."

The Communist New China news agency reports that about 200,000 people gathered to hear this historic pronouncement. All stood to attention when Mao hoisted the new flag of Communist China, five yellow stars on a red background, and the band played the new national anthem, "The March of the Volunteers." Guns fired 28 salvos, which echoed through the city.

◆

From 1927, there had been civil war in China between the Nationalists under Chiang Kai-Shek and the Communists, led from 1935 by Mao Zedong. The former had held the upper hand in the decade before the Second World War, when the two sides had joined to resist the Japanese. Afterwards, the Communists had steadily taken control of the country, with their opponents forced to retreat to the island of Taiwan.

The Communist victory committed the Party to revolutionary change for China, implementing Marxist ideals that included class struggle. Mao also wanted to industrialize a society that was still overwhelmingly rural and turned for guidance to the Soviet Union.

America had supported the Nationalists and refused to recognize Mao's government. The fall of China to Communism, which Mao had promised to export across the world, would shape much of the history of the next 70 years.

FESTIVAL OF BRITAIN

5 May 1951

In the Dome of Discovery the royal visitors ascended an escalator to a gallery in which the solar system is illustrated. From here they had a good general view of the vast building, and its layout was explained to them. They could also see below them at ground level a section of the crowd that had gathered and from whom cheers rose as the King and Queen came down to leave the dome. The King then went forward to the river terrace, on which is set the Skylon, to inspect a detachment of the 36th Army Engineer Regiment, Royal Engineers, by whom the Bailey Bridge connecting South Bank with the opposite side of the river had been built. Firemen of a fire float, moored off South Bank just beyond the terrace, dressed ship as the royal salute sounded.

The royal party then spent some time looking at the Skylon, which has already become one of the most popular symbols of the festival as enshrined at South Bank. The young princes in the party, like any other schoolboys, were intent on knowing "what it is" and still more intent on knowing "what it does" and were still listening to cautious explanations about the famous "vertical feature" as they moved off with their elders to the Transport Pavilion.

In the Transport Pavilion the King was keenly interested in the display of railway locomotives and had many technical points explained to him by the Lord Privy Seal, Mr Stokes. As the royal party moved on towards the downstream section of South Bank, by way of the arch under Hungerford Bridge, they paused to look at the mural painting depicting the peoples of the Commonwealth with which Mr. Feliks Topolski has brightly decorated the archway.

As the royal party walked towards the Lion and Unicorn pavilion the drizzle which had begun soon after their Majesties' arrival at the exhibition became more obtrusive. Queen Mary, who had been walking, received a helping hand up the steps to the pavilion, but inside she had the use of a wheeled chair.

About 10 minutes were spent here, after which the royal visitors departed by way of the television courtyard, where some of the equipment used in television broadcasts and a model studio are on view. The last call was at the Homes and Gardens pavilion, where their Majesties gave special attention to the sections illustrating small homes, while the young princes enjoyed looking at the toys.

Crowds swelled round the exit from this pavilion and in the forecourt of the Festival Hall to watch the departure. The royal cars, which were parked in the forecourt enclosure, slid forward into positions of readiness, with the king's car at the head.

The King and Queen drove away towards the Belvedere Road gate, while Queen Mary exchanged greetings with other members of the party before entering her own car. The National Anthem was played again as the King and Queen drove up the lined route to the exit.

The Earl and Countess of Harewood followed in the next car, and behind this was Princess Elizabeth's own dark-green limousine, in which she and the Duke of Edinburgh drove away to renewed cheering.

So a memorable occasion came to an end. Before leaving, the King and Queen told officials how much they had enjoyed their visit, and said that they would probably attend the exhibition again at a later date.

———◆———

The Festival of Britain was held, on the centenary of the Great Exhibition, to promote the nation's recovery from the war. With the country still in the grip of austerity, the intention was to look to the future by showcasing Britain's cultural and industrial strengths, and in particular its recent achievements in science.

Although there were events staged in other cities, the main site was on the South Bank in London, an area razed by bombing. The Royal Festival Hall was built for the occasion, while other attractions included the Dome of Discovery, which housed exhibits relating to exploration and technology. The Skylon was a thin, Zeppelin-shaped metal tower which soared 300 feet (91 metres) into the air, although this did not deter a student from climbing it and attaching a scarf. There was also a funfair located in Battersea Park.

The Festival, primarily promoted by Herbert Morrison, the Deputy Prime Minister, attracted controversy at the time. Critics suggested its budget would have been better used for new housing. It was a popular success, however, attracting eight million visitors, to whom it offered a glimpse of a less drab world to come.

THE KOREAN WAR

30 May 1953

The War Office issued the following communique yesterday on the Korea fighting:–

The "Hook" position in Korea was attacked last night by the enemy, estimated at brigade strength, who suffered a crushing defeat mainly at the hands of the Duke of Wellington's Regiment, The King's Regiment, and the Royal Artillery. No further details are yet available.

WITH THE BRITISH FORCES IN KOREA.

May 29. – Men of the battered "D" Company of The Duke of Wellington's Regiment to-day fought off hordes of Chinese on "Hook Ridge" and drove them back from blazing bunkers, though the British were greatly outnumbered. The attack started with a 10-minute barrage from the Chinese artillery.

"The moment it finished the Chinese were all over us," said a platoon commander. The British troops were driven back into a pocket on the hill and signalled by radio for reinforcements and for shrapnel to be placed on the hill.

MANY BRAVE ACTS

The Chinese, eagerly advancing for the "kill," were badly hit by the shell bursts. As soon as the barrage stopped the reinforced British troops stormed the hill, mopping up the Chinese who were left and recapturing their positions. Some of the bunkers had caved in and others were still burning from demolition charges set by the Chinese.

The bitter night of fighting saw many brave acts. A platoon runner dragged his lieutenant and sergeant out of a bunker when it collapsed under heavy shelling. Then, with radio and telephone contacts destroyed, he served as the sole link between the platoon and the rest of the company.

One machine-gunner, trapped in his weapon pit with only enough room to fire out of a narrow slit, decided to keep firing on his own all through the night and played a big part in breaking up the Chinese attack. A young Welsh signaller from Cardiff walked into two Chinese in his trench. "Come with me," one of the Chinese said in broken English, seizing his arm. The Welshman kicked and punched his way out and ran off with one of their sub-machine-guns before the Chinese could recover.

Another British soldier stopped to let three men pass him in a trench, thinking they were from his own company. As they squeezed past he realized they were Chinese, and the trench was soon humming with bullets. The Chinese all made off in different directions without capturing the British soldier.

The plucky performance of The Duke of Wellington's Regiment drew praise from the brigade commander, Brigadier D. A. Kendrew, who said to-day: "The attack on the Hook last night was the worst in all my experience. The 'Dukes' did all I asked. They held the Hook."

◆

Ruled since 1910 by Japan, Korea had been liberated at the end of the Second World War by America and the Soviet Union. It had then been divided in two, with the north under a Communist dictator and the south under a capitalist one.

In 1950, North Korea, which had support from both China and the Soviets, invaded the South. Many thought this was the beginning of a Communist bid to conquer the globe. The United Nations sent in an international force to shore up the South.

This included British troops but was dominated by the Americans, and when Chinese soldiers crossed over into South Korea, a wider confrontation seemed possible. The action at The Hook, a ridge on a tributary of the River Imjin, became one of the most celebrated battles of an exceptionally destructive war that claimed up to five million lives. Most of the dead were civilians.

The fighting was ended by a ceasefire in 1953, but the two countries remain in a state of war.

EVEREST CONQUERED

2 June 1953

A message was received by *The Times* last night from the British Mount Everest Expedition, 1953, that E. P. Hillary and the Sherpa Tensing Bhutia reached the summit of the mountain, 29,002 feet high, on May 29. The message added: "All is well."

Thus the British expedition, under its leader, Colonel H. C. J. Hunt, has succeeded in its enterprise. Hillary, a New Zealander, was one of the members of the 1951 expedition which, under the leadership of Eric Shipton, found the Western Cwm and so discovered the southern route to Mount Everest, by which the success of the present expedition was made possible. It was Tensing who, with Raymond Lambert, on the first Swiss expedition of 1952 reached the record height of 28,215 feet on May 28.

If the plans announced were followed, Hillary and Tensing formed the second assault party in this season's attempt. They were using portable oxygen apparatus of the "open-circuit" type. The first assault, made on May 25 with "closed-circuit" apparatus by Bourdillon and Evans, presumably failed. Both were made from Camp VII – "that vital camp," in the words of our Special Correspondent with the expedition, "established on the bleak plateau on the South Col, at 26,000 feet." – and the climbers must have returned safely on the day that they started.

The failure of the first assault was not a surprise. The closed-circuit apparatus, in spite of various advantages over the other, was found to have certain definite disadvantages and is, in any case, less well tried. If the second, now successful, attempt had failed, a third was to have been made this season after a 10-day withdrawal to the Western Cwm. Had this in turn failed, the arrival of the monsoon would have necessitated a postponement until the autumn. Plans for this eventuality had been made.

As reported in a message published yesterday, the timing of the assault was delayed, largely through obstacles, caused by bad weather, in the crossing of the difficult ice-covered Lhotse face, which leads to the South Col. This delay led to rumours in Katmandu – whence they were spread abroad – that the pre-monsoon assault had failed. Although there was some sickness among members of the expedition, as well as the obstacle of bad weather, there is no reason to think a withdrawal was contemplated at any stage.

---◆---

Edmund Hillary and Tenzing Norgay had reached the summit of Everest on the morning of 29 May. *The Times* had the only reporter embedded with the expedition, James Morris (who later became Jan Morris, the renowned travel writer).

Morris was chosen by the newspaper although he had never done any climbing before. After hearing the news of the successful ascent at Base Camp, which was at 18,000 feet, and where no radios were permitted, Morris dispatched a runner down the mountain to Namche Bazaar. There, a radio powered by a bicycle was used to transmit a message to the British embassy in Kathmandu.

To prevent the story from being scooped by other newspapers, the message was in code: Snow conditions bad stop advanced base abandoned May 29 stop awaiting improvement stop All well stop. This was at first decrypted incorrectly, with Hillary's name replaced by that of another climber, Tom Bourdillon.

But this was spotted by the Foreign Office before being relayed to *The Times*, which was able to break the news – in what seemed to many a symbolic coincidence – on the morning of the Coronation of Queen Elizabeth.

THE CORONATION OF QUEEN ELIZABETH II

3 June 1953

Queen Elizabeth II was crowned in Westminster Abbey yesterday, with traditional ceremony, in the presence of a great congregation that included many representatives of the Commonwealth.

Vast crowds had gathered on the route of the procession, and the Queen was acclaimed with enthusiasm as she drove to the Abbey with the Duke of Edinburgh and again when she returned by a longer route. The crowds were drenched in the afternoon by intermittent showers which at times were heavy.

The R.A.F. fly-past took place half an hour after the arranged time and in a modified form because of unfavourable weather. It was watched from the balcony of the Palace by the Queen and the Duke of Edinburgh, with whom were the Duke of Cornwall and Princess Anne.

Television gave some millions of people a close picture of the scene in the Abbey and along the route, and broadcasting again allowed the Queen to speak to her peoples at home and overseas.

In a broadcast address last night her Majesty emphasized the inspiration she had received from the loyalty and affection of her peoples. "Throughout all my life and with all my heart I shall strive to be worthy of your trust," she said.

The day was celebrated with rejoicing throughout the country and the Commonwealth, although the weather marred the festivities in many places at home.

CEREMONY SEEN FAR AND WIDE
OVATION FROM GREAT THRONG

A lustre which no clouds could dim and no torrent could tarnish glowed at the heart of yesterday's tremendous events. It was not the splendour of sovereignty so much as its high solemnity which enriched the long and lovely pageantry of the day and set the mood which held the multitude in thrall. That was the reward and fulfilment of the vigil gladly endured through many comfortless hours, a benison which all could share with the young Queen who came to her sacring so richly dowered with the prayers she had herself invoked from her people.

Seldom, surely, has a nation been so deeply aware of the religious reality which gives all the magnificence its meaning. The glitter of gold, the glow of scarlet, the trappings and embellishments of martial pride and gallantry were but the setting of the mystery enacted within the Abbey walls.

For the first time television brought many millions into the heart of that mystery, with consequences no one can measure, in this country and far beyond its shores. They were denied the glory of colour which blazed within the Confessor's great church, but they shared with the 7,000 privileged members of that glittering congregation the enormous significance of all that was done. Much of it indeed was more apparent in its detail and fullness to the viewers in their homes than to the guests of high dignity in state and Empire and from foreign lands who thronged the azure galleries of the Abbey.

◆

Queen Elizabeth had learned of her father's death, and of her accession to the throne, when she and the Duke of Edinburgh were in Kenya in February 1952. She was then 25. In order to allow her to mourn, and so officials had time to make the arrangements, the Coronation was held the following year.

More than any other event, it was the coverage of the ceremony that brought television into British homes. It is thought that at least half of the population watched the Coronation on a set – twice the radio audience – with many seeing television for the first time. It was also a landmark in international broadcasting.

There was still a place on the day, however, for age-old traditions. Eighty-two individuals and local authorities were given permission by the Ministry of Food to roast oxen to celebrate the occasion, providing they could prove that their forebears had done the same and on condition that the meat was distributed for free.

THE FOUR-MINUTE MILE

7 May 1954

R. G. Bannister accomplished at Oxford yesterday what a whole world of milers had recently been bracing themselves to achieve first – the four-minute mile. He did so in conditions which were far from promising, and he did better than even time, for he finished weary but triumphant and mobbed by an encircling crowd, in 3 minutes 59.4 seconds – three-fifths of a second less than the magic four minutes. On the way, at 1,500 metres he had equalled another world record, shared by Gundar Haegg, the previous holder of the world record of 4 minutes 1.4 seconds over the mile, Lennart Strand, another Swede, and Walther Lueg, of Germany.

The occasion was the annual match between the University and the Amateur Athletic Association which one fears was rather forgotten in the general excitement. For the record, the A.A.A. won by 64 points to 34 in the 16 events. The crowd might well have been larger but at least it did all it could to make up for lack of numbers by an intelligent enthusiasm which enabled many among them to realize when the last lap was being run and Bannister raced well ahead, that something big was about to be recorded by the time-keeper – almost certainly a world record – perhaps the four-minute mile itself.

The conditions have been described as unpromising because a strong gusty wind was bound to handicap the runners part of the time as they ran round the Iffley Road track and one or two early showers threatened worse things still. Actually, the weather was fine for the race. The match itself was not started until five o'clock in the evening and an uneasy hour passed, with little success for Oxford. C.E.E. Higham's excellent time of 14.8 seconds in the high hurdles only inches behind P.H. Hildreth, the A.A.A. champion, in spite of a slow start, was the best thing seen so far. I.H. Boyd's victory in the half mile to a great extent made up for his failures through unfitness in the university sports.

But all this was quickly forgotten when the mile was announced and the six runners lined up. Bannister, C.J. Chataway, W.T. Hulatt, and C.W. Brasher represented the A.A.A. and G.F. Dole and A.D. Gordon ran for Oxford. Bannister's great time of 4 minutes 3.6 seconds last year was well in mind and Chataway started as a university record holder, but nothing dramatic enough happened during the first two laps to excite more than the actual time keepers.

Brasher, always a gallant and willing runner – or steeplechaser – set the pace and the first quarter was completed with Brasher a stride or two in front of Bannister and Chataway about the same distance away, third.

Chataway went ahead about half way down the back-stretch during the third lap and Bannister went after him. Brasher dropped back and, one fears, became forgotten though he had deserved well of all concerned. At the bell, Chataway was still a little in front of Bannister and one had to wait again for the back-stretch to see a new and decisive phase in the race unfold itself. Bannister now lengthened his magnificent stride and, obviously going very fast, passed Chataway and raced farther and farther ahead.

Spectators now really sensed a triumph of above the average, and as Bannister broke the tape some 50 yards ahead of Chataway there was a general swoop on to the centre of the field. Bannister was encircled and disappeared from view, but somehow the news leaked out. There was a scene of the wildest excitement – and what miserable spectators they would have been if they had not waved their programmes, shouted, even jumped in the air a little.

◆

Roger Bannister had been among the favourites for the 1500 metres at the Helsinki Olympics in 1952 but had finished fourth. In search of renewed motivation to continue running, he set his sights on the first four-minute mile.

Achieving that time had long been regarded as impossible and doctors had told Bannister – himself a medical student – that trying to do so would ruin his health. The mark had become 'rather like Everest', observed Bannister, 'a challenge to the human spirit'.

Although running for the Amateur Athletic Association team against the university, Bannister knew the Iffley Road track well since he had studied at Oxford. The timekeeper for the race was a friend of his from those days, Norris McWhirter, who together with McWhirter's twin Ross, Bannister helped introduce later to Guinness when the brewer was looking for an editor for its new *Guinness Book of Records*. The twins edited every edition until 1975 when Ross McWhirter was assassinated by the IRA.

THE MISSING DIPLOMATS

13 February 1956

The missing former British diplomatists, Guy Burgess and Donald Maclean, showed themselves briefly on Saturday to several Soviet and British journalists, thus confirming reports that they went to Moscow when they disappeared from Whitehall. There is substantial reason to believe that it was decided to produce the two men at this time in anticipation of the visit to England by Marshal Bulganin and Mr. Khrushchev, which is tentatively fixed for April.

It was learned on good authority that the Soviet leaders had been advised that their sincerity might be doubted in Britain so long as Russia continued to insist that nothing was known about the missing pair. Before last night, the stock reply by the Soviet authorities to all questions concerning Burgess and Maclean was that nothing was known about the case, in spite of the British publication of the White Paper which indicated that they were in a Communist country.

FIRST DISCLOSURE
This morning the Moscow newspapers, including *Pravda*, *Izvestia*, and *Trud*, published the full text of the statement issued by the two men. As the case has scarcely even been mentioned in the Soviet newspapers, readers here may have some difficulty in comprehending the story.

The statement leaves many unanswered questions, even for persons who have closely followed the case. It leaves open such questions as precisely how the men left England, what work they are now engaged in, and the status of their families.

Both the English and Russian language versions of the statement appeared to have been written in some haste, as if the decision to produce Burgess and Maclean had been made suddenly and carried out equally quickly. This was indicated in the cumbersome language which produced such sentences as this: "Burgess, who some months previously had himself initiated arrangements to obtain a new job with a view to leaving the Foreign Office, was faced with the fact that the Foreign Office had independently and subsequently decided that they would no longer employ him."

The burden of the three-page statement signed by the two men was to assert that "we neither of us have ever been Communist agents," and to explain that they decided to go to the Soviet Union with the aim of seeking "better understanding between the Soviet Union and the West." They declared they grew disillusioned when they "became convinced from official knowledge in our possession that neither the British nor, still more, the American Government was at that time seriously working for this aim."

In addition to information available to your Correspondent, which indicates that the timing of the reappearance of the former diplomatists is connected with the London visit of Marshal Bulganin and Mr. Khrushchev, a hint to this effect is contained in one of the opening paragraphs of the statement. This declares: "It seems to us that doubts as to our whereabouts and speculations about our past actions may be a small but contributory factor that has been and may again be exploited by the opponents of Anglo-Soviet understanding." The reference to Anglo-Soviet understanding appears pertinent to the proposed visit of the Soviet leaders, who are apparently trying to avoid any complications in this connexion.

◆

By the early 1950s, the Americans knew from intercepted signals that several years earlier there had been a Russian spy based at the British embassy in Washington. Among those informed was MI6's liaison officer in America, Kim Philby.

Since Philby was himself a Russian agent, he knew the identity of the spy. Donald Maclean was a diplomat at the Foreign Office who, like Philby, had been recruited to the Communist cause while at Cambridge University. Alerted by Philby, Maclean caught the ferry to France one evening in May 1951 and subsequently vanished. He was able to make his escape because the staff of MI5 – which was tailing him – did not work at night.

Maclean took with him another member of the ring, Guy Burgess. Their disappearance sparked a commotion and much speculation in the press. It was only five years later, however, that Russia admitted that they had defected.

Philby was not unmasked as the 'Third Man' until, in 1963, he too slipped away to Moscow.

THE HUNGARIAN UPRISING

25 October 1956

Soviet troops and units of the Hungarian Army and security forces are to-night gaining the upper hand in the struggle for Budapest. The Hungarian Government claimed that the situation was well in hand, but admitted that "isolated nests of counter-revolutionary gangs" were still holding out. The rising began yesterday with student demonstrations demanding the return of Mr. Nagy as Prime Minister. Great crowds swelled the demonstrations far into the night, and firing began.

Mr. Nagy, who was deposed last year from office for his "Titoist" leanings, was swept into power again as a result of last night's demonstrations. He was asked to resume office as Prime Minister at an emergency meeting of the central committee of the Communist Party held during the night. Mr. Andras Hegedus handed over office to him on the spot, and from early this morning all announcements and decrees have been signed by Mr. Nagy.

Reports reaching Vienna speak of 200 dead and uncounted injured in Budapest alone, where Soviet tanks to-day fired at random into houses suspected of harbouring rebels. Machine-gun fire went on all day, and a squadron of Soviet jet fighters swept the city, seeking to locate rebel strongholds. The curfew imposed last night was extended until 6 a.m. to-morrow "to safeguard the peace-loving population."

Shops were closed and traffic was banned from the streets, which were given over entirely to tanks, armoured cars, and ambulances. Big fires were raging in various parts of the city to-night, and a spokesman admitted that looting had taken place and that the insurgents had done heavy damage. The centre of the fighting is reported to be the area on the Pest bank of the Danube between the National Museum and the West station, as well as around the famous chain bridge that spans the Danube.

In the suburbs rebels attacked factories and succeeded in capturing a number of them. The Government claimed that two of the biggest, the Ganz machine works and the Csepel iron works, were recaptured by Government troops after fighting that lasted for three hours. Insurgents also occupied one of the studios of Budapest radio, but surrendered it on being promised an amnesty.

In an appeal to surrender addressed to the rebels the Government offered a free pardon to all who gave themselves up by 2 p.m. to-day, and later extended the offer until 6 p.m. After that, the Government announced, anyone caught bearing arms or disobeying orders would be shot out of hand.

Throughout the day Budapest radio broadcast light music, constantly interrupted by items of news and announcements. Mr. Nagy, the Prime Minister, went to the studio this morning to broadcast on assuming office. He said: "Hostile elements have abused the peaceful demonstrations of Hungarian youth to direct a blow against the people's democracy. The first and main task confronting us now is to consolidate the situation."

Mr. Nagy called on the insurgents to surrender and to hand in their arms. He promised to present his reform programme in full at the earliest possible moment and to summon Parliament to discuss it.

◆

Hungary, which had sided with Germany for much of the Second World War, had been occupied at the conflict's end by the Soviets. The Communist Party then took power, but following the death of Stalin in 1953, Premier Imre Nagy had permitted the population a new measure of freedom.

His political opponents managed to secure his dismissal in 1955, but after Stalin had been denounced the following year by his successor, Nikita Krushschev, pressure for reform again mounted. Mass demonstrations in Budapest were met with violence by the security forces. When Soviet troops stationed nearby intervened, the protests became an uprising.

Nagy returned as Prime Minister and a ceasefire held from 28 October until 4 November as the Soviets withdrew from the city. Yet, when Nagy appealed – vainly – to the West for support and announced that Hungary would leave the Warsaw Pact, Krushchev changed his mind. Soviet tanks were sent onto the streets to crush the insurgency and up to 4,000 people were killed.

Thousands more were arrested and imprisoned as hardline rule was re-imposed, while Nagy was eventually executed in 1958.

SUEZ

⌁✣⌁

1 November 1956

In one way or another the air in official Washington to-day is thick with cries of "Perfidious Albion!" "Do we still regard Britain and France as our allies?" was one of the questions put to the White House to-night after word had been received of the air raids on Egypt; and the President has called for a full review of the situation at to-morrow's meeting of the National Security Council.

It might readily be imagined, as more extreme commentators aver, that the grand alliance was in shreds. An austere view, however, needs to be taken of this first flush of anger in the White House and State Department at the temerity of the British and French Governments in taking independent action to safeguard the Suez Canal after months of diplomatic effort to secure American agreement to anything that looked like a joint Western policy in the Middle East.

Open accusations of collusion with Israel and the hot resentment felt at the lack of advance information of the Anglo-French ultimatum might have been more measured had the crisis not exploded on the last crucial days of the American election, which for the past week or more has been swept from the headlines – almost from the front pages – by the succession of eruptions that have shattered the fond contemplation by Republican politicians of a benign "era of good feelings" bestowed by some magic touch in Washington on the world at large.

The argument is now readily advanced, of course, that a situation of such gravity provides all the greater reason for keeping President Eisenhower at the helm: but Mr. Stevenson finds cause to redouble his charges that events have flowed in logical progression from the

Administration's foreign policy of "threats, bluffs, foolish words, and alternate smiles and sabre-rattlings, of provocations and appeasements" – and he notes that the President the other day was talking of "good news" from the Middle East.

There can be no doubting from the outburst of condemnation that Anglo-American relations are under a severer strain on the official level than one remembers in contemporary times; but how far Washington's resentment extends to the country may be questioned. In private conversation some support is expressed for an action that would have won perhaps grudging admiration had it been taken at the onset of the Suez crisis. "It is time someone made a stand" is a fairly common attitude among intelligent people to the deteriorating situation in the Middle East – especially those who feel some concern for the validity of international contracts.

This impression was borne out to some extent by inquiries across the country, notably in Kansas City, Chicago, and Houston, Texas, where the chief topic of speculation was the possible effect of the crisis on next week's election. Little public reaction was discerned to the Anglo-French intervention, and in Houston one of the local candidates readily gave up his time on television to an explanation of the British and French positions by the two consuls.

◆

Together with the uprising in Hungary, which occurred at the same time, the outcome of the Suez Crisis confirmed the new balance of power in the world. Certainly, it marked the end of one age of empire, and arguably the start of another.

In July 1956, Egypt's leader, Gamal Abdel Nasser, who had Soviet backing, threw off what colonial influence remained in the country's affairs by nationalising the Suez Canal, conduit for much of the West's oil. Britain, which had formerly controlled Egypt, had already been requested to remove the garrison it maintained in the Canal Zone but had not complied.

Nasser's decision had 'put his thumb on our windpipe', objected Anthony Eden, the Prime Minister. A plan was secretly put together with France and Israel whereby the latter launched an attack first on the Canal, with Britain and France then sending in their forces on the pretext of ending the fighting.

The Americans had not been kept in the picture and a furious President Dwight Eisenhower threatened to impose economic sanctions on Britain. Eden was compelled to agree to a UN ceasefire and, having been unwell, resigned the following year. Britain's international standing was left just as diminished.

THE MUNICH AIR DISASTER

7 February 1958

Mr. Peter Howard, a *Daily Mail* photographer, who was stated to be the only one of the Press party to be well enough to describe the events, telephoned his newspaper last night after helping with rescue operations.

He said: "It was snowing when we landed at Munich. I was sitting in the front row of seats on the starboard side. When the pilot tried to take off there seemed to be some kind of slight fault with the engines. He stopped.

"Then he tried a second take-off. That did not seem satisfactory so he taxied back to the apron to get things checked up. It was on the third take-off that we crashed. I think we were about the end of the runway, only a bit above the ground.

"The plane suddenly appeared to be breaking up. Seats started to crumble up. Everything seemed to be falling to pieces.

"It was a rolling sensation and all sorts of stuff started coming down on top of us. There was not time to think. No one cried out. No one spoke; just a deadly silence for what could only have been seconds. I cannot remember whether there was a bang or not. Everything stopped all at once. I was so dazed I just scrambled about. Then I found a hole in the wreckage and crawled out on hands and knees.

"I turned and saw Harry Gregg, the goalkeeper. Gregg, Ted Ellyard, the two stewardesses, the radio officer, and myself went back into the wreckage. I saw Captain Thain, one of the crew, start putting out small fires with an extinguisher.

"It looked as though those who had been sitting in the forward part of the plane were the lucky ones who got out. The luckiest of all were those in backward-facing seats.

"Part of the engines of the airliner had gone forward for 150 yards and hit a small house which burst into flames but the fuselage did not catch fire."

News of the crash came as a tremendous shock to the football world. Mr. Jack Crayston, the manager of Arsenal, said last night: "All here are moved at this terrible blow." The board of directors of Wolverhampton Wanderers Football Club, who learnt of the crash shortly before a meeting to select their team to play Manchester United at Old Trafford on Saturday, issued a statement expressing "shock and grief."

◆

'The Busby Babes', as Manchester United's young side were known, after their manager, Matt Busby, stood on the cusp of greatness by 1958. Threatening to dominate both domestic and international football for the next decade, they were chasing their third league title in a row and had hopes of becoming the first British team to win the European Cup.

They had just secured their place in the semi-final of that competition by defeating Red Star Belgrade when, returning from Yugoslavia, their aircraft stopped to refuel in Munich. It crashed after losing speed on take-off and began to catch fire. When goalkeeper Harry Gregg regained his senses a few moments later, he assumed that he had arrived in Hell.

Gregg helped to rescue several survivors, including Bobby Charlton and a young girl and her pregnant mother. But 23 of the 44 people aboard died. Among them were eight United players, including Duncan Edwards, who promised to become the best player of his generation.

THE FIRST MOTORWAY

6 December 1958

With a suggestion of automation suited to the introduction of the motorway, opening a new era in road travel in Britain, the Prime Minister inaugurated the Preston by-pass to-day by pressing a button which caused a mechanism to cut the traditional tape.

Mr. Macmillan, Mr. Watkinson, Minister of Transport, and Mr. G.R.H Nugent, the Parliamentary Secretary to the Ministry, then drove along the motorway, incidentally breaking one of the regulations by getting out of their car at one point for a closer look.

However, this was a nicety that did not concern some 200 schoolchildren watching from one of the futuristic looking bridges that straddle the motorway. The children cheered the Prime Minister and were rewarded with a wave of his hat. Soon after the opening ceremony at 11 a.m. traffic began to flow in both directions. The eight and a half miles of motorway, with dual carriageways separated by a central reservation, connects with the A6 at large roundabouts at Broughton, north of Preston, and Bamber Bridge, south of the town.

This is the first section of the national north-south motorway to be completed. Two more sections are being constructed, to by-pass Lancaster and cross the Manchester Ship Canal by a viaduct east of Manchester. Within a few years the three will be linked to complete the northern part of the national motorway.

Mr. Macmillan managed a convincing Scottish accent to quote an observation by Robert Burns on roadmaking:

I'm now arrived – thanks to the gods!
Thro' pathways rough and muddy,

A certain sign that making roads
Is no this people's study:
Altho' I'm no wi' Scripture cram'd,
I'm sure the Bible says
That heedless sinners shall be damn'd,
Unless they mend their ways.

The motorway, said Mr. Macmillan, was a sign that we were determined to mend our ways – and no longer heedless sinners.

That it is possible to average speeds of up to 100 m.p.h. on the motorway in normal traffic conditions was demonstrated by a police car which, in less than 20 minutes, while another police car was being driven along the old route through Preston, made three journeys along the motorway at an average speed of over 80 m.p.h. and reached 107 m.p.h. more than once.

The Automobile Association stated last evening: "So far, traffic has been flowing in both directions on the motorway at a rate of some 400 vehicles an hour, and the average speed is now in the vicinity of 70 miles an hour." Drivers were maintaining excellent lane discipline, as set out in the new motorway code, and signalling had so far been "exemplary."

The A.A. also stated that the speed and density of the traffic would probably make the traditional salute from their patrols impracticable. For the most part service vehicles would be operating, but any A.A. motor cyclists who might have to use the motorway had been instructed to salute only when it was safe to do so.

◆

Such had been the increase in the speed and volume of traffic, that even before the war there had been plans for a national system of motorways that would not only cut journey times but also reduce accidents.

Fascist Italy, obsessed with looking dynamic, had started building fast roads in the 1920s. When Macmillan was conveyed along the Preston by-pass in an admittedly rather stately-looking Austin Sheerline, it seemed to many that Britain was at last embracing modernity.

The early motorways had only two lanes in either direction with no barrier in the central reservation. The first to be fully completed was the M1, linking London and Leeds, which was finished by the end of the 1960s. The Preston motorway eventually formed part of the M6.

Just over a month after it had been opened, it was closed for emergency roadworks.

MARILYN MONROE

6 August 1962

Miss Marilyn Monroe, the film actress, was found dead in bed in her Los Angeles home, early today. The local coroner said the circumstances indicated a "possible suicide". Miss Monroe, aged 36, had long been suffering from nervous trouble arising from both her professional and her personal life. The police said Miss Monroe was found by two doctors, who had to break a window to get into her room. She was lying nude in bed with the sheet pulled up to her neck and a telephone in her hand. On the bedside table were bottles of medicines, including an empty bottle of nembutal, a sleeping pill. The doctors were called to the house after the housekeeper, noticing that Miss Monroe's room lights remained on for several hours during the night, tried the door and found it locked.

The tragic circumstances of Miss Monroe's life, from her early days as a waif sent from one set of foster-parents to another, to her emergence as the "sex symbol" of America, are well known. What is less well known is that as a person she was warm-hearted, friendly and simple. Most people who met and spoke to her outside the glare of publicity (as your Correspondent did) found her a delightful person.

By a coincidence the latest issue of *Life* magazine carried an autobiographical article in which Miss Monroe tells how she felt about everything. She says: "Fame to me is only a temporary and a partial happiness – even for a waif, and I was brought up a waif. But fame is not really for a daily diet, that's not what fulfils you. It warms you a bit, but the warming is temporary.

"I was never used to being happy, so that wasn't something I ever took for granted. I did sort of think, you know, marriage did that." Her three marriages all ended in divorce.

◆

Everyone had an opinion about the most famous sex symbol of the twentieth century. The number of these increased still further after her suicide, as her affair with President John F. Kennedy was revealed and conspiracy theories about the manner of her death sprouted.

What was already known about the fragility of her health and the burdens she carried from childhood was commonly forgotten. Norma Jean Mortenson, as she was born, never knew who her father was. Her mother, who had already had two children taken from her by her first husband, was schizophrenic and spent much of her life in psychiatric institutions.

Abused by the adults who cared for her, Norma Jean was raised by evangelical Christians who forbade her to go to the cinema. She first married at 16, having already left school. By the time of her death, she had herself spent time in psychiatric care, had been fired from the set of her last film and, suffering from depression, was living as a recluse.

'Story of my life. I always get the fuzzy end of the lollipop,' as her character Sugar said in *Some Like it Hot*.

THE CUBAN MISSILE CRISIS

25 October 1962

The Administration is now seriously considering measures to reduce the risk of war, and proposing to the Soviet Union that direct communication be established between the White House, the Kremlin and the office of the Secretary-General of the United Nations. Other possible measures include an exchange of military missions between the United States and the Soviet Union and Nato and the Warsaw Pact countries. It is understood that officials were directed to consider such measures on Monday before President Kennedy announced that a partial blockade would be imposed on Cuba. This supports other information, as previously reported in this correspondence, that the President looks eventually to a summit conference to resolve problems such as Cuba and Berlin. The measures now being considered were first proposed in the outline of Basic Provisions of a General and Complete Disarmament Treaty, which the United States submitted to the 18-nation disarmament conference in Geneva on April 18.

Other measures proposed to promote confidence and reduce the risk of war are: advance notification of military movements and manoeuvres, observation posts at ports and rail and road crossings, and an international commission on the reduction of the risks of war. The possibility of establishing direct communication between President Kennedy and Mr. Khrushchev and exchanging military missions is being first considered because the Soviet Union agreed in principle to these measures at Geneva. They could therefore be quickly in force. It was emphasized here today that they are only being considered at present, and would probably be formally proposed only if the situation deteriorated further. Other measures, that would take longer to impose, are also being given some consideration. These would be more difficult, and there is no indication as yet that any progress has been made.

The American objective is to remove the missiles from Cuba. The hope is that this will be achieved as a result of negotiation at the summit or the Foreign Ministers' level, but it is conceded that some kind of an exchange would have to be agreed upon before the Soviet Union would back down. Reference to the American missiles in Italy and Turkey was received with small enthusiasm; while they have probably outlived their strategic usefulness, as have the Thor missiles in Britain, agreement would first have to be reached in Nato and it is possible that Turkey would lodge a strong protest. The partial blockade of Cuba was imposed at 10 a.m. today by Task Force 136, under the command of Admiral Alfred Ward, the commander of the United States 2nd Fleet. The fleet of aircraft carriers, cruisers, destroyers, and submarines, which had put to sea on Monday, was said to be in position and well supported by land-based reconnaissance aircraft. The Pentagon said tonight that no ships had been intercepted. The spokesman said that some communist ships had apparently changed course, but eastern block vessels were still steaming towards Cuba.

◆

In the autumn of 1962, the world appeared to come as close as it ever has to nuclear war. The crisis arose after America discovered in mid-October that the Soviets had installed ballistic missiles at sites in Cuba, fewer than 100 miles (160 kilometres) from Florida, and that more were on the way.

Cuba, allied with the Soviet Union since Fidel Castro's ascent to power, had accepted the missiles to deter further American attacks, following the Bay of Pigs Invasion. Nikita Krushschev, the President of the USSR, believed the deployment of missiles there would better balance the threat posed by America's own missiles based in Turkey.

The situation was more subtle than subsequently presented to the public. Kennedy knew that, contrary to what he had claimed, America had many more missiles than the Soviets. The Cuban missiles represented not a military threat but a political one. He could not afford to appear weak to American voters nor to other international leaders.

While it was the blockade of Cuba that convinced the world that Kennedy had stood up to Krushchev, the crisis was in fact defused by a secret deal whereby the Soviets removed the Cuban missiles while the Americans withdrew theirs from Turkey.

THE ASSASSINATION OF PRESIDENT KENNEDY

23 November 1963

The assassination took place as the presidential party drove from the airport into the city of Dallas. One witness said the shots were fired from the window of a building. People flung themselves to the ground as armed policemen and Secret Service agents rushed into the building. A rifle with telescopic sights was found there. The President was wounded in the head and collapsed into the arms of his wife. She was heard to cry, "Oh, no" as she cradled his head in her lap and the car, spattered with blood, speeded to Parkland Hospital. The President was still alive when he reached the hospital. He was taken into an emergency room where facilities were said to be adequate. Two Roman Catholic priests were called and the last rites were administered. Mr. Kennedy died at 2 p.m. Eastern Standard Time (7 p.m. G.M.T.), about 35 minutes after the shots were fired. Vice-President Lyndon Johnson escaped because his car, following the presidential vehicle, was delayed by the large crowds.

Mrs. Connally said afterwards that she thought that President Kennedy was shot first. She said that the President was in the right rear seat of the open car and Mrs. Kennedy was at his left. Mr. Connally faced the President on a jump seat. She herself faced Mrs. Kennedy. "They had just gone through the town. They were pleased at the reception they had received. They got ready to go through the underpass when a shot was heard. When the first shot was fired Governor Connally turned in his seat and almost instantly was hit. An assistant to the Governor said: "She does not know about the third shot, but it may have been the one that hit the Governor's wrist. Jackie grabbed the President, and Mrs. Connally grabbed Connally, and they both ducked down in the car." Two Secret service men were in the front of the car and one of them instantly telephoned to a control centre and said, "Let's go straight to the nearest hospital".

President Kennedy was shot through the throat and head, possibly by the same bullet, according to Dr. Malcolm Perry, the surgeon who attended him. Dr. Perry said that a tracheotomy was performed to relieve the President's breathing and blood and fluid were administered intravenously. Chest tubes were inserted, and Dr. Perry tried chest cardiac massage, but to no avail. President Kennedy began his last day in the fine humour which political occasions always aroused in him. He joked about his wife; he said that she was always late, but was worth waiting for. Then, in lovely autumnal weather, he drove off at the head of a large convoy of cars. The reception given to him on his arrival had been enthusiastic, and thousands of people thronged the airport and the streets. The President's journey to Texas, described as non-political, had been undertaken to bring some order to the state's faction-ridden Democratic Party. The electoral votes of the state were considered vital for his re-election next year. The state party was not only divided between liberals and conservatives, but also by the extreme right-wing.

◆

Kennedy had gone to Dallas to ease tensions between the Governor of Texas, John Connally, who recovered from his wounds, and other leading Democrats in the state. He was also seeking support for his forthcoming re-election campaign. He was the fourth President to be assassinated, following Lincoln in 1865, James Garfield in 1881 and William McKinley in 1901. Puerto Rican nationalists had attempted to shoot President Truman in 1950.

Forty-five minutes after the assassination, Lee Harvey Oswald, a former marksman in the US Marines, was stopped three miles away from the scene by a police officer, JD Tippit. Oswald resembled the description of a man seen leaving the Texas Book Depository, from where the fatal shots were thought to have been fired.

Oswald killed Tippit with a pistol and was subsequently arrested for that crime while hiding in a cinema nearby. It was only when he was being interrogated that evening about the Tippit shooting that an officer recognized his name as matching that of an employee of the depository, and he was not charged with assassinating Kennedy until the next day.

He was himself shot, by Jack Ruby, while being taken to prison a day later.

BEATLEMANIA

11 February 1964

The Liverpudlian singing Beatles were displayed on American television for the first time last night, and millions of Americans from coast to coast were able to satisfy their highly stimulated curiosities about these four remarkable young men. The overwhelming reaction, apart from those who were provoked into the private mental orgies that teenagers reserve for their latest heroes, was one of relief. "We can put away the spray-guns", one New York critic wrote today. "The Beatles are harmless." Quite what Americans had expected from the British quartet was never very clear. Rumour had it that the Beatles were a combination of Elvis Presley and an Anglicized Davy Crockett to the power of four, and American adult imaginations frankly boggled at the prospect. They feared that, because it has been some years since their teenagers adopted a universal craze, when one came it would be uncontrollable. The fears have proved groundless and there is as a result today a considerable feeling of gratitude towards Britain. It may even go some way towards compensating for the export of buses to Cuba.

The critic of the *New York Times*, Mr. Jack Gould, wrote: "Televised Beatlemania appeared to be a fine mass placebo, and thanks undoubtedly are due to Britain for a recess in winter's routine. Last night's sedate anticlimax speaks well for continuing British-American understanding. The British always were much more strict with children." Newspaper critics across the country were virtually unanimous in noting how modest and agreeable the performers were. "The Beatles are not such bad chaps after all", commented the

Washington Post. "They behaved in a more civilized manner than most of our own rock-and-roll heroes. Except for the outrageous bath-mat coiffure, the four young men seemed downright conservative . . . asexual and homely." Other critics have commented that the Beatles seemed aware that the performance of the audience was as important as that on the stage. The television studio for last night's Ed Sullivan show was filled with 750 lucky enthusiasts (more than 5,000 had applied for tickets) who screamed their pleasure in what must now be regarded as the conventional manner as the Beatles sang half a dozen songs.

As is the American way, those who are enthusiastic about the Beatles are being given ample opportunity to express it. Puritan Fashions Incorporated, which describes itself as "the only exclusive official licensed manufacturer of Beatle wearing apparel", is marketing T-shirts, sweat shirts, turtle-neck sweaters, tight-legged trousers, night shirts, scarves, and jewelry inspired by the Beatles, and there is of course an undergrowth of Beatle wigs for sale at $2.99 (one guinea) each. The *New York Times* today was one of the few newspapers to give serious attention to the nature of the music provided by the Beatles, and its critics disagreed with the music critic of *The Times*, who described it as pandiatonic. The *New York Times* prefers to regard it as purely diatonic. "The Beatles have a tendency to build phrases around unresolved leading tones", wrote Mr. Theodore Strongin this morning. "This precipitates the ear into a false modal frame that temporarily turns the fifth of the scale into the tonic, momentarily suggesting the Mixolydian mode. But everything always ends a plain diatonic all the same."

◆

Undisputed as the long-term impact of their music has been, the Beatles – and Beatlemania – also fashioned the template for the brief lifecycle of pop bands.

Almost unknown beyond Liverpool at the start of 1963, they had become such a phenomenon in Britain by the year's end that they were invited to appear on America's leading variety programme: The Ed Sullivan Show. With the nation still recovering from the Kennedy assassination, their first broadcast in February was watched by a record audience of 73 million – a third of the population. Few commentators appear to have recognized the American roots of the group's sound.

Teenage hysteria greeted their first concerts in America. Combined with exposure from more appearances on Sullivan's show, this led to the Beatles occupying, by April, the top five places in the singles chart.

The following year, huge numbers of fans saw them play Shea Stadium, New York. Yet, in 1966, the Beatles stopped touring, frustrated that their music could not be performed properly, so loud was the crowd.

More albums followed, of course, but by the end of the 1960s the band had in effect gone their separate ways. (See John Lennon, page 308.)

THE DEATH OF
WINSTON CHURCHILL

28 January 1965

On any random day Westminster Hall is resonant with memories that awe and move the mind of visitors, but its gaunt spaces can never have been more intensely charged with emotional remembrance than at this time, while the body of Sir Winston Churchill lies there for the rank and file of the people he served and led to take their last leave of him. For it is memory of some rare quality or idiosyncrasy of the man that everybody, except the very young, carries with him as he comes down the steps from St. Stephen's Chapel and in his turn moves slowly past the catafalque that is the still point of the turning world outside. No man, no woman who comes here is so poor as to be without the abundance of some personal memory of him, and none so rich as not to count his memory their best treasure.

He lies there now in a crowded quietude. In the middle of the hall, warming its chill, has been spread garnet-coloured carpeting. Rising from it is the platform, on which stands the catafalque 7ft high. The bier is covered in black velvet with edging of silver braid, and on it rests the coffin draped with the Union Flag. Sir Winston's insignia as a Knight of the Garter – collar, star, and garter – have been placed on a black silk cushion on the coffin. A golden cross rises at the head to catch the shifting light of tall, large candles burning at the four corners of the bier and sending up thin smoke towards the oak of the medieval roof. Now and then the heart of a nation's mourning floods with an almost theatrical light, for television will be served; it is kinder when the shadows and the mystery gather again around the oaken angels carved on the roof beams and on the austere walls. Day and night, until the cortege leaves the hall for the state funeral at St. Paul's Cathedral on Saturday morning, Sir Winston will have a guard of honour of officers drawn in turn from the three Services. Four members of each watch stand, heads bowed and hands crossed on the pommel of their swords, in motionless vigil at the corners of the bier, and a fifth stands at the head of the steps by which the relieving watch will soon enter the hall.

No spoken orders are heard or given. At 20-minute intervals a faint double tap of a sword on stone breaks the silence, and at that signal the guards change in slow, slow time. And there, as those of mark and name again rub shoulders with anonymity as they did years ago in acceptance of Sir Winston's leadership, personal memories begin. For each mourner it is an individual memory. A man is great indeed when his greatness can be shared out in so many fragments. Outside St. Stephen's entrance the moving crocodile of mourners stretches round the Palace of Westminster, over Lambeth Bridge, until at times they reach St. Thomas's Hospital on the south bank of the Thames. Each hour yesterday more than 4,000 men, women, and children passed into Westminster Hall, paid their tribute of memory, and then left by New Palace Yard.

There are Cockney women, many of them no longer young, who have rummaged in their wardrobes to find a black hat or scarf or a dark coat that would be apt for a mourner who knows what is seemly. Talk to them as they come, often moist-eyed, through the great doors of the hall and they will say, perhaps that they last saw Sir Winston standing among the ruin of their East End street and ruggedly symbolizing that it would not be the ruin of their hope. They remember particularly the grim set of his jaw, his compassion, his look of indestructibility, and the impishness of his V sign made with the first two fingers.

◆

Churchill died on 24 January. He was 90 and had suffered several strokes since recovering from the one in 1953 that had almost ended his second term as Prime Minister. Those had been the days in which a premier could still recuperate in secret for more than a month, being read to from the works of Trollope while the press obligingly hushed up the situation.

The wait to pay tribute to Churchill as his body lay in state in Westminster Hall averaged three hours. His funeral, which had been planned in detail a decade before, remained the largest international gathering of heads of state until that of Pope John Paul II 40 years later.

After the ceremony at St Paul's Cathedral, the coffin was carried by boat to Waterloo station. Even the cranes by the Thames were bowed in mourning. He was buried that afternoon at Bladon, hard by the seat of his ancestors, and his own place of birth, Blenheim Palace.

ABOLITION OF THE DEATH PENALTY

9 November 1965

The Royal Assent, given yesterday, to the Murder (Abolition of Death Penalty) Bill introduced by Mr. Sydney Silverman, M.P., as a private member's Bill, is the culmination of a century of political campaigning.

Important milestones in the history of reform:

1864. Royal Commission majority favoured recognition of degrees of murder, advocated death penalty where there was "malice aforethought" or in course of arson, rape, burglary, robbery or piracy. Recommendations failed.

1868. Public executions discontinued.

1908. Death sentence on children under 16 abolished.

1921. Howard League for Penal Reform founded.

1922. Infanticide by a distracted mother categorized as manslaughter.

1925. National Council for the Abolition of the Death Penalty founded.

1929. Parliamentary Select Committee recommended suspension of death penalty for trial five-year period. Not adopted.

1933. Minimum age limit for death penalty raised to 18.

1938. In free vote Commons passed motion in favour of abolition. Attempt to insert abolition clause in Bill defeated.

1948. Mr. Sydney Silverman's motion for abolition carried in Commons on a free vote by 245 votes to 222, but abolition clause in Bill heavily defeated in Lords. Compromise clause retaining death penalty for murders in course of robbery by three or more persons, of indecent assault, by explosives or systematic administration of poison, for second murders and for the murder by a prisoner of a police officer also defeated.

1953. Royal Commission under Sir Ernest Gowers recommended that juries should be given discretion as to penalties, doctrine of "constructive malice" should be abolished, an abettor should not be held Guilty of murder, and minimum age should be raised to 21. All main recommendations rejected.

1956. Commons motion in favour of abolition approved in free vote by 293 to 262. New Silverman Bill given second and third readings but again rejected by Lords 238-95.

1957. Homicide Act abolished doctrine of constructive malice, divided murders into "capital" and "non-capital". Capital murders were defined as those in course of theft, by shooting or explosion, and to prevent arrest; also murders of policemen and prison officers and second murders. Act also introduced defence of "diminished responsibility."

1965. Murder (Abolition of Death Penalty) Bill passed by both Lords and Commons.

———————◆———————

Until the early-nineteenth century, Britain was notorious for the sheer range and number of crimes – more than 200 – that attracted capital punishment. Although in practice the sentences were often commuted, petty theft and pickpocketing were punishable by death, and statutes decreed that even children as young as seven could be hanged.

As sentiment and morality changed in society, so attempts at reform began. Famously, Charles Dickens wrote to The Times in 1849 to decry the continuance of executions as a public spectacle. Children under 16 were spared death from 1908, and the killing of a newborn child by its mother was abolished as a capital crime in 1922.

Although the police believed the sanction for murder deterred criminals from using guns, miscarriages of justice and sympathy for crimes of passion further reduced public support for the death penalty. Silverman's Bill was sponsored by three other MPs: Michael Foot; Christopher Chataway, one of the pacemakers of the four-minute mile; and Jeremy Thorpe, later himself to be charged with conspiracy to murder.

THE WORLD CUP

1 August 1966

England, the pioneers of organized football and the home of the game, are the new World Champions for the first time. They are still pinching themselves.

So, too, are others of us, the sceptics, who from the start thought the feat beyond our reach. But it is no dream. If England, perhaps, did not possess the greatest flair, they were the best prepared in the field, with the best temperament based on a functional plan. Further to that, they built up to a peak. The timing of it was good.

West Germany, twice semi-finalists in other years and the surprise holders of 1954, when they upset the magnificent Hungarians, were beaten fair and square in a match of high drama. A squally afternoon of showers and sunshine was rich with excitement and some passing controversy that tested the stamina and willpower of both sides, to say nothing of the 93,000 crowd ranged around Wembley's steep banks and the 400 million others watching on television around the world.

The climax came in a punishing period of an extra half-hour after the Germans had first led and then saved their necks with an equalizing goal at 2-2 a mere 15 seconds from the end of normal time.

To have the Cup thus apparently dashed from their lips at the very moment of victory was a deep test of England's morale. Psychologically Germany should have had the edge in that extra time. But Moore and his men rose magnificently to the challenge. Only the two sets of actors down on that green stage could have truly felt the bitter disappointment or the elation of that moment.

But as England were yet girding themselves for the extended test, Mr. Ramsey, their manager, walked calmly among his men to say: "All right. You let it slip. Now start again!" They did. They reacted vigorously. How some of them found the resilience and the stamina finally to outstay a German side equally powerful physically, equally determined, equally battle-hardened, was beyond praise.

All were heroes: none more so than Moore as he drove his side on; than the little flame-haired Ball, a real ball of fire this great day, as he covered every blade of grass on Wembley's wide spaces; than the intelligent Peters, than Hurst – preferred to Greaves at the eleventh hour as a striker – who crashed in two goals during extra time to become the first man to hit the net three times in a World Cup final.

For Hurst, for Moore, the captain, and for Ramsey, the inscrutable manager, this indeed was a storybook ending. If there are no substitutes for gods, equally there are no substitutes for courage and temperament. England had those in full measure.

Thus the 1966 championships were crowned worthily in the presence of the Queen and the Duke of Edinburgh. Earlier irritations were forgotten and the best now lingers on. And never has Wembley itself provided a more emotional setting. From early afternoon the atmosphere was electric. It fairly crackled. The terracing was a sea of waving flags, the standards of two nations; the noise was a wall of sound that drowned the flutterings of one's heart. High in the stands there came the beating of a drum, a deep, pulsating thud, almost tribal.

It set the mood of a throbbing match, climaxed in the sunshine of the end when the Germans, honourable losers, made their own farewell lap of the stadium to a warm reception and followed amid thunderous roars as the stadium rose to Moore holding the golden, winged trophy in triumphal circuit. Honour and justice were done in that proud moment beyond many dreams.

———◆———

Alf Ramsey had publicly predicted his England team would win the tournament. In retrospect, when their victory is so familiar it seems preordained, what is surprising is how easily things might have gone awry – and that without querying whether England's third goal did cross the line.

In the build-up to the World Cup, Ramsey struggled to find the right blend of forwards. Martin Peters made his international debut just two months before the competition, and only came into the team in the second group match after Ramsey felt his conventional wingers had failed to shine. The 'wingless wonders' were born of necessity.

It is often forgotten that Ramsey's first-choice striker was Jimmy Greaves. He was injured in the last group game and only then replaced by Geoff Hurst. Moreover, arguably the true foundation of England's triumph was its defence, which conceded a single goal before the final, and that a penalty. Yet, what if Ray Wilson had not overcome the back strain that immobilized him for four days on the eve of the tournament?

And what would Bobby Moore have held aloft had the Jules Rimet trophy – stolen in March 1966 – not been found a week later, on his Sunday walk, by a collie named Pickles?

ABERFAN

22 October 1966

A death roll of about 200 is feared in the disaster at the Welsh mining village of Aberfan, Glamorgan, where yesterday morning a rain-soaked 800 feet slag tip slipped and engulfed a school, a row of terraced cottages, and a farm. Early today known deaths totalled 85.

The slag was part of a colliery tip linked to the Merthyr Vale colliery. Two days of heavy rain are stated to have caused it to give way. Last night while 2,000 men and women worked under floodlights, using shovels, picks and their hands, the slag was still moving slowly. Several rescue workers were injured.

The south-western division of the National Coal Board said last night that the fall away ran for about half a mile before it engulfed the school and other buildings.

Casualty figures announced early today were:–

Children dead	76
Adults dead	9
In hospital	36
Missing	about 80

The school, Pantglas infants' and junior, was overwhelmed as the boys and girls were about to start their first lesson. The children were aged seven to 11 years.

Rescuers found the bodies of 14 in one classroom. Bulldozers and earth-clearing equipment were brought in. Mothers worked deep in mud as they tried to find their children.

Hundreds of volunteers – including many miners – shifted coal slurry by bucket chain. When faint cries could be heard there were shouts of "Quiet!". Bulldozers stopped and a hush fell upon the rescuers. The cries were pinpointed, digging and shovelling were resumed, and the bulldozers started up again.

The body of Mr. D. Beynon, the deputy head teacher, was found near midnight. A rescuer said: "He was clutching five children in his arms as if he had been protecting them."

A woman and her two grandchildren died in the farm engulfed by the slag. A woman who lost a son in the disaster was taken to hospital to give birth to a child.

ABNORMAL RAIN BLAMED BY COAL BOARD

Few people saw the slag tip move when the disaster occurred here today, but those who did, agree it came with frightening suddenness. There was a rumbling noise, and suddenly the village was engulfed in black dust.

People who arrived on the scene first could hear cries from those trapped on the fringe of the tip. Wreckage was strewn over a quarter of a mile.

Pantglas School was almost demolished. Many children had been in the playground, which is now under 45 feet of slag. Some had just filed into their classes for roll call.

As soon as the alarm was given police, firemen, civil defence workers, Red Cross and other volunteer groups were rushed in. The police sealed off most approach roads and set up an emergency headquarters in Merthyr Tydfil.

At first rescuers were hampered by fog. Then when they arrived they had to spend precious minutes leading away dozens of weeping women who were clawing at the slag.

The shifts at two collieries nearby were immediately stopped, and miners, their faces still covered with coal dust, joined in forming chains to carry buckets of slag.

The National Coal Board said tonight in an official statement that abnormal rainfall had caused the tip to move.

About 50 children coming from the neighbouring village of Mount Pleasant by school bus were delayed by fog. Many got out to walk, but it is thought most arrived 10 minutes late.

Merthyr Tydfil's Chief Constable, Mr. Thomas Griffiths, in charge of the massive rescue operations, told a press conference that his biggest problem was getting vehicles through to the site, which is in a cul-de-sac. A broken water main which runs to Cardiff had flooded most of the area and turned the slag into mud.

For miles around clusters of ashen-faced people stood watching scores of trucks shunting to and fro carrying loads of slag. Some of the drivers were working turns of six hours or more. Indeed, many of the miners who toiled to shovel the slag clear had worked nonstop for 10 hours. One, whose little daughter is believed to be dead, was still digging at 6 o'clock in the evening. He had run three miles to get to the scene.

◆

Although the industry was already in decline, coal mining was still central to life in South Wales in the 1960s. Some 8,000 men worked in the mines near Aberfan, in the Merthyr Valley, and vast spoil heaps formed of the waste from the diggings were familiar sights.

That sited on the hill above Pantglas Junior School was more than 100 feet (30 metres) high. The dangers of the tips were well known. They retained heat from the sun and this made it hard for grass to grow, causing them to erode and become unstable. The National Coal Board (NCB), which operated the mine, had been warned about the location of the heap but had taken no action.

When heavy rain led to water building up inside the tip, some 140,000 cubic yards of waste slid down onto the village, engulfing it in black mud so that only the chimneys could be seen. Twenty-eight adults and 116 children died. The inquiry that followed held the NCB responsible. One of the Queen's main regrets of her reign is said to be the decision not to visit Aberfan until eight days after the disaster.

PARIS '68

4 May 1968

The battles between students and police which occurred today in Paris's Latin Quarter were probably the most violent since the end of the Algerian war. At least 20 police were injured – one with a fractured skull – as well as a still unknown number of students.

Two hundred and fifty students were arrested, some of them carrying weapons such as iron bars, pick handles and hatchets. When it was over, thick clouds of tear gas floated above the Boulevard St. Michel, which was left looking like a battlefield strewn with missiles.

The Rector of the University, M. Jean Roche, has decided provisionally to suspend all courses at the Sorbonne and at the Censier annexe which is also part of the Arts Faculty. It is the first time this has ever happened in the history of the faculty.

The students originally assembled in the Sorbonne courtyard to call a mass demonstration for next Monday, when six students from the faculty of letters at Nanterre, in the western suburbs, are to appear before a disciplinary commission. Among the six is an anarchist student, Daniel Cohn-Bendit, of German origin, who was said to be one of the leaders of today's demonstration and is believed to have been arrested. Known to some as "Red Dany", both because of his politics and the colour of his hair, he first gained attention in January by insulting M. François Missoffe, the Minister of Youth and Sports, who had come to Nanterre to open a swimming pool.

Since then many left-wing students, who at first condemned M Cohn-Bendit, have come to support him against what they regard as "fascist repression" by the university authorities and the police. He is generally regarded as the leader of the March 22 Movement – a loose coalition of Nanterre's extreme left factions.

This movement provoked the closing of the faculty yesterday by organizing a three-day campaign against "imperialism". In particular, its members occupied a lecture room and prevented a history lecture from taking place.

Today this climate was transferred to the Sorbonne, where leaders of the March 22 Movement, supported by those of the National Union of French Students (U.N.E.F.), occupied the courtyard and tried to take over a lecture room. In the afternoon the police surrounded the Sorbonne, while a number of extreme right-wing students attempted to march on it armed with clubs, iron bars and even a meat-axe. Several were arrested.

Then, with the written permission of the Rector, the police used tear gas to clear out the courtyard. About 1,000 left-wing students assembled on the pavement outside jeering at the police. Some of them tore up paving stones and pieces of railing to use as missiles. Eventually the police made repeated and violent charges, and made numerous arrests.

◆

The violence of 3 May was merely the prelude to riots that were to shake France to her foundations. The students' initial grievance was a decision by the University of Paris to prevent couples from spending the night in the same dormitory.

The riot police's heavy-handed response to a request by the Sorbonne to clear those protesting seemed to embody everything French youth, in thrall to Che Guevara and influenced by news of the Vietnam War, claimed was wrong with society.

More students took to the barricades, notably during the running battles of 10 May, and the following week they were joined by many of the country's workers as it was gripped by strikes. Tear gas, baton charges and a hail of cobblestones became the abiding images of the time.

Fearing revolution, President Charles de Gaulle lost his nerve. On 29 May, he suddenly disappeared from the Elysée Palace and, with his aide-de-camp navigating from a road map, had himself flown by helicopter to Germany.

Reassured by the French forces there that the Army supported him, he called a general election. With wage concessions, this quickly ended the demonstrations. De Gaulle won the vote by a huge majority but resigned the following year.

PRAGUE SPRING

22 August 1968

About 175,000 troops, the great majority of them Russian, were last night occupying the major cities of Czechoslovakia. Six top Czechoslovak leaders, including Mr. Dubcek, were taken by troops to an unknown destination after being detained all day in the Central Committee building in Prague.

Soviet troops entered the National Assembly after deputies meeting there in emergency session had unanimously approved a categorical demand that the foreign armies should withdraw.

A curfew was imposed on Prague last night with a warning that anyone on the streets would be shot on sight.

In a radio address to the nation last night President Svoboda said the occupation of Czechoslovakia was illegal and undertaken without the consent of the Czechoslovak authorities. "The situation must be solved rapidly and the troops must depart", he said.

Cetka, the official news agency, which throughout the day referred to the Russians as "occupation forces", sent out an urgent message late last night stating that it had been occupied by foreign troops. After that the line went dead.

More than 20 people were reported dead as anti-Russian protests mounted throughout Czechoslovakia. Heavy firing was reported in Prague, where seven people were killed and nearly 200 injured in clashes with Soviet troops.

Crowds of people, many of them students, roamed through the capital chanting support for Mr. Dubcek and hurling abuse at Soviet troops. Tanks were overturned and set on fire. Machine gun and rifle fire echoed through the streets.

All road, rail and air links between Czechoslovakia and the outside world have been cut. Clandestine radio stations loyal to Mr. Dubcek continued to broadcast messages of support and appeals for calm.

A Czechoslovak Note to the governments of the five Warsaw Pact countries that took part in the invasion called for an immediate end to the "illegal occupation".

U Thant, the U.N. Secretary-General, described the invasion as a "serious blow to international order and morality". He appealed to the Russians and their Warsaw Pact allies to "exercise the utmost restraint".

Announcing that both Houses of Parliament had been recalled for 2.30 p.m. on Monday, Mr. Stewart, the Foreign Secretary, said that what had happened in Czechoslovakia "puts at risk the rights of every small country".

President Johnson said the Soviet Union and its allies had invaded a defenceless country "to stamp out a resurgence of ordinary human freedom". The tragic news had shocked the conscience of the world.

General de Gaulle attacked the Russian intervention as an infringement of Czechoslovakia's rights and likely to obstruct the European detente.

Mr. Ceausescu, the Rumanian party leader, said the invasion was a "grave error". He announced the immediate creation of an armed national militia to defend the country's independence. President Tito of Yugoslavia said the Soviet Union had unilaterally annulled the Bratislava agreement and violated the rights of a sovereign state.

In a statement issued by Tass the Soviet Union said its troops and those of its four closest allies had occupied Czechoslovakia to prevent a foreign-backed counter-revolution.

It had intervened at the request of a group of Czechoslovak Government and Party leaders. Tass appealed to the Czechoslovak people to cooperate with the occupying troops. These would be withdrawn as soon as the "lawful" authorities in Prague considered they were no longer needed.

For the first time in its history, the French Communist Party publicly dissociated itself from the action of the Soviet Government. The invasion was also sharply condemned by the British and Italian parties.

———————◆———————

'Socialism with a human face' was what the new leader of the Communist Party in Czechoslovakia, Alexander Dubček, promised when he was elected in January 1968. Reforms followed in April, including less censorship of the press, greater freedom of travel and more powers for the Slovak part of the nation.

It was this reduction of central authority that particularly angered the Soviets, prompting President Leonid Brezhnev to send in Warsaw Pact tanks and 500,000 troops to end hopes of democratization.

Resistance was not crushed at once and demonstrations continued for several months. In a notorious incident in January 1969, a student, Jan Palach, set himself on fire in protest in the centre of Prague and died of his burns.

Dubček was removed from office in April 1969 and control by hardliners was re-imposed. He returned to politics 20 years later, after the Velvet Revolution had brought about the end of Communism in Czechoslovakia, but he died in a car accident in 1992.

CONCORDE'S MAIDEN FLIGHT

3 March 1969

The Anglo-French Concorde supersonic airliner took off on its maiden flight from Toulouse today. It was in the air for 27 minutes, and the flight was described as faultless.

The test flight reached 10,000 feet, but the Concorde's speed never rose above 300 m.p.h. – eventually it will fly at more than 1,300 m.p.h. The pilot decided to return to the airport because of worsening weather conditions. Beaming with pleasure on his return to the airport, M. André Turcat, the 47-year-old Sud Aviation chief test pilot, who was at the controls, said: "Finally the big bird flies, and I can say now that it flies pretty well."

M. Turcat, with his crew of co-pilot and two flight engineers watching over 12 tons of test equipment, had taken Concorde up to 10,000 feet, made a practice landing approach at high altitude, and then brought the revolutionary aircraft straight back to the runway without any further tests.

The decision to return direct to the airport was taken by the test pilot because of a mounting wind from the wrong direction, which had kept the first flight in doubt throughout the day.

Conditions when Concorde did eventually take off, shortly before 3.30 p.m., were marginal for such an important mission. The first indication that the 500 representatives of the world press and thousands of Sunday afternoon sightseers who had swarmed in from all over the Midi region had that M. Turcat had decided to take off was when the two photographic chase aircraft which were to keep close company with the Concorde in the air, a Meteor fighter and a six-seat Paris executive jet, sped down the runway. The flight had been postponed on two successive days.

After a 20-minute technical delay in the starting of the first of the four engines, Concorde taxied sedately and deliberately to the end of the runway. A cloud of black smoke billowed upwards as the jets were run up. Then, laden with 6,500 gallons of fuel, and weighing 110 tons, she began to roll.

As the speed built up, Concorde quickly lifted her tall stalk of a nosewheel leg off the ground. Balanced on her main landing bogies, and with her long nose surmounted by the "snoot" angled down at 12 degrees to give the pilot better vision, she looked like a great white bird of prey.

As the aircraft reached and flashed past the press stand all wheels by now just off the ground, there was a spontaneous burst of applause, immediately drowned by the thundering backwash of the quartet of Olympus 593 engines, built jointly by the Bristol division of Rolls-Royce and the French Snecma organization.

But although the noise from the engines, each developing 13,000lb of thrust and together producing one and a half times as much energy as Battersea power station, was enormous at so close a range, it was not as stupefying as many people had feared.

Lateral noise nuisance from Concorde as it takes off from the world's airports when it goes into airline service in 1973 has been thought by many as possibly presenting an even greater problem than that of the supersonic boom. From this early test, it appeared to me that the fears may be greatly overrated.

On his return to the airport, M. Turcat put the Concorde down gently, with only a puff of smoke from burning rubber on the wheels to show that he had touched the ground. He deployed the braking parachute and reversed the thrust of the engines to bring the aircraft to a smooth halt.

Instead of the 130 passengers who will disembark from the production models in four years' time when they cut the flying time between London and New York from seven hours 40 minutes to three hours 25 minutes, and that between London and Sydney from 24 hours 35 minutes to 13 hours, the small and rather lonely looking figures of M. Turcat and the three members of his crew appeared at the top of the steps. A slight pause, and then the chief test pilot bounded down the ladder, giving the thumbs up signal with each hand as he did so.

◆

Even though it first flew several months before the Moon landings, Concorde was so futuristic looking that it seemed at the time to inaugurate the space age. The project to develop the supersonic passenger aircraft ran for 15 years, ran enormously over budget, and only yielded two customers – British Airways and Air France.

Yet while it never made their money back for the British and French governments, its breakthroughs influenced the whole airline industry. Nothing would ever rival its paper-dart shape for sleekness, but it was also the first production aircraft to use computers and electronic control systems to such an extent, the first to be flown not manually but digitally, or 'by wire'.

It could carry 128 passengers between London and New York in 3½ hrs, cruising at 60,000 feet, from where the curvature of the Earth could be clearly seen. Concorde still holds the record for the greatest distance flown at supersonic speed.

After the fatal crash of an Air France Concorde in 2000, it returned to service briefly. Its first landing in New York was on 11 September 2001, shortly before the attacks on the Twin Towers. It was retired soon afterwards.

THE MOON LANDINGS

21 July 1969

It was 3.56 a.m. (British Standard Time) when Armstrong stepped off the ladder from Eagle and on to the moon's surface. The module's hatch had opened at 3.39 a.m.

"That's one small step for man but one giant leap for mankind", he said as he stepped on the lunar surface.

The two astronauts opened the hatch of their lunar module at 3.39 a.m. in preparation for Neil Armstrong's walk. They were obviously being ultra careful over the operation for there was a considerable time lapse before Armstrong moved backwards out of the hatch to start his descent down the ladder. Aldrin had to direct Armstrong out of the hatch because he was walking backwards and could not see the ladder.

Armstrong moved on to the porch outside Eagle and prepared to switch the television cameras which showed the world his dramatic descent as he began to inch his way down the ladder.

By this time, the two astronauts had spent 25 minutes of their breathing time but their oxygen packs on their backs last four hours.

When the television cameras switched on there was a spectacular shot of Armstrong as he moved down the ladder. Viewers had a clear view as they saw him stepping foot by foot down the ladder, which has nine rungs. He reported that the lunar surface was a "very fine-grained powder ".

Clutching the ladder, Armstrong put his left foot on the lunar surface and reported it was like powdered charcoal and he could see his footprints on the surface. He said the L.E.M.'s engine had left a crater about a foot deep but they were "on a very level place here".

Standing directly in the shadow of the lunar module, Armstrong said he could see very clearly. The light was sufficiently bright for everything to be clearly visible. The next step was for Aldrin to lower a hand camera down to Armstrong. This was the camera which Armstrong was to use to film Aldrin when he descends from Eagle.

Armstrong then spent the next few minutes taking photographs of the area in which he was standing and then prepared to take the "contingency" sample of lunar soil. This was one of the first steps in case the astronauts had to make an emergency take-off before they could complete the whole of their activities on the moon.

Armstrong said: "It is very pretty out here." Using the scoop to pick up the sample, Armstrong said he had pushed six to eight inches into the surface. He then reported to the mission control centre that he placed the sample lunar soil in his pocket.

The first sample was in his pocket at 4.08 a.m. He said the moon "has soft beauty all its own", like some desert of the United States.

Armstrong then started to prepare to guide Aldrin out of the lunar module as he emerged backwards through the hatch on to the porch. By this time Armstrong and Aldrin had used up 45 minutes of their oxygen supply.

Armstrong told Aldrin: "I feel very comfortable and walking is very comfortable. You've got three steps to go and then the long one." Seconds later Aldrin dropped down on to the lunar surface and Armstrong said: "Isn't that wonderful."

It was 4.15 when Aldrin stepped on to the surface. One astronaut was heard saying "magnificent desolation". Armstrong and Aldrin then carried out a number of exercises. Armstrong could be seen jumping up and down while Aldrin, clutching the ladder, was doing what looked like a knees bend.

Armstrong appeared to move rapidly across the moon's surface but only seeming to take short steps. Sharp contrast between light and shadow made the television picture partly obscure, but early overall transmission was good. One of the astronauts reported that the rocks had a powdery surface and were rather slippery.

One of them said that he tended to lose balance in one direction but recovery was quite natural. He said you had to lean in the direction you wanted to go. The astronauts reported to mission control that their steps tended to sink down about quarter of an inch. All the time the two astronauts could be seen moving around in front of the lunar module. Their movements were slow and they seemed to lope.

They then unveiled the plaque which contained President Nixon's signature and with an inscription saying:

"Here men from the planet earth
"First set foot upon the moon
"July, 1969, A.D.
"We came in peace for all mankind."

◆

Following the Soviets' launch of Sputnik, the first satellite, in 1957, the 1960s saw the Cold War become the Space Race as Russia vied with America for technological dominance and international prestige. When the Russians increased their lead by sending Yuri Gagarin into orbit in 1961, President Kennedy responded by committing America to putting a man on the Moon by the end of the decade.

Neil Armstrong later said that the most stressful moment of the mission had not been stepping out of the Eagle lunar module but landing it. As he began the descent, the computer began to sound loud alarms. The astronauts had overloaded it by forgetting to switch off a radar, which was not a major problem if nonetheless a distracting one just at that moment.

Advances in computing were central to the success of the Apollo 11 mission, and much of the programming was overseen by a woman, Margaret Hamilton. Even so, by modern standards the onboard computer was not powerful – mobile telephones today have processing speeds 100,000 times faster and up to seven million times more RAM memory.

THE SEVENTIES AND EIGHTIES

DECIMAL DAY

15 February 1971

After a foretaste of the change to decimal currency, which begins fully today, Southern Region of British Rail were able to report last night that all had gone smoothly. "In fact it is proving rather simple," an official said.

Many public houses and shops which open on Sunday also took the opportunity to use decimal coinage ahead of the official D-Day.

Customers at a London public house took the change in their stride, pausing to convert the price of their pint, to check their change at the suggestion of the bar staff, and then carry on as usual except to wonder if the tiny ½p would drop through a hole in their pocket.

The Decimal Currency Board said: "We know of no hitches. Nobody seems to be worried. We have had a few people ringing in, but it has been much quieter than we expected."

Today signals the beginning of the change-over period, fixed at a maximum of 18 months but likely to be completed in less than one year.

Lord Fiske, chairman of the board, went to Euston Station to see how British Rail was coping. He spent 10p on two tickets to Kilburn, 2p (5d.) for a platform ticket and 4½p (11d.) for a cup of British Rail tea.

At the end of his tour of the station he said there was no trouble as far as he was aware, although he had difficulty in identifying the 1p and ½p among his small change.

Referring to a reported rush to stockpile goods by housewives he said: "There has been slightly more buying, but I do not think it has been much.

"Monday is not much of a shopping day and I think the real test will come on Thursday and Friday, when people will have had two or three days to get used to it and will have to go out shopping for food."

One of the ticket office clerks at Euston Station, Mr. Jock Donald, said the operation had been going without trouble. "People are better educated than we thought, but this station has been decimalized as far as tickets are concerned for some time."

In the canteen Mr. Nigel Pavey, the station catering manager, said that queries had come from only about 5 per cent of their customers. "All could be solved, and there have certainly been fewer inquiries than I expected", he said.

If the results of yesterday's small-scale excursion into decimalization were encouraging the board knows that its moment of truth really starts today, and that the next 10 days or so will determine the success of its £1.25m. publicity campaign, boosted by another £78,000 to fill the gap created by the non-delivery of some five million copies of *Your Guide to Decimal Money*.

Britain is one of the last countries to go decimal.

Several others, including the Republic of Ireland, and Malawi, as well as the Isle of Man, Jersey and Guernsey, are switching at the same time. Only Nigeria, Malta and the Gambia, which is changing over later this year, will then have non-decimal systems. Although Malta has plans to adopt a decimal system, the Central Bank of Malta has declared Britain's new decimal bronze coins, the ½p, 1p and 2p, unacceptable as legal tender in Malta.

———◆———

There had been campaigns to decimalize Britain's currency since the mid-nineteenth century, Russia having been the first nation to adopt the system in 1704. But even as other countries followed, influenced chiefly by Napoleonic France, many Britons saw their money as one of the traditions which differentiated them from Europeans.

Pounds, shillings and pence harked back to Roman times, when a pound of silver yielded 240 *denarii* or pennies. There were 20 shillings to a pound, and therefore 12 pennies in a shilling, which is why generations of schoolchildren had to learn their twelve times table.

Guineas, half-crowns, florins, tanners and threepenny bits were swept away when Harold Wilson's government decided in 1966 to go decimal as part of its drive to modernize Britain. Banks were closed for several days to process transactions in the old money, but the changeover was smoother than anticipated for most people, in part because three of the new coins had already been in circulation for a year.

Pre-decimal pennies are still vital to the working of one symbol of Britain that has not changed: a stack of them is used to correct the weight regulating the pendulum of Big Ben's clock.

BLOODY SUNDAY

31 January 1972

More than 200 heavily armed parachutists this afternoon stormed into the IRA stronghold of Bogside, Londonderry, and a hospital official stated tonight that 13 people had been shot dead and 17 others, including two women, wounded in a brief but fierce gun battle.

The Altnagelvin Hospital said that three of the injured were in a serious condition.

One of those badly hurt was a young girl who had been run over by an armoured car.

A soldier was slightly wounded and two others were injured by acid bombs thrown from the roof of some flats as the troops moved in.

It was by far the worst day of violence seen in this largely Roman Catholic city since the present crisis began in 1969 and Bogsiders were tonight complaining that troops had fired on unarmed men, "including one who had his arms up in surrender".

A photographer who was directly behind the parachutists when they jumped down from their armoured cars said: "I was appalled. They opened up into a crowd of people. As far as I could see, they did not fire over people's heads at all."

An Army spokesman at Northern Ireland headquarters said: "It is not true we fired indiscriminately into the crowd – we were fired on first."

The trouble began as a big civil rights procession defying the Stormont ban on parades and marches, approached an Army barbed wire barricade near the bottom of William Street, on the edge of the Bogside. The demonstrators, who formed up on the Creggan estate, had intended to hold a meeting in the Guildhall, where Lord Brockway was among the listed speakers.

Stewards leading the march, estimated at between 7,000 and 10,000 strong, appealed for calm as the mainly younger elements, some carrying banners with the names of local internees printed in black, began shouting at the soldiers and chanting: "IRA . . . IRA."

Then a few bottles, broken paving stones, chair legs and heavy pieces of iron grating were thrown at the troops of the 2nd Battalion, The Royal Green Jackets, who were manning the barrier.

Stewards, probably realizing that the troops would retaliate, again shouted at the hecklers and missile-throwers to stop. But after a brief lull the barrage of primitive artillery became much heavier and within a few minutes the area behind the barricade was covered by stones, bricks and iron of all shapes and sizes. Glass was strewn all over the area.

Then senior officers called up a water cannon, which was filled with dark purple dye. This was sprayed on the demonstrators, who immediately retreated, but two canisters of CS gas which appeared to have been thrown from the demonstrators' ranks exploded.

One of them went off under the water tender, whose driver was badly affected. The other one exploded in Waterloo Street, near by, where another barrier was in position.

Within a few minutes the demonstrators, many of them soaked with dye, but numbering only a few hundred at the most, began pelting the troops again. This time the soldiers replied with rubber bullets, fired in several volleys totalling about 60 or 70.

Undeterred, the demonstrators, many wearing white handkerchiefs over their faces in case the security forces lobbed CS gas into their midst, continued their barrage.

A few minutes later "snatch squads" from the 1st Battalion, The Parachute Regiment, which had been standing by in case they were needed, leapt over the barricade and chased the demonstrators, who fled.

The barricades were quickly opened and eight armoured vehicles, each full of other parachutists, went into the Bogside as reports came in that a sniper had been seen on a roof and another was thought to be hiding in the attic of a three-storey building overlooking William Street.

Other parachutists stormed the Bogside from two other directions and the demonstrators found themselves in the centre of a three-pronged attack.

———◆———

In the late 1960s, there was an upsurge in violence between Catholics and Protestants in Northern Ireland. The Protestant-dominated police force was viewed as partial and the Army was sent in to maintain order, but its efforts to do so led to a deterioration in relations with the Catholic population.

Increasing numbers of soldiers were killed in attacks in 1971, including nine in Northern Ireland's second city, Londonderry. This led to the imposition in August of internment without trial. The procession that triggered the shootings on Bloody Sunday was a protest by Catholics against this policy.

Even within the Army, the choice of the Parachute Regiment to deal with trouble at the march was regarded as risky, as it had a reputation for unwarranted aggression. The soldiers sent into the Bogside to make arrests fired 100 shots in 10 minutes. Twenty-six people were hit, of whom 14 died. No troops were injured.

In 2010, the Saville Inquiry found that, on balance, the soldiers rather than paramilitaries had fired the first shots, that none of those killed posed a serious threat and that their deaths were unjustifiable. David Cameron, the prime minister, subsequently apologized on behalf of the government and the country.

MUNICH MASSACRE

6 September 1972

The Mayor of Munich, Herr Kronawitter, announced early today that all Israeli hostages, four of their Palestinian terrorist captors, and a West German policeman were killed during a gun battle last night at Fürstenfeldbruck, 24 miles from here.

The Mayor's announcement stunned newspapermen who had been told earlier that the hostages had survived the shooting at the airport where the Palestinians had taken them after a day-long attempt to obtain the release of some 200 political prisoners in Israel in exchange for their lives.

The mayor said that three other Palestinians were still at large and that a pilot at the airport was also seriously wounded in the shooting. They mayor himself had just left the airport. He described the scene there as "terrible" – Agence France Presse.

Late last night Reuter sent this report from Munich:–

Eyewitnesses at the airport said that a Boeing 707 of the West German airline Lufthansa was waiting on the airstrip as the helicopters bringing the terrorists and their hostages from the Olympic village landed.

As the hostages and the guerrillas walked towards it, the marksmen, hidden in the darkness behind the airliner, opened fire.

The guerrillas fired back, and the exchange of fire continued for several minutes.

A Government spokesman in Munich said tonight that Herr Brandt, the West German President, had a long telephone conversation with the Egyptian Prime Minister shortly before the helicopters took off from the Games village. He did not give any other details of the conversation.

Earlier tonight, the Olympic Games had been suspended.

The guerrillas, all belonging to the Black September extremist Palestinian group, had killed two Israelis when they occupied the team's headquarters in the Olympic Village at dawn today.

They threatened to kill others if their demands for the release of 200 named Palestinian prisoners held in Israel jails were not met. At their request an aircraft was drawn up ready for takeoff on the tarmac at Munich airport.

Herr Willy Brandt, the West German Chancellor, returned from Kiel to Munich to take charge of negotiations between the West German authorities and the guerrillas. He took over from Herr Hans-Dietrich Genscher, the Minister of the Interior, and the head of Munich police, Herr Manfred Schreiber.

The Egyptian team announced that they were withdrawing from the Games. A spokesman said that they were unable to take part in the "present difficult circumstances."

Mark Spitz, the American swimmer, who is a Jew, left Munich hurriedly taking his record seven Olympic gold medals with him. He said he was afraid he might be the object of a further Palestinian attack.

The announcement that the Games were being postponed was made by Mr Avery Brundage, the outgoing President of the International Olympic Committee. "The Olympic peace has been broken by an act of assassination by criminal terrorists. The whole civilized world condemns this barbaric crime, this horror", he said.

———◆———

The memory of the Munich Olympics should have been of the seven gold medals won by Mark Spitz, the American swimmer, and of 17-year-old Olga Korbut, whose performances transformed the popular standing of gymnastics.

Instead, what transfixed television audiences was the sight of men in ski masks on the balcony of the Israeli team's apartment. Early on 5 September, a group of Palestinian terrorists had burst into the building, taking nine athletes and coaches hostage and killing two more.

The group, which belonged to the Black September organisation, demanded freedom for more than 230 Palestinians in Israeli prisons, as well as for the two German leaders of the Baader-Meinhof gang.

The fact that the athletes were Jewish increased pressure on the Bavarian authorities, who subsequently bungled an attempt to kill all the terrorists when they believed they were to be allowed to fly to Egypt.

The police marksmen had no special training or equipment, and in the chaos and darkness all the hostages died together with five terrorists. Three more were captured but released the following month in exchange for a hijacked jet.

The Games continued after a pause of 24 hours.

BRITAIN JOINS THE EEC

1 January 1973

In a discordant fanfare, the party leaders spoke yesterday of their hopes and fears on the eve of the United Kingdom's entry into the European Economic Community.

Mr Heath, in a radio interview recorded before his departure for Ottawa, spoke of the exciting prospects for improving the standard of living of the British people and for Europe to create a fresh balance with the United States and Japan in trade and monetary affairs.

Mr Wilson, the Opposition leader, condemned the Government for taking Britain into Europe "without the support of the British people" and on terms which he thought would be utterly crippling for Britain.

Mr Thorpe, the Liberal leader, welcomed the new era and said that Liberals could take pride in the fact that over the past 20 years they had been totally consistent in their support for European unity.

Mr Heath acknowledged that some British people feared entry to the Community, but said he had been most impressed by parents who told him they thought that for their children and grandchildren the change was going to be all important.

"I think, in their phlegmatic and pragmatic way, the British are now waiting for action and, as we in the Community together take action, more and more they will respond to it."

If the standard of living was to be improved, it was necessary constantly to seek opportunities and to find ways of seizing them, and to "educate our young people so that they can hold their own. If you allow yourself to be bedevilled by your fears you are paralysed by them."

Mr Heath said he felt the degree of European unity now achieved, with nine partners in the Community, "is something for which people have longed, really, for centuries and even in the last two decades... people have been working so hard for it.

"But this is only the first stage. The work is not completed. Indeed, I think probably the more exciting time is now beginning, of working together within this unity to achieve our next objectives."

Businessmen would find themselves going to and from Europe much more, there would be an exchange of ideas in all sorts of fields, and in the universities, professions and technology we should be working more closely together. Firms would be coming together for large-scale enterprises which no country could create on its own.

The monarchy would not be affected in any way, Mr Heath assured his questioner, Mr Gordon Clough, on *The World This Weekend*. "As far as the sovereignty of Parliament is concerned, what people want today is to see that we are running our affairs in the best possible manner, and if we are going to run them jointly with other countries they are sensible enough to recognize that, in that case, you share your sovereignty."

Britain's accession to the European Economic Community (EEC) was, by a distance, the major achievement of Edward Heath as prime minister. It came at the third time of asking, previous applications to join having been blocked by Charles de Gaulle, France's president, who doubted that Britons shared his commitment to the European project.

Indeed, many British politicians did not. But by the time de Gaulle left office in 1969, Britain had exited still further from empire. With the economy stuttering, business leaders heaped on pressure to engage more closely with the nation's main group of trading partners.

For party reasons, Labour opposed membership, although its position would probably have been different had it been in power. Nor was sovereignty undiscussed. Yet there had been no referendum on whether to join and few opinion-formers seemed sure what ordinary people thought.

'A majority remain trepid and apprehensive', *The Times* reported, citing polls. 'The future for Britain in Europe cannot be accurately forecast and assessed at this stage.' There was, however, perhaps already one pointer: the Union Flag unfurled in Brussels that first morning was flying upside down.

NIXON RESIGNS

9 August 1974

President Nixon tonight announced his resignation. It will take effect tomorrow when Vice-President Gerald Ford will be sworn in as thirty-eighth President of the United States.

The unprecedented midterm transfer of power was forced upon Mr Nixon by the knowledge that Congress was certain to impeach him and remove him from office for his crimes in the Watergate conspiracy.

Speaking in a final national television broadcast to the nation he has led for nearly six years, he said he would resign at noon tomorrow, and that Mr Ford would take the oath at the same time in the Oval Office. Calmly and deliberately, Mr Nixon said: "I have never been a quitter. To leave office before my term is completed is abhorrent to every instinct in my body. But as President, I must put the interests of America first."

He went on: "America needs a full-time President, and a full-time Congress." His family had unanimously urged him to fight on "but the interests of the nation must always come before personal considerations". As long as there had been the base of political support he felt it had been justified to continue the constitutional process – meaning, but not saying it, towards his trial in the Senate. But the disappearance of the base of support, he reasoned, meant "the constitutional purpose had been served and there is no longer a need for the process to be prolonged".

Because of what he called "The Watergate matter" he suggested he "might not have the support of the Congress" for vital policy decisions ahead. Mr Nixon made a most cursory apology for all the scandals that have afflicted and finally destroyed his administration. Still less did he admit any real measure of guilt.

Expressing deep regret for injuries caused is [not] quite the *mea culpa* which might have induced some of the people he has wronged and deceived to forgive him. The scant contrition might affect Mr Nixon's chances with Congress for immunity from legal process. He regretted deeply any injuries done during his presidency, and he then said he had no bitterness against those who had opposed him.

Considering the enormity of the charges pending against him, and the years of lying to the people over Watergate, his one admission of wrong struck an incongruous and paltry note. He said: "I would say only that if some of my judgments were wrong, and some were wrong, they were made in what I believed at the time were the best interests of the nation".

◆

Early one morning in June 1972, a security guard at the Watergate building in Washington spotted that the latch on a door had been taped over, so that it appeared locked even when open. From that moment, Richard Nixon's path to doom was set.

Police arrested a team of men inside the complex who appeared to have been gathering secrets in the offices of Democrat politicians. At first, no direct link could be made to the President and by the time he was re-elected later that year the burglars had been jailed.

From there, they began to claim there had been a cover-up. Soon, it emerged that the administration had been party to illegal operations to prevent leaks of information and to help Nixon retain power.

Most damning were recordings of Nixon in the White House that made it clear he knew of at least some of this and that revealed his personality to be more calculating than that projected to voters.

His achievements, including withdrawing America from the war in Vietnam and improving relations with China, could not save him, and he became the only president to resign while in office.

SAIGON FALLS

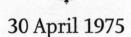

30 April 1975

Vietnamese desperate to get out of Saigon ahead of the communists clawed their way over the 10-foot wall around the United States embassy today despite the barbed wire on top of it. American Marines and armed American civilians used pistol and rifle butts to smash the fingers of Vietnamese trying to climb over the embassy gate. The Marines in their battle gear pushed all the people they could reach off the wall, but the mass of people was so great that scores got over. Some jumped and landed on the barbed wire, cutting themselves in countless places. A middle-aged man and a woman were lying on the wire, bleeding in numerous places. While the Vietnamese fought the embassy guards and each other, United States Marine helicopters were lifting more than 50 evacuees from the roof of the embassy building. Across the street, soldiers, police and teenage youths were stripping and stealing the scores of abandoned embassy cars, calmly picking door locks and rigging the ignition wires so they could get them started. American reporters who had been taken to Tan Son Nhut airport earlier in buses could not be evacuated from there because Vietnamese guards would not let the buses into the air base. The buses returned to the embassy, and the newsmen climbed over the wall themselves, beating off Vietnamese who tried to cling to them. Some people held up their children asking Americans to take them over the fence. Teenagers climbed over low roofs in the French embassy compound next door and leaped into the American compound. More people in cars and on motorcycles poured into the area. Meanwhile, thousands of Vietnamese were stripping the apartment buildings in which the fleeing Americans lived. Soldiers, police and civilians joined in collecting household goods, bathroom fixtures, books, furniture and food.

◆

Vietnam had been torn by war for almost 30 years, since Communists had led the bid for independence from French colonial rule. Fearful of the 'Red Tide' washing through the region, the Americans had steadily increased their military aid to the South during the 1960s, as it fought against a North supported by China and the Soviets.

In 1973, having lost about 60,000 troops and public confidence in the conduct of the war, America pulled out of Vietnam. By then, the fighting had spread to the neighbouring countries of Laos and Cambodia, where the Khmer Rouge came to power in 1975. That same year, the forces of North Vietnam finally captured Saigon, the capital of the South. Up to three million Vietnamese soldiers and civilians had died in the conflict.

Some of the most memorable images of the era showed Vietnamese desperate to flee the Communists being evacuated by helicopter from the American embassy in Saigon. Over the next decade, millions more attempted to escape by boat, with as many as 250,000 dying at sea.

ELVIS PRESLEY DIES

18 August 1977

Thousands of people crowded round the gates of Graceland, Elvis
Presley's Tennessee mansion, this afternoon, to catch a glimpse of his
body lying there. Some 50 people had to be given emergency treatment
on the lawn as they jostled for their last 10-second glimpse of the man
who, in the late 1950s, pioneered an overtly sexual style of singing which
remains in vogue today. Some parents had brought young children to
see the body, which was dressed in a cream suit, blue shirt and striped
silver tie. Wreaths lined the drive to the house and hundreds of cars
jammed Elvis Presley Boulevard outside. People had been arriving at
the house ever since the announcement of his death late yesterday.
The mood of idolatry at the scene has been matched by extensive
tributes and news reports on radio and television. Some radio stations
have been playing nothing but Elvis Presley records since yesterday,
and record shops all over the country report that they are selling out
fast. The television networks cobbled together special programmes
last night composed largely of clips from Mr Presley's films. Although
many of them were in black and white, dating back up to 20 years, it was
remarkable how well his style has worn, how similar his gyrations, his
gestures and his pouts were to those of many of today's popular young
performers. Interviewers went out into the streets and found dozens
of people in their thirties who gave emotional expression to their
sorrow and surprise at the death of a man whose records, films and
performances had set a style which shaped their entire adolescence.
In the late 1950s Mr Presley had been regarded as a symbol of youth
and iconoclasm, of rebellion against established order. As he and his
fans became less young and less rebellious his reputation changed,
but did not diminish. He became highly regarded by professionals
as a genuine pioneer of a musical fashion. Tributes came yesterday
from many of his contemporaries. Sammy Davis Jr made a perceptive

remark about the sexuality of his performance: "There was something just bordering on rudeness about Elvis", he said. "He never actually did anything rude, but he always seemed as if he was just going to. On a scale from one to 10, I would rate him 11." Carl Wilson of the Beach Boys singing group described the impact Mr Presley made on his generation: "His music was the only thing exclusively ours. His wasn't my Mom and Dad's music." The circumstances surrounding Mr Presley's death at 42 remain partly mysterious. Doctors say death was caused by an irregular heartbeat but give no real reason for this, beyond saying that he had been receiving treatment for circulatory difficulties and excess weight. Suggestions that the singer may have taken a drug overdose have been denied by everyone concerned. The funeral will be tomorrow. It is planned that it should be private, but the demands of the media are likely to make it far from that. Memphis: The postmortem examination showed no evidence of abnormal drug abuse, the Shelby county medical examiner said today. – AP.

Peter Godfrey writes: Mr Todd Slaughter, secretary of the British Elvis Presley fan club, said: "One or two fans have talked about ending it all". He urged the club's 12,000 members "not to go overboard". Thousands of them will be flocking to the Palais de Danse, Nottingham, this weekend to pay tribute to the "king" of rock and roll. Mr Presley's legendary standing among British fans is almost by default: despite endless invitations, the only time he set foot on British soil was at Prestwick airport on his way to do army service in Germany.

◆

Seventeen white Cadillacs and 100,000 mourners formed the cortège for the King of Rock'n' Roll as his body was brought to Forest Hill Cemetery in Memphis from his home, Graceland, where he had died on 16 August. He was 42.

Despite the initial denials, it became clear that drugs had at least contributed to the decline in Presley's health. His personal doctor was found to have prescribed him thousands of pills, to which he had become addicted as much as he was to junk food. Perhaps no other person had done as much to popularize the idea that young people should have their own culture. Nor would that have a more famous victim.

After the White House, Graceland now attracts more visitors than any other home in the United States. Presley remains the best-selling solo singer in history, with annual earnings of £30 million even 40 years on from his death.

STAR WARS

10 February 1978

I have been to see Star Wars, and a wretched disappointment it was. It is technically inferior to 2001, and lacking in imagination by comparison, too; moreover, the plot is incoherent and much of the dialogue unintelligible, and it is equipped with the least attractive hero and heroine I have ever seen in any film not actually called The Uglies. Three things rescue it from complete unendurability; the presence of Sir Alec Guinness, whose part is a diluted version of Gandalf, the benign wizard of The Lord of the Rings; a lovable little robot, which in turn is reminiscent of the famous Robby in Forbidden Planet; and an equally lovable ape, presumably suggested by King Kong, which introduces the only touches of humour in what is otherwise a trackless desert of self-important seriousness. Yet Star Wars has at the very least a sociological interest, and at the most an interest a good deal deeper than that. For the extraordinary success it has had in the United States (it does not appear to have caught fire here in the same way) needs explaining, and since the success is inexplicable on its cinematic merits, it must be sought elsewhere. The first thing we notice, in pursuing the search, is that a clear ethical distinction is drawn between the two warring sides, and that this distinction is more than the usual cops/robbers, cowboys/Indians or Nazis/Allies dichotomy that has been the staple of so many films in the past. A space empire of unqualified evil is being challenged by a group of rebels, who are making war upon it in the name of freedom, but of freedom extended into a fully moral dimension. Once, we are given to understand, the moral principles of the universe were guarded by a company of Samurai-like knights, of whom there are now only two survivors. One of them is the character played by Guinness; the other has forsworn his allegiance to virtue and thrown in his lot with the totalitarian empire. (He, too, incidentally, can be found in *The Lord of the Rings*; his black helmet and visor, with no face to be seen, bring to mind immediately the Lord of the Nazgul: The Black Rider flung back his hood, and behold! he had a kingly crown; and yet upon no head visible was it set. The red fires shone between it and the mangled shoulders vast and dark. From a mouth unseen there came a deadly laughter. And the echo can be heard even more clearly when, in the film, this figure fights a duel with Guinness-Gandalf, the latter having to keep him at bay until the rebels' victory, close at hand now, is secured, just as Gandalf must ensure that Gondor holds out until the rescuing Rohirrim arrive.) But there is more to this theme than unambiguously recognizable good and evil, though that is now sufficiently rare, in a film of any pretensions, to be refreshing. (Again, that lack of ambiguity is not only one of the most valuable and attractive things about Tolkien's book, but accounts, I am sure, for much of its immense popularity, particularly among young people searching, often without knowing that they are searching, for moral certainties in an adult world of equivocation and relativism.)

◆

Perhaps not being as clever as *The Times*'s columnist, Bernard Levin, most of the audience for *Star Wars* enjoyed it chiefly for its cinematic merits. With the exception of *Gone with the Wind*, it became the biggest box-office success in American history, despite the doubts of director, George Lucas, and the studio, 20th Century Fox, that it would be a hit.

Lucas and his friend Steven Spielberg, who was making *Close Encounters of the Third Kind*, each expected the other's film to do better. And they thought both would be overshadowed by the forthcoming surfing drama, *Big Wednesday*.

With *Jaws* in 1975, Spielberg had inaugurated the age of the blockbuster – exciting films that would generate wider cultural expectation. Yet, it was *Star Wars* that turned this development into a phenomenon that forever altered the film industry.

This was partly due to its revolutionary special effects, but also because of the possibilities it demonstrated for selling huge quantities of merchandise. Demand to see it helped as well to popularize home video recorders.

Star Wars not only transformed mass entertainment for the 1970s; it determined its future form for the next 20 years, too.

THE TEST-TUBE BABY

27 July 1978

The birth of the Browns' test-tube baby was recorded on film by the Government's Central Office of Information. It intends to sell the film for use on television.

The Government said yesterday that the film was made as a record of an historic medical event and to assist in the evaluation of the baby's behaviour at birth. It was made with the agreement of the parents, Mr Steptoe and the hospital authorities, and the Central Office of Information expects it to be a "best seller".

There was apparently some dispute over the film with Associated Newspapers, which had bought the syndication rights to the story of the birth. The Department of Health and Social Security said last night: "Ministers have decided that they cannot accept the agreement with Associated Newspapers made last night in so far as it relates to restrictions on the release of the film made by the Central Office of Information.

"Subject to the views of the parents, they are prepared to make the film available commercially for television viewing. The parents' solicitor is accordingly being approached."

Sir John Dewhurst, President of the Royal College of Obstetricians and Gynaecologists, said the birth carried hope for certain childless women, but he doubted whether the technique would ever be easy.

Dr Anne MacLaren, director of the Medical Research Council's mammalian development unit, said there was no evidence that children born by the technique would run a risk of greater deformity than children born normally.

Our Medical Correspondent writes: The birth of this baby is the culmination of more than ten years' research by Mr Steptoe and

Dr Edwards; but while it offers some hope to infertile couples the technique is unlikely to be used widely. It does, however, open up the prospect of surrogate motherhood in which a "foster-mother" could take over the burden of pregnancy.

A test-tube baby differs from a normal conception in that the fertilization of the ovum by the sperm takes place in a laboratory instead of inside the mother. Once fertilization has occurred and the ovum begins the process of cell division it is returned to the mother's body and grows inside the uterus.

This method benefits only some infertile couples. Though one marriage in every 10 is involuntarily childless, the cause is as likely to be in the man as in the woman.

The technique developed by Mr Steptoe and Dr Edwards provides an alternative for women in whom surgery has failed. The woman is given a short course of treatment with hormones to cause several ova to mature at the same time. A laparascope, a narrow tube like a telescope, is then passed into her abdomen and the ova are removed. They are mixed with spermatozoa from the man in a culture fluid.

One ovum or more is likely to be fertilized, and after a few days it will have become a small ball of dividing cells, a blastocyst. This very early embryo can then be placed inside the uterus so that implantation can occur.

The procedure sounds simple but in practice there have been repeated failures. Human ova were cultured successfully as long ago as 1965, but since then progress has been slow. Either the ova have stopped dividing after a few hours, or they have failed to "take" when replaced in the uterus. Two years ago Mr Steptoe reported a successful pregnancy, but the blastocyst became implanted in the lower end of the tube instead of the uterus and the pregnancy miscarried.

———◆———

Louise Joy Brown was born by caesarean section at Oldham General Hospital, Lancashire, and weighed 5 lbs 12 oz (2.6 kg). Her middle name was suggested as being apt by the two pioneers of in vitro fertilization (IVF), Patrick Steptoe and Robert Edwards.

The moment of fertilization had been observed under a microscope as early as 1879 but it had taken another century for techniques to advance sufficiently to allow scientists to sustain an embryo. Even then, Steptoe and Edwards faced opposition from leading biologists, who queried both the ethics and worth of their research. Edwards had to give up his position with the Medical Research Council as it would not fund his work. He was awarded the Nobel Prize in 2010 (Patrick Steptoe had already died).

Louise Brown's mother, Lesley, had blocked fallopian tubes. Four years after Louise's birth, she gained a sister, Natalie, who was also conceived via IVF and who subsequently became the first person born by that method to give birth to her own child. More than eight million children worldwide have now been born with the help of assisted reproduction.

THE ELECTION OF
POPE JOHN PAUL II

17 October 1978

The smoke blew strong and unmistakably white tonight from the improvised chimney above the Sistine Chapel, sweeping away centuries of tradition in this amazing election which has brought to the Papal throne a Polish cardinal with still nearly two years to go before reaching his sixtieth birthday.

The new Pope until his election this evening was Cardinal Wojtyla, Archbishop of Cracow, who has taken the name of John Paul II. He appeared on practically nobody's list of likely candidates.

To choose a non-Italian, the cardinals had to reach back in history to 1522, the year of the election of Hadrian of Utrecht, a short and featureless reign which remains famous in the annals of the Papacy only because it led to the Italian monopoly of the Holy See.

The feeling in Rome tonight is a quite extraordinary emotion at this step of such towering importance to the papacy at a delicate moment. The official Vatican press office came out with a statement to the effect that the church had once again expressed "all its richness and inexhaustible vitality" in making this choice.

The surprise was all the more complete because of the undoubtedly distasteful speculation about the political bargaining supposed to be going on behind the walls of the Conclave. This speculation was in part caused by the behaviour of some of the cardinals in statements and interviews before they met beneath the huge fresco in which Michelangelo depicts the consequences of good and of bad decisions on Judgment Day.

They made up their minds quickly. They needed a day more than the August Conclave from which emerged John Paul I but it was still not a long affair by normal standards except to the impatient crowds gathering twice a day in St Peter's Square.

Pope John Paul II has a gentle smile and it was there tonight for all to see as he stepped on to the central balcony of St Peter's to receive his ovation and give his first blessing as Pope. But his face is noticeably strong and quiet strength is the most striking first impression that he gives.

He could not provide a greater contrast with the easy smile of his immediate predecessor which became so quickly famous. The adoption of the same name must nevertheless be regarded as an intention to follow what John Paul I had pledged to do, in developing the policies laid down by the Vatican Council and to apply them in the way that Paul VI did throughout the 15 years of his crucial Pontificate.

The Roman Church has not only a strong Pope now, but a young one. The cardinals have once again broken with tradition in electing a man so young by ecclesiastical standards.

The shock of this change, too, could be felt amidst the elation and amazement tonight at the presence of this tense and serious figure among the theatrical aspects surrounding a Papal election; the huge crowds, the floodlit palaces, the ancient ceremony of the smoke, the marching troops led by a detachment of the Swiss Guard with helmets and halberds shining, followed by representatives of all the Italian armed forces.

Shortly before his appearance tonight Cardinal Karol Wojtyla suffered the private suspense, not only of hearing that he has reached the required number of votes to be made Pontiff, but of being asked the dramatic question whether or not he accepted and, immediately after giving his acceptance the question by what name he wished to be called.

Then the Papal master of ceremonies, acting as notary with two assistant masters of ceremony acting as witnesses, in accordance with the regulations laid down by Paul VI drew up a document "concerning the acceptance by the Pontiff and name taken by him."

The new Pope is the son of a worker and while still a student worked in a chemical factory in Cracow. He was already actively talking Christianity at the work bench before moving into the main seminary in the city.

He comes from what has been frequently described as the most Catholic country in the world and the beautiful city of Cracow is itself one of the leading centres of Poland's religious and intellectual life.

He will bring, too, a joint experience which is quite unique: First, having to carry out his pastoral duties under a communist regime; and secondly of doing so within the ranks of a national hierarchy which has been dominated for years by the personality of Cardinal Wyszynski, the Polish Primate.

There can be little doubt that he did not always agree with the Primate's behaviour but whatever their personal relationships, in public he has been totally loyal to the head of his hierarchy.

The experiment of a Pope whose total experience is with a communist state will be a fascinating one to follow as he takes on the international responsibilities of the Papacy.

It was known that the new Pope was particularly close to Paul VI on the question of relations with the communist world, which clearly will be one of the principal issues of his reign. He summed up what he feels on this question in an article which he published in February, 1976, in the *Osservatore Romano*. He said: "One can understand that a man may search and not find; one can understand that he may deny: but it is not understandable that a man may have imposed on him 'it is forbidden for you to believe'."

———◆———

On 26 August 1978, the Patriarch of Venice, Albino Luciani, was elected Pope and took the name John Paul, honouring his two immediate predecessors. Just over a month later he was dead of a heart attack, his pontifical reign among the shortest in history.

So the cardinals returned to the Sistine Chapel for their second conclave that year. The favourites were thought to be – as usual – two Italians. Cardinal Siri, the Archbishop of Genoa, represented the traditionalists and had been in the running before. The reformers backed the Archbishop of Florence, Cardinal Benelli. After three votes there was deadlock, with neither close to the two-thirds majority required. Accordingly, a compromise was suggested: Karol Wojtyla.

Habemus papam. Few Italians, however, had heard of the relatively young Archbishop of Krakow or knew of his ability to get his message across.

'I don't know if I can express myself well in your – in our – Italian language', said the new Pope in his first words from the balcony of St Peter's. 'But if I make a mistake, you will correct me!' So began one of the most momentous (and longest) of all papacies.

THE WORST OF TIMES

14 November 1979

As soon as our backs were turned, events seemed to start happening at twice the normal pace. In Iran, Kampuchea, South Africa, Uganda and many other countries (not to mention Westminster, Edinburgh and New Printing House Square) the scene last November seems an epoch away, not just a year. These transformations reinforced the sense of disorientation apt to be felt in this office during the hiatus in our own affairs.

At first we had to repress a sense of incredulity that time could continue when *The Times* did not. But before long it was hard to avoid the impression that our paper must have served as a kind of pendulum to world events which, deprived of its restraint, were rattling away with an absurd and unrealistic rapidity. The events of the interim, not fully legitimate as part of recorded history by inclusion in our columns, could quite plausibly have been spread over two or three years without giving the least impression of thinness.

It would have been easy enough, admittedly, to predict Mrs Margaret Thatcher – but not the baleful Ayatollah – not military hostilities between China and Vietnam – not the spectacle of Dr Julius Nyerere proving a mightier man of war than Idi Amin – not Vorster disgraced, with a new South African Prime Minister speculating about the future of the laws against miscegenation – not the Pope in Phoenix Park – not British Leyland agreeing to build Hondas – not the virtual extinction of the devolution issue – not Chairman Hua Guofeng at Claridges.

It will be recalled that when we were interrupted, Mr James Callaghan was riding high. Only shortly before, at the peak of his confidence, be had burst publicly into song to deride eager election-date tipsters. In retrospect, the decision not to go to the country in the autumn appears the first sign that his sureness of touch, or his luck (much the same thing in politics), had left him.

In December the Government's 5 per cent wages policy melted away at the first test. Industrial action at the BBC seemed likely to black out Christmas programmes, including the first televised screening of *The Sound of Music*. Greatly concerned at this threat to the British Christmas (ironically, in view of the stoic public reaction to the very intermittent availability of television in the months to come), the Government recommended reference to the Central Arbitration Committee, which, acting in providential fashion reminiscent of the Official Solicitor, precipitately awarded not 5 per cent but 12½.

The stampede that followed settled the outcome of the election. Regardless of political consequences, unions in many fields set out frankly to use their muscle. Lorry drivers mounted pickets far and wide, uncollected rubbish blocked the pavements, trains were halted, a thousand schools were closed and scores of hospitals barred all but emergency admissions. Repeated stoppages by customs officers enabled returning travellers to bring brandy and cigars home unchallenged, while at least one of the hundreds of bereaved families distressed by a cemetery workers' strike turned to and dug the necessary grave themselves.

The winter, meanwhile, was the worst for 15 years, with snow, floods, gales and ice in Dickensian quantities. Mr Callaghan's luck required him to visit the West Indies for a summit conference, an affair in which shirtsleeves, sunshades and long cool drinks unavoidably figured, as we all jealously observed. Returning, suntanned, he ill-advisedly tried to strike the unflappable note at an airport interview, and an entire nation nursing its chilblains yearned as one to stuff him head first into a snowdrift.

———◆———

The particularly cold winter of 1978–79 brought to a head again many of the problems that had plagued the British economy for much of the decade. Among these were unemployment, inflation – which had touched 27% a few years before – and seemingly intractable disputes over pay.

The price of oil surged following the Revolution in Iran, a National Day of Action saw more workers walk out than at any time since the General Strike, and in London the dustmen refused to collect rubbish. Many people thought the country in thrall to the unions. When the Prime

Minister, James Callaghan, played down matters on his return from a Western powers conference in Guadeloupe, the press translated his words into a famous headline: 'Crisis? What crisis?'

That did not appear in *The Times*, which was not immune from strife and where the attempts of management to change age-old working practices and technology led to the newspaper not being printed for almost a year. When it returned, perhaps for the benefit of those readers who had been elsewhere during the 'Winter of Discontent', it reviewed the news it had missed, including the assassination of Lord Mountbatten, the fall of the Shah, and the election of Margaret Thatcher.

INDEPENDENCE FOR ZIMBABWE

18 April 1980

At the stroke of midnight Zimbabwe became independent. Rhodesia, the land that was named after its imperial founder, Cecil John Rhodes, made its way into history.

The former British colony, whose white minority vainly tried to stem the tide of black nationalism in Africa, became the fiftieth independent state in black Africa. It has also become the forty-third member of the Commonwealth.

The transfer of power took place at an independence ceremony held at the Rufaro Stadium in the Harare black township of Salisbury.

A crowd of 20,000 cheered as the Union Jack was lowered for the last time and replaced by the new red, green, black and gold Zimbabwean flag.

The Prince of Wales, representing the Queen, handed over the constitutional instruments – the symbols of independence – to President Canaan Banana, who had been sworn in as the country's first head of state.

A few hours earlier Prince Charles, Lord Soames, the Governor, and other British dignitaries had quietly watched the British flag being lowered for the last time in the grounds of Government House, with the sound of the Last Post filling the cool autumn air.

The ceremony not only symbolized an end of an era for Britain but also for the African continent. There are no longer any colonies left in Africa, apart from Namibia which is not a colony in the true sense of the word. The independence process, begun in Ghana in 1957, has now come to an end. During that period 15 African nations over which the British flag once flew have gained their sovereignty.

In an address broadcast to the nation last night, Mr Robert Mugabe, the Prime Minister, said that April 18, Independence Day, was "the birthday of great Zimbabwe, the birthday of its nation. Tomorrow, we shall cease to be men and women of the past and become men and women of the future. It's tomorrow then, and not yesterday, which bears our destiny".

The independence ceremony was similar to many which had been witnessed in other parts of Africa. Apart from the raising and lowering of flags, an independence flame was lit which will be carried by runners to the Salisbury Kopie (hill) today in time for a service for fallen heroes. Musical accompaniment was provided by a Scottish pipe band, Hindu dancers, a choir made up of Zanla guerrillas as well as Mr Bob Marley, the Jamaican reggae singer.

However, there were also several unique factors about last night's ceremony. First was the swearing in of the new President, the Rev Canaan Banana, by Mr Justice Macdonald, the Chief Justice. Mr Justice Macdonald, who is to retire shortly, was a prominent supporter of UDI. Second, was the presence of a joint guard of honour comprising the Rhodesian security forces and elements from the Zanla and Zipra guerrilla armies. Four months ago these men were killing one another.

In his broadcast, Mr Mugabe called on all Zimbabweans to follow the example of the integrated forces. By marching in step together, he said, they heralded a new era of national unity and togetherness. The whole ceremony was orderly and good-humoured and was only marred when police threw tear gas to disperse a crowd.

Representatives from almost 100 nations were attending the celebrations. They included four heads of state, six heads of government, and 23 foreign ministers. Other guests included Mr Pieter van der Byl, who was in Mr Ian Smith's Government and was one of the staunchest opponents of majority rule, and Bishop Abel Muzorewa, the former Prime Minister. Mr Smith was not present; he is lecturing in South Africa.

In messages from the Queen, the British Prime Minister, and Mr Mugabe, delivered at last night's ceremony, emphasis was placed on the need to look to the future and not to the past and also for close ties between Zimbabwe and Britain.

In his broadcast, which like previous broadcasts was notable for its moderation and spirit of reconciliation, Mr Mugabe called on all Zimbabweans to adapt themselves intellectually and spiritually to the reality of the political change that had taken place and to relate to each other as brothers. "The wrongs of the past must now stand forgiven and forgotten", he said. Oppression by blacks should not be allowed to replace oppression by whites.

———◆———

British involvement in Zimbabwe had begun a century earlier, when Cecil Rhodes obtained mining concessions that led gradually to his gaining control of the country. Now named for him, Southern Rhodesia, as it was, officially became a colony in 1923.

As the move to self-determination swept across Africa in the Sixties, however, Rhodesia's prime minister, Ian Smith, who was White but saw himself as African rather than British, unilaterally declared independence from Britain in 1965. The last colony to do so had been America.

Yet as Whites, who formed 5% of the population, still dominated the administration and the economy, this led to a civil war involving two Black nationalist movements, headed ultimately by rivals Joshua Nkomo and Robert Mugabe. The agreement brokered by Britain at Lancaster House led to the brief re-imposition of government from London before Zimbabwe was formally constituted.

Mugabe subsequently came to power and ruled in an increasingly dictatorial manner until he was ousted in 2017.

THE SAS STORM THE
IRANIAN EMBASSY

6 May 1980

A team from the Special Air Service Regiment stormed the Iranian Embassy in London last night under cover of explosions and rescued the surviving 19 hostages held by Iranian gunmen. Two other hostages had been shot dead earlier in the day.

Three of the gunmen died in the SAS attack, one was injured, and another captured outside the embassy.

The three Britons held by the Iranian gunmen, including PC Trevor Lock, the embassy police guard, were among the hostages who staggered from the building as smoke and flames enveloped it and automatic gunfire echoed in the street. At one stage in the afternoon, as the terrorists began to talk about killing hostages at the rate of one every half hour, the police brought in a mullah to plead with the men inside.

A fire was still raging on the second floor of the embassy at midnight last night.

A porter working in a building nearby said that during the attack three SAS men climbed down ropes at the rear of the building, hurled grenades through the windows, and stormed into the embassy. He said all three wore balaclava helmets and carried handguns.

Ninety minutes after the siege had been lifted Mr William Whitelaw, the Home Secretary, said he had ordered the SAS to strike after talking to Sir David McNee, the Commissioner of the Metropolitan police.

Mr Whitelaw said: "The operation, and I think the people of this country and many in the world will think so too, was an outstanding success, and it showed we in Britain are not prepared to tolerate terrorism in our capital city."

The Prime Minister paid tribute to the team from The Special Air Service Regiment. Mrs Margaret Thatcher and her husband visited the SAS men at 9.45 and stayed with them at a barracks in London for about half an hour. She congratulated them on the success of the operation.

The attack by the SAS, whose men are specially trained as a weapon of last resort in such situations, came on a day which started with police optimism which later turned to extreme pessimism for the safety of the hostages. Negotiations began in the morning, then around 2 pm it appears that things went seriously wrong.

While the negotiator was on the field telephone talking to the embassy, a number of shots were heard and these later turned out to be the executions of two of the hostages. Deputy Assistant John Dellow, the officer in charge of the police operation, said later the atmosphere in the embassy had changed "by way of suggestions of instability and irritation".

It is likely the police learned of that through the sophisticated microphones and miniature television cameras which they got close to the embassy during the six days of the siege.

◆

The terrorist attack at the Munich Olympics in 1972 forced governments of Western nations to confront the likelihood that they would soon have to deal with similar crises. Britain's response to it burst into the public consciousness on a Bank Holiday Monday evening, as television coverage of the Embassy World Snooker Final suddenly went off air, to be replaced by the dramatic live broadcast of another sort of final at another kind of embassy.

Six days earlier, gunmen had seized control of the Iranian Embassy in London and taken 26 hostages. These included not only diplomatic staff but also the police officer on guard and two BBC journalists who were applying for visas. The terrorists were Arabs seeking autonomy for the oil-rich and predominantly Arab Khuzestan region of Iran.

Negotiations with the group continued until one of the Iranian diplomats was killed. The police believed another had been shot and that more were at risk. A team from the SAS, then a little-known part of the Army, was sent in to rescue the hostages. The images of the black-clad soldiers transformed the regiment's profile and helped to make the Thatcher government appear competent and decisive.

THE DEATH OF JOHN LENNON

10 December 1980

Hundreds of mourners, chanting "All You Need Is Love" and other songs of the Beatles clustered today outside the Dakota apartment building in New York where John Lennon was shot dead last night.

Lennon, aged 40, was writer, singer and guitarist in the fabulously successful Liverpool singing group of the 1960s. He and Paul McCartney composed most of their hit songs.

Mark Chapman, a 25-year-old visitor to New York from Hawaii, was charged today with killing Lennon with a .38 revolver as the singer and his wife, the Japanese artist Yoko Ono, returned from a recording session just before 11 pm. Mr Chapman had been lurking round the building for days and earlier in the evening had asked Lennon for his autograph.

Lennon shouted "I'm shot" and staggered into the building's entrance booth. He was driven to a hospital nearby in a police car, but was dead when he arrived.

"Tell me it isn't true", Miss Ono sobbed, as the news was broken to her. Mr Chapman made no attempt to flee.

When the doorman asked him whether he knew what he had done, he is alleged to have said: "I just shot John Lennon."

When Mr Chapman was formally charged this afternoon, Miss Kim Hogrefe, the assistant district attorney, said that he had borrowed money to come to New York specifically to kill Lennon. The judge ordered him held without bail pending a psychiatric examination, which his court-appointed lawyer had requested.

The lawyer said Mr Chapman had twice in the past attempted suicide and had been committed to mental institutions.

Miss Hogrefe said that Mr Chapman had $2,000 (about £800) in cash on him when he was arrested a few minutes after the shooting.

Police denied earlier reports that Mr Chapman had a record of arrests, including armed robbery.

Mr Chapman, who has lived in Hawaii for the last few years, grew up in Georgia. A police source suggested that his motive may have been dissatisfaction with the scribbled autograph Lennon had given him a few hours earlier, but this would not tally with Miss Hogrefe's allegation that the killing was planned in advance.

People who knew Mr Chapman in Georgia said that he had been an amateur guitarist. He became interested in religion at school and had worked since as a security guard.

An extraordinary upsurge of grief overwhelms America today. Scores of radio stations are playing non-stop recordings from the Beatles' heyday in the 1960s when they became, according to the *Guinness Book of Records*, the most successful recording group in history.

Sorrow over the loss of a prodigally talented musician is mixed with horror that, once again in America, an assassin has found it a matter of absurd simplicity to destroy a life at whim. In the immediate aftermath, the killing is being compared with the murder of President Kennedy in 1963, immediately prior to the Beatles' greatest success. It may not be as unbalanced a comparison as it sounds. Both Lennon and Kennedy represented, in their different ways, the aspirations of a generation, which a quick squeeze of a trigger helped to destroy.

◆

John Lennon's killing led to a wave of grief sweeping the world. Huge crowds gathered in New York, where the singer was cremated, and his music once again topped the charts. He had only recently released his first songs for several years. To publicize the album, he had that afternoon posed nude, curled around his wife Yoko Ono, for the photographer Annie Leibovitz. The image would become one of the best-known of the couple.

Mark Chapman, who had shot Lennon four times in the back, was sentenced to at least 20 years imprisonment and has never been paroled. His motive for the murder remains unclear. He had been a fan of the Beatles but claimed that he had been angered by Lennon's statement that the group was 'more popular than Jesus'.

He had also been influenced by the character of Holden Caulfield in *The Catcher in the Rye*, the novel by J. D. Salinger. Chapman hoped, too, that killing one of history's great songwriters would make his own name immortal, much like Herostratus, the ancient Greek who burned down the Temple of Artemis at Ephesus.

THE BRIXTON RIOTS

13 April 1981

After three days of violent confrontation between hundreds of police and black youths the streets of Brixton, south London began to quieten early this morning, leaving the memory of the worst public disorder seen in mainland Britain for years.

The first reaction of the Government is expected to be the announcement today of a public inquiry into the reasons for the riots which led to over 200 casualties, more than 150 arrests, and scenes of desolation after looting and arson.

The worst damage occurred on Saturday night and yesterday there were hopes that the violence had subsided. But as evening approached, trouble broke out again with sporadic running battles.

The new violence came as the local community was still trying to repair the damage left by Saturday night's riot, in which 192 people were injured, 106 people arrested and well over £1m worth of property was destroyed by arsonists or stolen by looters.

Scotland Yard said last night that 90 people had been arrested in yesterday's clashes. Six civilians and 28 policemen were injured.

Police had cordoned off the Brixton area throughout the day and were keeping a watch from a helicopter hovering constantly overhead. They were ready to move, often in up to 12 vans, at the slightest sign of trouble.

Then trouble flared as the police in force appeared to be trying to arrest youths who had been seen making trouble earlier and also responding to isolated attacks made on them for no apparent reason.

In one incident around 5 pm, a police van was reported to have been overturned outside a public house in Atlantic Road, and later skirmishes started outside the town hall, where a crowd of at least a thousand people, including many sightseers, had gathered.

A snatch arrest of a black youth took place on the corner of Coldharbour Lane and Atlantic Road. A bystander, who appeared to have some authority over many of the young people who were hanging about, said that the arrested man had been very excited, but had done nothing wrong.

In the Railton Road area police coaches were attacked and police with riot shields met a hail of bricks and stones. As police in one part of the road were busy talking to residents trying to calm the situation, bricks and bottles from the supply of ammunition that still carpeted the devasted area were hurled at coaches, smashing windows.

Police with riot shields and dustbin lids for protection pushed the crowd back, splitting them into sections and driving groups of running black and white youths away into the side streets before regrouping around the mass of police vans parked along the road.

After about two hours of intermittent clashes, police with riot shields succeeded in clearing many of the youths down Effra Road. They surged back towards Railton Road where most of the youths seemed to be bent on congregating.

A man with a megaphone called on the crowds to assemble in Railton Road, scene of the previous night's riots.

In one incident five policemen and one policewoman, none carrying riot shields, tried to arrest a black youth outside a disused church now a community centre, opposite the town hall. The group was immediately surrounded by crowds who hurled bricks at the officers and police reinforcements ran quickly to their aid.

Many of the people on the streets were in their teens. Blacks and whites were there in equal numbers, often running in groups of a dozen or more, carrying missiles in their hands, which they threw away as soon as police arrived.

Others in the approaches to Brixton, down Coldharbour Lane and Brixton Road itself, stood quietly but clearly expecting a renewal of Saturday's violence. Both blacks and whites could be seen walking around as if it were a normal Sunday evening.

———◆———

The riots caused widespread shock not only because of their scale but because to many people they were unexpected. Superficially, the children of the Windrush generation of Black immigrants, born and raised in Britain, appeared well assimilated.

Yet, the unemployment rate of young Black men in the area was 55 per cent and there were longstanding tensions with the police, who were under pressure to reduce the similarly high rate of crime. Use of the 'sus law', whereby those deemed to be acting suspiciously could be arrested even if they had committed no crime, was particularly resented by Black youths, who felt disproportionately targeted.

The riot was sparked by rumours that a young Black man had been beaten by police while being taken away; in fact, they had been trying to get him to hospital to treat a knife wound. More than 300 people were injured in the violence – the great majority police officers – and £7.5m of damage done.

A report by Lord Scarman acknowledged that 'racial disadvantage was a fact of current British life' and recommended changes to policing. By the time it was published, however, there had been further riots in other inner cities, notably in Liverpool.

THE SHOOTING OF JOHN PAUL II

14 May 1981

An operation to save the Pope's life was successfully completed tonight five hours after a man had opened fire in St Peter's Square, hitting him at close range with several bullets.

Dr Giancarlo Castiglioni, head of surgery at the Gemelli Clinic in Rome said: "The Pope was hit in the abdomen by two bullets. The first exited immediately. The second was removed by surgeons during the operation." The Pope also had two slight wounds on his right arm and one on his left hand.

None of the vital organs had been touched, although the bullets had grazed arteries and the aorta, the main artery carrying blood from the heart.

A risk of infection remained, Dr Castiglioni said, but "we have a pharmaceutical arsenal at our disposal sufficient to limit such risks". He added that the Pope's robust health was his best guarantee in these circumstances. After the 4-hour, 10-minute operation and blood transfusions, the Pope was transferred to the hospital's emergency care unit where he was expected to remain for the next 48 hours.

The Pope, who is 60, had been rushed from St Peter's to the hospital, where the operation was performed by three surgeons, a cardiologist and three anaesthetists. When taken into the theatre, he was still conscious and a male nurse reported that he asked in a weak voice: "How could they do it?"

Two tourists among the estimated 10,000 in the square were accidentally hit in the shooting. An American woman, Anne Odre, aged 60, from Buffalo, New York State, was seriously wounded in the chest by a stray shot and was undergoing surgery in another Rome hospital. A Jamaican woman, Rose Hall, aged 21, was hit in the left arm but was not seriously hurt.

Mgr Agostino Casaroli, the Secretary of State and administrative chief at the Vatican, was on a flight to the United States when the shooting occurred. Vatican officials said he was informed by radio and would be taking the first flight back to Rome from New York.

It was at 5.19 pm when the shots rang out as the Pope in his open white Jeep was making his familiar gesture of welcome to the crowds. He fell forward, bleeding from his wounds, into the arms of his Secretary Don Stanislaw Dziwisz.

The Pope had just completed his first round of contacts with the crowd at the general audience, clutching hands as he passed, waving affectionately to groups of children and drawing almost to a stop to talk to enthusiastic pilgrims and visitors drawn up to sense the aura of protective strength which John Paul II was so adept at giving to the crowds who flocked to see him.

When he was shot his Jeep was moving towards the chair placed in front of the steps of the Basilica where the Pope was due to sit and read his discourse.

The driver immediately took the Jeep back into the Vatican through the Arch of the Bells and minutes later an ambulance left the Vatican by another exit – St Ann's Gate – taking the wounded pontiff to hospital.

Eye-witnesses later began to tell their stories. Caterina Damiani of Rome, who was about 30 feet from the Pope said: "I saw two streams of blood. They were clearly visible on the Pope's white silk vestments. The Pope was still for a moment, then he fell."

◆

There was no mystery as to the identity of the would-be assassin of the Pope. Mehmet Ali Ağca was a 23-year old Turk with a piercing gaze and connections to Far Right groups in his home country. He had escaped from prison in Istanbul while on trial for the political murder of a newspaper editor.

Yet, that was almost all that ever became clear about the attempt on John Paul II's life. The more investigators and journalists pored over Ağca's movements and motives, the more muddied the waters became.

It was never ascertained for certain if he was acting alone or was a hired gun. Different theories connected him to Palestinian terrorists, Turkish criminals and the Bulgarian intelligence service. Many saw behind the shooting the hand of the KGB, worried at the Pope's influence on

Solidarity, the trade union movement in Poland that was standing up to the communist regime.

Ağca was given a 40-year sentence but was freed after 20 at the request of the Pope, who had visited him in prison and forgiven him. Ağca, who then spent a further 10 years in jail in Turkey, changed his own story many times. Was he a lone gunman? Did he really believe he was a manifestation of Jesus Christ? Only he knows.

THE HEADINGLEY TEST

22 July 1981

England's victory in the third Test match, sponsored by Cornhill, at Headingley yesterday was greeted by the kind of scenes reserved for great sporting occasions. After Australia, needing only 130 to win, had been bowled out for 111, the crowd massed in front of the pavilion, cheering their heroes and waving the Union Jacks they were saving for the Royal wedding.

While at one end of the balcony Brearley and his victorious team were being serenaded, at the other Alan Border, who had not long before been out for nought, was to be seen with his head buried in his hands. It was a moment of disaster as well as of triumph.

Kim Hughes, even so, was gracious in defeat, giving credit where it was due and saying that, whereas from tea-time on Monday the luck had gone mostly England's way, before that the Australians had had the greater share of it.

If Botham's unforgettable innings made the recovery possible, it was Willis who crowned it with a marvellous piece of bowling after Australia had got to within only 74 runs of their target with nine wickets standing. When play started yesterday morning the chances seemed to be that Willis was playing in his last Test match. He had bowled below his best in England's first innings and it was not until his second spell now, after he had changed ends, that he caught the wind.

That was where Brearley came in. His return to the England side had not only released Botham to play his game unhampered by the burden of captaincy; it meant that England, with so few runs to play with, were under the command of a supreme tactician. To everyone on the ground, except those who wanted Australia to win, it was a great reassurance to see Brearley handling the situation with calm and understanding.

After England's last wicket had added only another five runs at the start of the day, Brearley opened the bowling with Botham and Dilley, England's third different new ball partnership of the match. His reason for this was partly psychological: Botham and Dilley having shared such a decisive partnership with the bat, it was worth seeing whether they could repeat it with the ball.

In the event Dilley, though he was to hold a great catch later in the innings, was taken off after two unimpressive overs. Although in his second over Botham had Wood caught at the wicket he looked hardly in the mood to move another mountain. That Willis was the man to do this, at the age of 32, and with knees that have often had to be supported by sticks, was a mark of rare courage. He had started with five rather laboured overs from the Football Stand End. At 48 for one, half an hour before lunch, Brearley gave him the breeze, the decision which launched him on his devastating spell.

It was noticeable even in his first over from the Kirkstall Lane End that Willis was bowling faster than in his earlier spell; not only that, he was making the ball lift as well.

◆

England's near-miraculous victory was only the second time that a side had won after being made to follow on in a Test. The previous occasion, which involved the same nations, had been in 1894. The feat has since been achieved by India in 2001, with Australia completing the hat-trick of being the losers each time.

The match was won by Bob Willis, who took 8 for 43 as England triumphed by 18 runs. The series, however, belonged to Ian Botham.

Having given up the captaincy after defeat and a draw in the first two matches, and with his own form poor, Botham found himself at the crease in the second innings at Headingley with England seven wickets down and 92 runs short of making their opponents bat again. One bookmaker gave odds of 500-1 on an England victory.

Botham's assault on the Australian bowlers, as he made 149 not out, was said to have led to crowds gathering to watch outside shops that sold televisions. It was enough to give England their chance. Then in the next match, Botham took five wickets for a single run to deny Australia certain victory and set England on course to retain the Ashes.

THE ROYAL WEDDING

30 July 1981

A princely marriage is the brilliant edition of a universal fact and, as such, it rivets mankind. When the couple fluff their lines, the universal fact becomes instantly and poignantly human.

Charles Philip Arthur George, Prince of Wales and heir to the Throne, and Lady Diana Frances Spencer, were married before the altar of St Paul's Cathedral at 11.20 am yesterday, she having promised to take Philip Charles Arthur George, and he having omitted to mention that the goods with which he endowed her were worldly ones.

It was the most public of all private moments, watched by 3,500 guests inside Wren's light and majestic cathedral, heard over loudspeakers by one million people lining the processional route, and seen by another 750 million throughout the world on the most popular television programme yet transmitted.

The marriage ceremony, conducted according to the simple rite of the Church of England, was the core and the purpose of a great ceremonial occasion that assumed the gaiety of carnival rather than the gravity of state, with the participation of more crowned heads and commoners than London has seen since the Coronation.

In a grey world, for a troubled nation smarting from a crown of social and political thorns, it was a day of unbridled romance, colour, and celebration, shared with half the globe. But the realities of the times were obliged to intrude discreetly with 4,000 policemen, many of them armed, lining the route, marksmen atop buildings, detectives mingling with the crowds, and two armed police sergeants disguised as footmen riding with the royal coaches.

But there were no unhappy incidents. Even the dismal English summer allowed itself a dry day of close, muggy heat, sunshine, and occasional cloud.

Nevertheless, recent attempts, real or imagined, on the lives of public figures, culminating in the firing of shots in the presence of the Queen at the start of the Trooping the Colour ceremony, have enforced the need for a degree of security uncharacteristic of great British public events.

The day was one of worry, and immense organization, for Sir David McNee, the Metropolitan Police Commissioner. Once the royal couple were safely out of his domain he revealed that the use of police sergeants as footmen had been an arrangement between his force and the Palace, not so much to add to an already weighty security apparatus, as to provide the Royal Family with a feeling of comfort.

But the day ended in relief. All missing persons were found, and in the City of London there was a single arrest, for street trading.

Crowds, drawn from many of the nations over which the British Throne holds titular sway as well as lost colonies such as the United States, had begun to camp along the two mile processional route on Monday, the most favoured vantage point being opposite the door of St Paul's. By yesterday morning every yard was packed by a red, white and blue multitude cheering everything that passed, be it a duchess or a dustcart.

From Buckingham Palace to Ludgate Hill there processed representatives of eight of the nine monarchies remaining in mainland Europe, the King and Queen of Spain having declined their invitation over the issue of Gibraltar's being used as a honeymoon calling place. They were followed by the British Royal Family in strength, led by the Queen in aquamarine, and ending with the bridegroom in the full dress uniform of a naval commander.

But it was for the procession from Clarence House that the ultimate accolade was reserved. Lady Diana, riding in the Glass Coach, sat almost hidden in her spectacular wedding creation of ivory taffeta and old lace. Only when she stepped from the coach on the arm of her father at the cathedral steps was its true magnificence revealed: a wildly romantic gown with 25ft of train that cascaded like a river behind her down the steps of St Paul's.

———◆———

They were not, of course, destined to live happily ever after. Yet, as was frequently said at the time, even by Archbishop Runcie during the service, the wedding of Prince Charles and Lady Diana Spencer seemed to be the stuff of fairy tales.

Like a modern Cinderella, the bride arrived in a glass coach in a dress made of ivory silk taffeta embroidered with 10,000 pearls. (It was Queen Victoria who is said to have started the fashion for women to wear white on their wedding day.)

The 25-foot train was the longest in royal history, while on her unseen feet Lady Diana wore, if not glass slippers, then low-heeled shoes with the couple's initials painted on the arch.

Everything had been thought of. The shoes' soles, for example, were made of suede to stop her from taking a tumble, although she spilled perfume on the dress and when on camera had to cover the patch with her hand.

It was, everyone agreed, the 'wedding of the century'. Few recalled all the Archbishop's words: 'Fairy tales usually end at this point...This may be because fairy stories regard marriage as an anti-climax after the romance of courtship'.

THE FALKLANDS WAR

15 June 1982

The Prime Minister told an elated and packed House of Commons last night that large numbers of Argentine soldiers had thrown down their weapons and were reported to be flying white flags over Port Stanley.

A deafening cheer from the Government benches greeted her statement that the British and Argentine commanders in the field were holding talks about the surrender of the Argentine forces on the East and West Falklands.

It seemed to take longer for the Opposition benches to believe that Mrs Thatcher might be announcing the end of the Falklands war, two and a half months after the invasion. But the Labour benches too were cheering by the time Mr Michael Foot rose to congratulate first the armed forces and then, in the warmest terms, the Prime Minister herself.

The Prime Minister, with other members of her inner Cabinet beside her, shuffled her handwritten notes as the House filled. MPs had been drawn to the Chamber by the rumour that a minister would have something definite to tell them. Few expected anything so dramatic.

She rose to cheers, to give the latest information about "the battle of the Falklands", and said:

"After successful attacks last night General Moore decided to press forward. The Argentines retreated. Our forces reached the outskirts of Port Stanley. Large numbers of Argentine soldiers threw down their weapons. They are reported to be flying white flags over Port Stanley.

"Our troops have been ordered not to fire except in self-defence. Talks are now in progress between General Menendez and our deputy commander, Brigadier Waters, about the surrender of the Argentine forces on East and West Falklands".

Up to now the Prime Minister had spoken with marked self-control, slowly and clearly, but now she relaxed and smiled broadly, in obvious relief, as she told the Speaker that she would report further to the House today.

Mr Foot was every bit as relieved. He began by thanking Mrs Thatcher for coming to the House to give the news, particularly because the news was so good for all concerned. It appeared, he said, that what she had said meant that there would be an end to the bloodshed "which is what we have all desired".

If the news was confirmed, as he trusted, there would be great congratulations to the British forces. Then came his words for the Prime Minister.

"I can well understand the anxieties and pressures that must have been upon her during these weeks and I can understand at this moment those pressures and anxieties may be relieved, and I congratulate her upon it".

The Conservative ranks cheered Mr Foot for this generosity and Mrs Thatcher was moved by it. Mr David Steel, the Liberal leader, added his congratulations to the forces and the Government "in bringing this sad matter to a satisfactory and peaceful conclusion". And Dr David Owen, for the Social Democrats, congratulated the armed forces and those ministers who had played a major role in the achievement of an extremely successful outcome.

———◆———

The Falkland Islands, in the South Atlantic, had been governed by Britain since the early-nineteenth century, but Argentina had long claimed sovereignty over them. The war began at the start of April 1982 when, to boost its domestic popularity, Argentina's junta invaded the Islands and stationed 10,000 troops there.

Despite the difficulties of mounting operations 8,000 miles from Britain, the government sent a task force by sea to retake the islands. (The Americans provided significant logistic support, not least with secret intelligence.) After aerial and naval engagements, including the sinking of the Argentine cruiser *General Belgrano* and the loss of several Royal Navy warships, British forces landed on the islands.

A series of hard-fought actions, notably at Goose Green, enabled the infantry to advance and dominate the high ground around the capital at Port Stanley, leading to the Argentine surrender. Three civilian Falkland Islanders, 255 British servicemen, and 649 Argentinians lost their lives during the conflict.

The defeat led to the fall of the junta the following year, while conversely Margaret Thatcher rode a wave of patriotic pride to a landslide victory in the 1983 General Election.

THE MINERS' STRIKE

19 June 1984

Mr Arthur Scargill the miners' leader, was detained in hospital last night after being injured in violent clashes between thousands of pickets and police at the Orgreave coking plant near Sheffield.

Eighty people were hurt and more than a hundred, mostly miners, arrested during hours of running battles between some 6,500 pickets and 3,300 police. It was the worst violence in a British industrial dispute since the war.

The police were at first overwhelmed by the pickets, but then re-grouped to advance under a hail of stones, bottles and bricks, until the demonstrators retreated behind a barricade of burning cars, lamp posts and stones from a wall they had demolished.

Late last night those arrested appeared before two sittings of Rotherham magistrates in special session. They were charged with unlawful assembly and were remanded on bail for one month on condition that they do not go within a mile of the Orgreave plant. Some faced additional charges including assault.

Mr Scargill, wearing his familiar baseball hat, was with the miners when policemen with truncheons drawn drove them back across a railway bridge.

He was found sitting on the ground by a burning barricade, his head in his hands, and he was clearly badly shaken. He said: "All I know is that these bastards rushed in and this guy hit me on the back of the head with a shield and I was out."

Mr Scargill sustained head, leg and arm injuries and was taken to Rotherham Hospital where he was detained overnight for observation. Police cheered as he was led to an ambulance.

Mr Scargill's claim to have been struck with a riot shield was denied by Assistant Chief Constable Tony Clement, of South Yorkshire, who was in charge of the police operation at Orgreave.

Mr Clement, who was with officers in riot gear who chased demonstrators across the bridge to a position close to where Mr Scargill was injured said: "He slipped off the top of the bank and hit his head on a sleeper. If he was injured before that I know not. .

"Mr Scargill slipped, rather than fell. I do not know whether he had been hit before that. He was not near a riot shield. The officers with shields were on the road and Mr Scargill was off the road. They did not come within seven or eight yards of him."

Mr Steve Howell, a miner from Silverwood colliery, South Yorkshire said Mr Scargill had been standing in front of his men when the police ran towards them. "My impression was that he was getting leathered by truncheons."

Mr Clement had said earlier: "Scargill's presence is always provocative. When he arrives everybody gets excited. I wish he would stay away."

The union has made the Orgreave plant a target in an attempt to stop the daily convoys of lorries taking coal to the Scunthorpe steelworks. Ironically, news that the British Steel Corporation was suspending shipments for Orgreave came after most of the miners had left.

The British Steel Corporation said the Scunthorpe furnaces had been restored to stable operating levels, and although the efforts to damage the steelworks by the mass picketing of Orgreave had been unsuccessful, supplies would be terminated temporarily because stocks of coal would have been exhausted. They would be resumed when stocks had been replenished and it was judged appropriate to resume them.

The police expected a massive picket yesterday, because they said the demonstration was being advertised at the Wakefield gala at the weekend as the "Saltley" of the dispute.

To try to avert trouble, the police had requested licensing magistrates in Sheffield and Rotherham to shut all public houses and off licences within two miles of the Orgreave plant. It was the first time the magistrates had granted such a request in an industrial dispute.

But even though they were prepared for a big turnout the police were still surprised by the size of the demonstration and the scale of the violence.

———————◆———————

A decade earlier, miners' strikes for higher pay had undermined the authority of Ted Heath's government. With coal unable to reach power stations, electricity had to be rationed and the nation reduced to a three-day working week. Heath had called an election to determine 'who governs Britain?'. It turned out that it was not going to be him.

He was replaced as Conservative leader by Margaret Thatcher. The coal industry, nationalized after the war, was subsidized by the state and needed to shed jobs if it was to become more efficient before its planned privatization.

The news that 20 pits were to close prompted a mass strike by the National Union of Mineworkers, led by the combative Arthur Scargill. He had come to prominence during a turning point of the 1972 dispute, the picketing of a fuel depot in Birmingham known as the 'Battle of Saltley Gate'.

There had been no national ballot before the 1984 strike, as was required, and it split many communities. Confrontations, particularly between police and miners, were marked by violence. When the strike was ruled illegal by the courts, the miners returned to work in 1985. Thatcher's government had shown it would not bow to the unions.

THE BRIGHTON BOMB

13 October 1984

It was the last night of the Conservative Party conference. There had been many parties, many arguments. By 2.45 am yesterday most of the representatives were in bed. There were some late-night drinkers in the hotel lounges; a few more were walking along the Brighton promenade.

The three days of debate had been talked over and over. By now the main point of discussion was the leader's speech, the traditional end to a Conservative conference. The leader herself was writing that speech in the first floor Napoleon suite of the Grand Hotel, the Victorian pile that so often served as party conference headquarters.

Mrs Margaret Thatcher remembers clearly the moment she knows she will never forget: "I was working. I had just finished doing something when I looked at the clock. It was a quarter to three and I started on another paper. My husband was in bed."

The bomb went off just before three. The windows of the Prime Minister's suite overlooking the sea were blown in. Her bathroom, according to her husband Denis, looked as "if it had been blitzed".

Only a few moments before, Mrs Thatcher had been in the room which had suffered such damage that nobody in it at the time of the blast would have survived the impact.

In adjoining suites on either side were Sir Geoffrey Howe, Foreign Secretary, and Mr Leon Brittan, Home Secretary.

Police with guns drawn ran to Mrs. Thatcher's suite. Officers stood guard at the windows as more police arrived with Mr Brittan, Sir Geoffrey and his wife, Elspeth, whose rooms were even more badly damaged than the Prime Minister's. Mrs Thatcher, a police officer reported, "remained icy calm throughout".

Within five minutes of the explosion, police, who were later to face questions about security at the hotel, had sealed off the roads in a three-mile radius of the Grand. Firemen, ambulances and medical teams arrived as dazed guests scrambled to safety, many of them through holes in what had once been the walls of their bedrooms.

Immediately after the explosion it was as if time had been suspended. The explosion blew Mr Harvey Thomas, the conference organizer, from the seventh to the fifth floor. He recalled the moment from his hospital bed: "I was sound asleep and I felt a tremendous noise and crashing. I thought it was an earthquake. Then I realized that you do not have earthquakes in Brighton, at least not during a Tory Party conference."

Mr Thomas, whose wife is expecting a baby this weekend, was trapped for about an hour and a half. He said: "I was in rubble up to my nose and I kept on wondering how long the air would last. I prayed.

"I almost lost consciousness but not quite. We were freezing cold and water from the hotel tanks was pouring all over us."

On every floor at the front of the hotel, which had been ripped open by a bomb the IRA later said consisted of 110 pounds of gelignite, the emergency services were struggling to release men and women trapped under the rubble.

The most public rescue was for Mr Norman Tebbit, Secretary of State for Trade and Industry, who had been in bed with his wife in an upper room of the hotel. His wife, Margaret, had been taken to hospital suffering from neck injuries, but Mr Tebbit was trapped against a wall above one of the main exits in the hotel foyer.

Firemen had to cut the main power supplies as they cut away plaster and concrete with their hands to get to Mr Tebbit, who is 53. The only light available was from a BBC television outside broadcast unit.

Four hours after the explosion television viewers across the country saw Mr Tebbit being gently lifted by firemen on to a stretcher. He had been conscious throughout and had refused pain killers. He moaned quietly as a medical team gave him oxygen and a saline drip for the ambulance journey to the Royal Sussex County Hospital.

Clearly in pain, Mr Tebbit was suffering from shock, cuts and broken ribs. An emergency operation was carried out soon after he had been admitted to hospital. His work at the Department of Trade and Industry will be shared among the seven ministers who report to him. He made his first telephone call to them shortly before lunch yesterday.

Out of sight of the cameras the rescue continued. From time to time officers in the emergency services would report progress. Around 10 am a fire officer said that they had uncovered two hands, one warm, another cold.

◆

The bomb that went off in the Grand Hotel, Brighton, had been intended by the IRA to kill Margaret Thatcher while she was staying there during the Conservative Party Conference. She had just finished looking at papers about the Liverpool Garden Festival when the explosion occurred. She heard two sounds, the second being falling masonry. At that stage, she did not realise that the blast had occurred inside the hotel and thought it was a car bomb.

The device had been concealed a month before by a member of the IRA, Patrick Magee, in a bathroom five floors up from Mrs Thatcher's suite. When it went off, it killed five people and 34 others were hurt. Among those left disabled by their injuries was Margaret Tebbit. Magee was caught and convicted of the bombing in 1986. He was released after the Good Friday Agreement in 1999. (See Good Friday, page 384.)

Thatcher impressed many with her fortitude, insisting that she make her speech at the Conference as planned. She revealed later, however, that her husband, Denis, had subsequently bought her a new watch to remind her of her escape that night. 'This is to tell you,' he had said, 'that every minute counts'.

LIVE AID

15 July 1985

Although its ostensible purpose was to bring balm to a far-off people, at times the Wembley leg of Saturday's extraordinary Live Aid concert felt like the healing of our own nation. After the weeks of troubled self-examination that followed the tragedy in the Heysel Stadium in Brussels, here the British seemed to be proving that their young people could gather peacefully in great numbers, drawn as much by a "good cause" as by the chance to worship the gods of popular entertainment.

As the venerable Beach Boys appeared by satellite from Philadelphia, their image on the giant screens and the sound of their carefree summer pop music provoking cheers and community singing around Wembley, the irony deepened. They sang "Surfing USA", written and recorded in 1963, when Danny Blanchflower was captain of Tottenham Hotspur and Chuck McKinley won the Wimbledon championship. Who in 1963 would have dared predict that while sport could lead young people towards violence in the guise of nationalism, pop music would present them with the opportunity of showing compassion across continents?

Bob Geldof of course, was the catalyst, and the day belonged to him. Even more rumpled than usual – unlike many of his peers, Geldof is a man who sleeps in his hair – and rendered practically transparent by fatigue, he was still to be found at four in the morning, haranguing a BBC camera in a West End nightclub, asking for the umpteenth time the question to which he would most like an answer: how, with millions starving, can the developed world justify the destruction of food surpluses?

There may be some sane and plausible answer, but it would have taken a brave politician to present it to Geldof yesterday morning.

Sometimes the day resembled what passes for normal life at a big rock concert. The stars arrived by limousine or helicopter and paraded for the bucket lenses of the paparazzi. Fans jammed up against the crush-barrier in front of the stage were sprayed with hoses in the ferocious heat, and some passed out.

At other moments, though, it seemed wholly original. For the stars, there was a magical hour in which they could compete for proximity to the Prince and Princess of Wales in the Royal Box, perhaps getting close enough – while Status Quo's "Rocking All Over the World" put the first sixpence in Geldof's "global jukebox" – to exchange views on contemporary culture with the Princess, as David Bowie appeared to do.

For the fans, there was the marvellous game invented during a lull between performances, when the random throwing of an orange teddy bear high into the air led spontaneously to the massed hurling of every available soft object. And when the rain came, warm and light, during Elton John's appearance, the multi-coloured umbrellas and polythene sheets merely added to the gaiety of the scene. Television could not have conveyed the crowd's good humour at such moments.

A little bit Woodstock, a little bit *Tiswas*, the style of the Wembley event was also an appealing throwback to the days of package tours, when a dozen acts were sent on the road together each performing their two or three hit songs. Indeed, Elvis Costello and Howard Jones produced performances the more striking for being confined to a single song. Similarly intimate in conception was the half-hour slot shared by Phil Collins and Sting, whose collaboration seemed to constitute the world's biggest living-room jam session.

Others saw things more conventionally. Bryan Ferry, Sade, Spandau Ballet, Dire Straits and U2 produced the expected goods, to varying degrees of rapture. The Who came back together after three years for a short set that would probably prove to have been their last word: the sight of Roger Daltrey and Pete Townshend falling over each other during the climax "Won't Get Fooled Again" spoke volumes for the minutes of rehearsal they had devoted to the reunion. Still, as Daltrey pointed out, Bob Geldof's offers are impossible to refuse.

Queen, by contrast, had devoted three days to preparing their short programme, with the result that beneath Freddie Mercury's preposterous preening lay stagecraft that dominated the audience.

◆

The concert had grown out of the effort the previous year by Bob Geldof, lead singer of The Boomtown Rats, and fellow musician, Midge Ure, to raise funds to alleviate a severe famine afflicting Ethiopia.

Moved by the images of starving people in a report about the disaster by the BBC journalist Michael Buerk, the duo had co-opted other stars of the day into singing on a hastily recorded charity disc. To their surprise, *Do They Know it's Christmas?* became the best-selling single in UK chart history.

A global audience of at least one billion watched the concert at Wembley and that staged by chiefly American acts the same day in Philadelphia. Tens of millions of pounds were donated by viewers. The rate of giving increased following the screening of footage of starving infants matched to the song *Drive*, by The Cars.

Its lyrics were used out of context but seemed apposite: You can't go on/thinking nothing's wrong. A few weeks before, 39 people had died following clashes between Liverpool and Juventus fans gathered for the European Cup final at the Heysel Stadium, Brussels. At the least, Live Aid gave the lie to those who said the young and their idols cared nothing for others.

THE CHALLENGER DISASTER

29 January 1986

The US shuttle Challenger, carrying a crew of seven, yesterday exploded in a fireball over the Atlantic 90 seconds after blast-off from the Kennedy Space Centre in Florida in the worst ever space disaster.

Wreckage plunged into the sea a few miles offshore from Cape Canaveral. Rescue ships and helicopters raced to the area but were held back for an hour by the rain of burning debris. All crew members, including the two women – one of them the first teacher in space – are presumed dead. Medical personnel were waiting to parachute into the crash area.

Vice-President George Bush rushed into the Oval Office to tell the President of the disaster. Mr Reagan immediately broke off his meeting with top advisers and hurried next door to watch live television pictures. The White House spokesman said he was stunned and close to tears. The House of Representatives held prayers and immediately adjourned.

President Reagan postponed his scheduled State of the Union address to Congress until Tuesday. He ordered Mr Bush to Cape Canaveral to express his sympathy to the families of the shuttle astronauts.

In a five-minute nationwide broadcast President Reagan vowed that the shuttle programme would go on despite the disaster.

"We will continue our quest in space. There will be more shuttle flights... More teachers in space. Nothing ends here. Our hope and our journeys continue."

Mr Reagan paid a moving tribute to the seven astronauts, comparing their bravery with that of Sir Francis Drake, who died exactly 390 years ago yesterday.

Speaking quietly and sombrely, Mr Reagan said the seven had a special grace, a hunger to explore the universe. They were pioneers, pulling the United States into the future. "We will continue to follow."

To the schoolchildren who watched the tragedy Mr Reagan said it was hard to understand painful things, but this was part of exploration and discovery. "The future doesn't belong to the faint-hearted, it belongs to the brave."

The Soviet Embassy in Washington expressed "deep condolences and sympathy" for the deaths of those killed in the "enormous tragic" explosion. The spokesman said the statement was for the American people and members of the victims' families.

The tragedy, watched by millions, including the families of the crew, came without warning after a perfect lift-off. A solid rocket booster apparently exploded nine miles up just as ground control instructed the crew to throttle up. A blazing multi-coloured ball of fire engulfed the shuttle, which then seemed to spin out of control, breaking up as it fell.

It happened so fast that ground control had no time to put into effect the emergency procedures practised before the mission. The crew was not equipped with ejector seats.

◆

In 1981, NASA launched *Columbia*, the first reusable spacecraft or space shuttle. Aircraft-like in form, it was propelled into orbit by its three engines and two booster rockets. It would perform tasks such as deploying satellites before gliding back to *terra firma* at the end of its mission. As a marvel of engineering, it justifiably became a source of pride to Americans.

Its successor, *Challenger*, was making its tenth flight when, at 10 miles up and three times the speed of sound, catastrophe struck. On what was an unusually cold morning in Florida, one in five Americans was watching coverage of the lift-off. Among the crew was Christa McAuliffe, a teacher who was set to become the first civilian in space.

An investigation determined that the cause of the disaster had been a leaking seal on a booster. This would fail at low temperatures, allowing burning gas to reach the external fuel tank. The flaw was known to NASA but the risk posed was not sufficiently appreciated.

The space programme resumed in 1988 with *Discovery* but in 2002 *Columbia* was also lost, together with its crew. Space shuttle flights came to an end in 2011, although in 2020 SpaceX became the first private company to send astronauts into orbit and to the International Space Station – and to bring them back.

CHERNOBYL

29 April 1986

A massive radioactive leak at a Soviet nuclear power station has caused casualties in what may be the world's worst nuclear accident. The leak was so large that it prompted a full-scale alert nearly 1,000 miles away in Sweden, including the evacuation of 600 workers from a Swedish power station on the Baltic coast.

Finland reported radiation levels six times higher than normal, Denmark five times higher than normal, and Norway 50% up as a result of the accident. "We have registered radiation just about everywhere we have looked," said Mr. Ragnar Boge, of the Swedish Radiation Institute.

Soviet atomic energy authorities at first told the Swedish Embassy in Moscow they were unaware of any nuclear accident on Soviet territory that could cause a leak to reach Sweden.

But later Tass reported that an accident had taken place at a nuclear power station at Chernobyl, north of Kiev, and there were some casualties.

It said measures were being undertaken "to eliminate the consequences of the accident" at the plant, where a reactor had been damaged. Aid was being given to those affected by the leak, it added.

Swedish scientists at first believed a leak had occurred at their own nuclear plant at Forsmark, on the Baltic coast about 60 miles north of Stockholm, and evacuated the 600 workers there. After the evacuation radiation levels were checked at other areas of the country, including the capital.

These all confirmed a higher degree of radioactivity than normal, and further tests at Forsmark led the Swedish authorities to conclude that the discharge had come from the Soviet Union.

Some Swedish nuclear experts said they believed the Soviet accident was caused by the overheating of nuclear fuel. A "considerable explosion" would be the result of such overheating and could have led to a "meltdown" of the nuclear core of the reactor, they said. The Swedish Energy Minister, Mrs Birgitta Dahl, said all Russian nuclear reactors should be placed under international control.

"We must demand that Soviet Union improve their security, and inform the rest of the world of such accidents in good time," she said.

The first stage of the Chernobyl nuclear plant was put into service in September 1977, followed by two more stages in 1980.

A government committee of inquiry had been set up by the Soviet Union into the accident, Tass said.

The Swedish Defence Ministry said an abnormally high level of radioactivity had been recorded on Monday afternoon by several monitoring stations in Finland, Sweden, Denmark and Norway.

The ministry said that at a rate of "a few millirems an hour" the level was not thought high enough to warrant the evacuation of the local population at Forsmark. It would not be a danger to human beings, although regional specialists said the level was twice as high in Finland as in Sweden and Norway.

A millirem is a unit of ionizing radiation that gives the same biological effect as one thousandth of a standard unit of X-rays.

Since Mr Mikhail Gorbachov came to power in March 1985 there have been repeated calls in the Soviet press for more open reporting of disasters inside the Soviet Union.

The Tass statement was seen as a quick propaganda move ordered by the Kremlin to counter any international criticism of safety measures taken inside the Soviet Union, which has traditionally surrounded details of its nuclear programme with secrecy.

◆

The accident at Chernobyl – the Ukrainian word for wormwood – is still regarded as the most serious in the history of nuclear energy. Although its true causes were concealed at first by the Soviet state, these were a mixture of the faulty design of the plant and failings in operating procedures during a safety drill that went terribly wrong.

It took longer than anticipated to restore power to the reactor after electricity to it was cut off in a test, leading to instability there that provoked a devastating explosion and fire. More than 100,000 people had to be evacuated from the area around Chernobyl. About 135 deaths were directly attributable to radiation poisoning but estimates of those across the areas of Europe affected by the fallout range as high as 16,000.

The plant was subsequently entombed in several layers of concrete. Clean-up of the site, which has cost tens of billions of dollars, is scheduled to finish by 2065.

WAPPING

7 February 1987

The year-long dispute between the print unions and News International is officially over. The National Graphical Association informed the company yesterday that it was prepared "unconditionally" to call off its picketing. After meeting at its Bedford headquarters, the union decided to follow the same course as Sogat '82, which decided on Thursday that it would abandon the dispute.

The NGA decision was given to the company shortly before News International solicitors were due to activate High Court proceedings for contempt of an injunction granted last July which banned mass picketing outside its new plant at Wapping, east London. If the action had gone ahead, the 126,000-strong craft union faced the possible sequestration of its assets.

Last night, Mr Bill O'Neill, the company's managing director, said: "The NGA's action signals the end of the dispute. We can now get on with a normal relationship with the community."

Mr Tony Dubbins, general secretary of the NGA, said that picketing and demonstrations by his members would end immediately. "Sogat's decision played a very major part in our own decision. Bearing in mind that NGA members formed only 20 per cent of the sacked print workers, it would have been impossible for us to continue the dispute on our own. It was the most difficult decision I have had to recommend to the executive in 15 years. What has upset them is the fact that by the threat of legal action by News International they have not been able to take part in a secret ballot."

Mr Dubbins, who accused the TUC of "letting down" the print unions, said the NGA had lost about £1.5 million during the dispute through legal costs and dispute payments.

Miss Brenda Dean, general secretary of Sogat '82, denied that her union's decision to pull out had been "in any way responsible" for the NGA move. "I was not surprised by the NGA decision because they were in the same legal boat as us. I am not prepared to accept any responsibility for another union's decision," she said. "It's been a very sad two days for all of us. We now plan to let things settle down for a few days before the leaders of both unions get together again."

Mr Kenneth Clarke, the Minister for Employment, said the NGA's move had shown that "even the most hardline and militant unions" had to comply with the law.

"Little direct good ever comes out of a dispute of this kind – it's a fairly sad story – but I think the lasting effects may be beneficial," he said on Channel 4 News. He hoped "fringe groups" would not now continue causing violence outside Wapping. "Most people will be glad that the law has been upheld, and that even the NGA have at last accepted that these laws are there to protect public order and make sure disputes are conducted in a more sensible way," Mr Clarke said.

The NGA began its dispute with the company after 939 of its members employed by News International went on strike over the issue of jobs for life and were dismissed. Since then 207 have received termination payments of up to £30,000. The remaining NGA members will be able to apply for termination payments of four weeks' pay for every year of service following a decision by the company to reopen the offer until March 10. A small minority of hardline Sogat members have said they do not accept the decision taken by their national executive by 23 votes to nine but they have been warned they could be dismissed from the union if they continue to picket the plant.

Sogat branch officers in Fleet Street, who were in the forefront of organizing demonstrations at Wapping and marches to the plant, met last night and said that they would announce on Tuesday whether they accepted the decision of their national executive. The National Union of Journalists, which is also in dispute with the company, will decide its position next week at a meeting of its national executive committee. Most of the journalists working for the four national newspapers published at the plant, The Times, The Sunday Times, The Sun and the News of the World, ignored instructions not to cross picket lines and 95 have been fined £1,000 for doing so.

In the 1980s, *The Times*, like many British newspapers, was still being produced by printing processes a century old. Closely controlled by the unions, these required (or were said to require) many more operators than newer technology, at rates of pay similarly outsize.

Production was often subject to stoppages and disruption. Yet, managers were reluctant to engage in a trial of strength with the unions as, once an edition was lost, there was no way to recoup the sales forfeited.

Rupert Murdoch's News International wanted to move *The Times* and its three other newspapers from Holborn to a new plant at Wapping, in London's Docklands. There, journalists would use computers to create pages themselves. Negotiations with the unions about their future terms of employment broke down and a strike was called.

Six thousand workers walked out and were replaced at Wapping by 600 from another union. There were violent clashes between police and those picketing the plant, but the papers were produced and distributed throughout 1986 without interruption.

As with the miners, the defeat of the print unions was a significant blow to the power of the unions, not least as they could no longer show members they were able to protect their jobs.

THE LOCKERBIE BOMBING

22 December 1988

In Britain's worst air disaster, about 300 people were killed last night when a Pan American Boeing 747 flying from London, Heathrow, to New York crashed and exploded on the small town of Lockerbie in Scotland.

Flight 103 with 258 people on board came down in flames and in pieces after a mid-air explosion that aviation experts last night said could only have been caused by massive structural failure, or a bomb.

Trailing flames, spewing burning aviation fuel and scattering wreckage over 10 miles, the doomed aircraft fell from the sky, hit a small hill east of the town and broke up, somersaulting across the main A74 London-Glasgow road before crashing into houses and the petrol station in the town centre.

All those on board were killed. At least 20 of the townspeople, possibly more, also met their deaths.

Forty houses were destroyed when the wreckage fell, it emerged early today. The 747's engines are thought to have landed on two rows of houses, smashing them to the ground. The RAF rescue co-ordination centre at Edinburgh said at 2.20am: "A rescue situation does not exist anymore – we are just recovering bodies."

A fireball 300 feet high lit up the sky as the aircraft blew up. Houses in the town (population 3,000) – 10 miles east of Dumfries and 15 miles north of the Scottish border – simply disappeared in the explosion. Others were set ablaze or had their roofs blown off. Pieces of the wreckage carved a huge hole in the A74, blocking the route through the town, and cars driving past were set on fire.

A fleet of rescue services – helicopters, ambulances, fire engines and police – sped to the scene from all over Scotland and the North of

England, but only five casualties had been taken to the Dumfries and Galloway Royal Infirmary in Dumfries by early today – an indication of how severe the crash was.

A Buckingham Palace spokesman said last night: "The Queen was shocked and appalled by the news of the air crash and is being kept informed." In the Commons, both Mrs Thatcher and Mr Neil Kinnock expressed their deep sympathy. The Prime Minister was being kept fully informed of developments through the night. Mrs Thatcher, who said she was "shocked by this terrible disaster" and expressed her deepest sympathies to all the bereaved families, also sent her sympathies to Mr Charles Price, the retiring US Ambassador in London, who flew to the scene late last night.

Mr Malcolm Rifkind, the Secretary of State for Scotland, who also flew to the scene, plans to report back to the Prime Minister this morning, when Mr Paul Channon, Secretary of State for Transport, will make a full statement to MPs. Mr Donald Dewar, the Shadow Scottish Secretary, accompanied Mr Rifkind and Sir Hector Monro, Conservative MP for Dumfries, on the flight to the scene.

A 10-man team from the Department of Transport's Air Accidents Investigation Branch arrived within hours of the crash to look for the "black box" and cockpit voice recorders and to sift through the wreckage. Experts from the US Federal Aviation Administration and from Pan Am are expected to join them.

But last night one theory – a mid-air collision, suggested in early reports – was ruled out by both the RAF and the Civil Aviation Authority and by air traffic controllers who played back tapes of the radar returns and of the conversation between the ground and the flight deck. The only possible causes could therefore have been either a bomb or a major structural failure.

◆

The attack on Pan Am Flight 103 was the deadliest act of terror to have taken place in Britain. Two hundred and fifty-nine passengers and crew, most of them Americans returning home for Christmas, died when a bomb exploded their aircraft above Lockerbie. Eleven more people were killed there as large pieces of debris fell to earth.

As the blast had occurred at 30,000 feet, wreckage was scattered over some 845 square miles of Scotland. One of the abiding images of the disaster was that of the aircraft's cockpit, which had come to rest on its side, seemingly almost intact, on a hill outside the town.

Several theories about the bombing were put forward, in particular by relatives of the passengers who had died, but the joint investigation by the Scottish police and the FBI found it had been carried out by Libyan agents.

One, Abdelbaset al-Megrahi, was convicted in 2001 by a Scottish court, sitting in the neutral venue of the Netherlands, and sentenced to life imprisonment. He was released in 2009 when terminally ill and died in 2012. Libya, which had had a series of confrontations with America in the 1980s, formally admitted responsibility for the attack in 2003.

TIANANMEN SQUARE

6 June 1989

At noon yesterday, when tanks and armoured personnel carriers started moving eastwards along the main Changan Avenue in Peking, I watched as a man in a white shirt ran from a crowd.

He ran in front of the leading tank. Tank commanders have not flinched from crushing people, but this one shifted direction.

The tanks could not advance. The leading one hesitated and tried to move around the man. He followed it, then clambered up onto its turret to talk to the soldiers.

No effort was made to knock him off, but a machinegun opened fire nearby. He clambered down and stood in front of the tanks for about five minutes, before three men pushed him across the road.

A British eye-witness who returned last night said: "At first the army moved down the street firing tear gas. Some of the crowd attacked soldiers. I was hit with clubs when I tried to stop one group attacking a teenage soldier – in the end, they dropped rocks on his head until he did not have a face anymore.

"When I went into a hotel where several soldiers lay dead or dying, I tried to take pictures and was attacked by plainclothes officers. I saw an old woman in a block of flats shouting 'fascists' at the troops. Suddenly, there were shots and she fell to her death."

A caller to the International Society of Human Rights said soldiers went into a hospital and "took students, some in great pain, outside the hospital and shot them dead".

The reality of bodies stacked up in hospitals around the capital made a macabre contrast to Peking radio's evening broadcast, which said that not one person had been killed in Tiananmen Square.

In the decade after the death of Mao Zedong in 1976, China abandoned the extreme course steered by the 'Great Helmsman', which had wrought such damage to its economy. The adoption of a market-based system began to lift millions out of poverty. Yet, the changes did not please everyone. Some thought they departed too much from communist ideals. Others felt they did not go far enough. Many felt left behind, especially when officials made the most of opportunities for corruption.

The funeral in April 1989 of Hu Yaobang, the reform-minded general secretary of the Communist Party driven from office by hardliners two years before, became the focus for protests by students. They and others who had spent time abroad demanded China become more democratic.

Although demonstrations continued in many cities, that which attracted most coverage was the occupation of Tiananmen Square in Beijing, where more than one million people gathered. China's leaders were at first divided about how to react but eventually declared martial law. Tanks were used to clear the demonstrators, with the incident described memorably captured in photographs.

As many as several thousand protesters were killed, bringing an end to hopes for greater freedom in China.

THE FALL OF THE BERLIN WALL

10 November 1989

In an historic announcement which rendered the Berlin Wall irrelevant, East Germany declared last night that its citizens could leave the country at all crossing points through the Wall and over the 1,000-mile border with West Germany.

Herr Gunter Schabowski, the Politburo member responsible for the media, said that the new ruling came into effect immediately – 43 years after Winston Churchill proclaimed, in a speech in Fulton, Missouri, that an "Iron Curtain" had descended across Europe.

Herr Schabowski also promised "free democratic and secret elections" and admitted for the first time that East Germany was "a pluralist society in which there are a variety of interests which we did not previously recognize".

As a first step the prohibition on the New Forum opposition group was lifted yesterday by the Ministry of the Interior.

In a startling acceleration of previous travel proposals, Herr Schabowski announced that all citizens could now be issued with visas for purposes of travel or visiting relatives in the West. But the Wall would stay as a "reinforced state border", he said.

Later, East German radio reported that exit visas would be issued from 8 am today, ending unchecked crossings through the Berlin Wall.

Within hours of yesterday's announcement, the centre of Berlin took on a festive air with thousands moving back and forwards through the previously formidable barrier.

The first East German couple to test the new ruling strolled across the border at the Bonnholmerstrasse crossing at 9.25pm. Guards allowed them to cross without a visa and reassured them that they could return later.

There was evident confusion about the new regulations. At the Invalidenstrasse crossing point guards turned people away, telling them to collect a stamp from their local police station first.

East German television stations were inundated with calls from viewers stunned by the announcement and anxious to hear it repeated. A flustered announcer had to interrupt programmes several times to repeat the news.

The relaxation also applies to would-be emigrants who will now be given exit visas to cross at any point on the German border and from East into West Berlin "without delay", the statement said.

More than 200,000 have left East Germany so far this year, about half of them legally. West German officials estimate that between 1.2 million and 1.4 million East Germans have applied to leave. West Germany is prepared to take all those coming across the border, the Interior Ministry said last night.

At Checkpoint Charlie, the Allied crossing point, border guards huddled around a radio set to hear the news. One guard grinning broadly said: "I have stamped other people's passports for four years, and I never thought I would stand on the other side of the counter. I can't believe it." His colleague joked: "We will soon be out of a job here."

———◆———

The Berlin Wall had been built in 1961 to stop the flood of those leaving the East for life in the West. A physical manifestation of the 'Iron Curtain', it was heavily guarded and hundreds were killed trying to escape across it.

When the Soviet Union – compelled by the parlous state of its economy – began to introduce reforms in the mid-1980s under the leadership of Mikhail Gorbachev, this piled pressure on the regimes that ruled its satellites in Eastern Europe.

Encouraged by changes in neighbouring countries such as Poland and Hungary, East Germans began to stage mass demonstrations. The government tried to save itself by allowing travel to the West but the Politburo spokesman who made the announcement, Günter Schabowksi, had not been told of the intention to carefully vet applications for visas. Accordingly, he said the new policy was effective immediately. The regime lacked the nerve to subsequently correct the mistake.

A country, and a continent, divided for half a century had been reunited by accident. Astonished East Berliners came out onto the streets in their dressing gowns to check the news was true and within half an hour were crossing freely through checkpoints. By the end of the year, the rest of Eastern Europe had gained its liberty and the Cold War was over.

MODERN TIMES

NELSON MANDELA

12 February 1990

Nelson Mandela emerged from more than a quarter of a century in jail last night to tell tens of thousands of supporters that the armed struggle against apartheid must continue.

There could be no negotiation until the state of emergency was ended and all political prisoners were freed, he told a rally of 50,000 cheering people in Cape Town.

"Our resorting to the armed struggle in 1960 was a purely defensive action against the violence of apartheid," he said. "We have no option but to continue."

As Mr Mandela spoke, jubilant blacks across South Africa danced in the streets, but the celebrations were tinged with violence, and 19 people were reported killed in various clashes. One was shot by police as groups of youths waiting to hear Mr Mandela looted shops in Cape Town.

When he finally appeared at the City Hall, Mr Mandela appealed for calm and after his speech urged the crowd to disperse peacefully.

He called on his supporters to intensify and redouble their campaign against apartheid and urged overseas states to continue sanctions against the Nationalist regime. Most South Africans, black and white, recognized that apartheid had no future: "It has to be ended by our decisive mass action. We have waited too long for our freedom.

"Our struggle has reached a decisive moment. Our march to freedom is irreversible. Now is the time to intensify the struggle on all fronts. To relax now would be a mistake which future generations would not forgive."

But he also said that President F. W. de Klerk was a man of integrity and he hoped a climate conducive to a negotiated settlement would be created soon, making the armed struggle unnecessary. "We call on our white compatriots to help us in reshaping a new South Africa," he said.

Mr Mandela's first words to the cheering crowd contained a message of peace. "I greet you all in the name of peace, democracy and freedom for all," he said. "I stand here before you not as a prophet, but as a humble servant of you the people."

He concluded by reiterating his statement at his trial in 1964, when he declared: "I have fought against white domination and I have fought against black domination. I have cherished the ideal of a democratic and free society in which all persons live together in harmony and with equal opportunities. It is an ideal I hope to live for and achieve, but if needs be, it is an ideal for which I am prepared to die."

Mr Mandela had been an angry young revolutionary when he first spoke those words before being bundled into prison. Yesterday, aged 71, he walked free as a distinguished elder statesman, but hopes that he would be welcomed in a dignified manner were dashed when the rally degenerated into bloodshed. One person was shot dead and three were said to have died from heart attacks as the assembly overflowed a parade ground in front of the City Hall.

◆

In the late 1950s, at the height of apartheid in South Africa, Nelson Mandela had been the leader of the African National Congress (ANC), which campaigned for the rights of the country's Black population. After 69 people were shot dead by police at Sharpeville, tensions rose further, the ANC was banned and Mandela went into hiding after vowing to bring down the White regime.

Descended from royalty, Mandela had been born in the eastern Cape in 1918 and was given his first name by a Methodist teacher. At his trial in 1964, he was sentenced to life imprisonment. He spent much of the next 26 years doing hard labour on Robben Island, as efforts steadily intensified around the world to free him and end apartheid.

When, in 1993, he won the nation's first multi-racial elections and succeeded F. W. de Klerk as president – having shared the Nobel Peace Prize with him – Mandela used his remarkable personal charisma to promote reconciliation and a new image of South Africa. He died in 2013.

THE FALL OF
MARGARET THATCHER

23 November 1990

A POLITICAL era ended yesterday when Margaret Thatcher announced that she would resign next week as prime minister. The foreign secretary, Douglas Hurd, and the Chancellor, John Major, immediately entered the Conservative leadership battle.

The prime minister, tears in her eyes, told the cabinet at 9 am: "I have concluded that the unity of the party and the prospects of victory at a general election would be better served if I stood down to enable cabinet colleagues to enter the ballot."

She had decided overnight that she did not have the troops to win and urged cabinet colleagues to unite in electing one of their number to replace her, underlining her determination to stop Michael Heseltine.

Mrs Thatcher's departure brought her party an immediate opinion poll bonus. First results of a snap On-Line telephone poll of 760 voters for *The Times* last night showed that if Mr Heseltine were at the helm, 47 per cent would support the Tories, compared with 42 per cent for Labour. Under Mr Major, the figures were 45-44 and under Mr Hurd, the Tories would trail 44-45.

Of the three bandwagons, the one that appeared to be gathering speed fastest last night was that of Mr Major. His team was swiftly into action and his supporters were quickly joined by Norman Tebbit, who said: "I am convinced that both left and right should unite under the leadership of John Major." He hoped the 80 to 90 who had promised to support him, had he stood, would now opt for Mr Major.

Mr Heseltine was one of the first to acknowledge the prime minister's "awesome achievements". He said: "The important thing today is to pay tribute to the premiership of Margaret Thatcher.

It has by any standards been remarkable. Perhaps the very fact that I at one moment found it impossible to continue in cabinet makes it particularly fitting for me to record the admiration and gratitude of the Conservative party for what she has achieved, and what so many of us worked so hard to help her bring about."

President Bush telephoned Mrs Thatcher from Saudi Arabia last night, thanked her for all that she had done and signed off with the words: "We love you." In the Commons and outside, MPs paid tribute to her as "the greatest peacetime prime minister this century". Even Neil Kinnock told her during question time that she amounted to more than those who had turned upon her.

The prime minister then put up a bravura performance in the censure debate, which ended with a 367-247 government victory. She was crisp, combative and humorous, winning universal cheers from Tories who could hardly believe that her reign had ended so messily. There were recriminations from hard-core supporters who felt she had been betrayed by senior party figures.

Her decision to go has thrown the contest wide open. Mr Heseltine was continuing to win support yesterday, including that of the party deputy chairman, David Trippier. But some who voted for him in the first round did so only to ensure a second round involving Mr Hurd or Mr Major. Mr Heseltine now faces a battle to increase his first-round vote of 152 to the 187 required.

◆

Margaret Thatcher had so utterly dominated British politics, and for so long, that her sudden downfall seemed astonishing. Yet there had been signs for some time that she was losing the support of Conservative voters, especially over her plan to introduce the poll tax. Tory MPs and the Cabinet, meanwhile, were frustrated by her unwillingness to heed the views of others.

The trigger for the rebellion was a speech made to the Commons in early November by Sir Geoffrey Howe after his resignation as Deputy Prime Minister. He had become exasperated by Thatcher's public undermining of her ministers' policies, notably his own work when Foreign Secretary on monetary union with Europe.

Howe's call for others to consider their continued loyalty to Thatcher prompted a leadership challenge from Michael Heseltine, who had long aspired to the premiership. The first vote among Conservative MPs was held while Thatcher was at a summit in Paris. She came top, but not with a decisive lead. She told waiting reporters: 'I fight on: I fight on to win'.

Yet, overnight, it became clear the Party thought that what had been leadership was now divisiveness and made her an electoral liability. She resigned and John Major succeeded as Prime Minister.

DESERT STORM

18 January 1991

THE missile exploded out of nowhere, kicking up a white, mushroom cloud over the ancient Ottoman fortress. If this was meant to be the start of the "mother of battles" as President Saddam Hussein had declared confidently yesterday, the first engagement did not open well for Iraq.

Hundreds of soldiers, waiting for transport to take them to the battle field, scattered and our driver, a veteran of many fierce battles himself, smiled at his passengers' discomfort and swerved to miss the panic-stricken traffic speeding across the intersection in front of him.

"No problem," said a young man hurrying down the pavement where we had taken cover. "What you have to be careful of are the bullets from the anti-aircraft guns, not the aircraft."

When the second missile hit in precisely the same place, the Abbasid Palace – the former Turkish and British Army barracks and now part of Iraq's defence ministry – disappeared behind a mask of blue smoke and dust which trailed away down the Tigris river.

The third explosion minutes later set ablaze the entire building, which the Baghdad fire brigade decided to let burn rather than risk putting out and being caught themselves in another strike.

Never before in its violent modern history has this Arab city seen so much destruction in only a few hours and never have the Iraqi people, hiding in shelters or manning defences, felt so powerless to protect it. The capital's communications centre is destroyed, hit by four precision missiles. The Presidential Palace lies half in ruins and in the distance the rumble of heavy air bombardment suggests that the outlying districts are taking an even heavier toll in the relentless attack. The hundreds of anti-aircraft guns and missile batteries, located on every tall building and beside every strategic site in the city, provided a spectacular fireworks display, which left orange tracer rounds and chaff lighting up the Mesopotamian sky yesterday morning when the first wave of bombers struck. However, the aircraft appeared to be flying well out of range for most of Iraq's air defences. It is becoming increasingly clear that Iraq's much-vaunted military is almost powerless to stop the war planes, whose sophistication renders the contest more like the Battle of Omdurman, when Kitchener's technological superiority defeated a larger force under the Mahdi, than the more evenly-matched battles Iraq was accustomed to fighting with Iran.

The Iraqi capital is now deserted and those who have not fled are making plans to do so. Even government ministries, key components of the Iraqi war effort, are abandoned, their officials, so confident just a day ago, seemingly taken by surprise at the swift onslaught.

Whatever the damage to morale among civilians and soldiers, the two waves of air attack in Baghdad did not initially appear to dent Saddam's resolve, and at dawn he made a call to the "Sons of our great Iraqi people, to the glorious Arab nation and our heroic armed forces."

He said on Baghdad Radio: "The devil Bush, aided by criminal Zionism, has launched the mother of battles between victorious good and the forces of evil."

What particularly infuriated Saddam was that Saudi war planes had taken part in Operation Desert Storm. He denounced them as "treacherous criminals" who would be overthrown as part of a liberation that would embrace Jerusalem, the Golan Heights and Lebanon.

◆

In August 1990, Iraq had invaded Kuwait, one of the main suppliers of oil to the Western world. Saddam Hussein, Iraq's leader, cited grievances including that Kuwait had drilled into Iraqi reserves. However, it was thought that his real ambition was to take control of those belonging to Kuwait's neighbour, Saudi Arabia.

Iraq had one of the world's largest armies, built up in part with American support during its long conflict with Iran. With backing from the UN, America put together a huge coalition of forces from 40 nations, including Britain and Saudi Arabia, initially to protect the latter.

The campaign to liberate Kuwait – Desert Storm – began in January 1991 with six weeks of air attacks. Iraq itself was blitzed on 42 consecutive nights. It was the world's introduction to a generation of weapons that appeared to have sprung from video games, including laser-guided bombs, stealth aircraft and Cruise missiles.

The subsequent ground assault took only 100 hours to chase the invaders from Kuwait, although the decision was taken to stop General Norman Schwarzkopf's troops from pushing on and deposing Saddam. That would lead in time to the Gulf War of 2003.

THE FIRST BRITON IN SPACE

27 May 1991

HELEN Sharman, the first Briton in space, floated safely down to the deserts of Soviet Central Asia yesterday after a mission of eight days in which she travelled three million miles.

The Soyuz TM11 capsule touched down at 11.04.48am London time near the area of Dzhezkazgan, 74km northeast of Baikonur cosmodrome, where the historic Juno mission was launched on the afternoon of Saturday, May 18.

Miss Sharman, commander Musa Manarov, engineer Viktor Afanasyev and their capsule were retrieved by Soviet military helicopters before being flown from Leninsk airport, Kazakhstan, to Star City training centre, Moscow, for quarantine, medical checks and a traditional "bread and salt" welcome. She is expected to spend ten days in isolation before returning to Britain in the second week of June.

Christopher Hayes, a spokesman for the Moscow Narodny Bank, the mission's organisers, said yesterday that the touchdown had been flawless and that Miss Sharman, aged 27, appeared in excellent health.

Miss Sharman's family, who had an open telephone link from their home in Sheffield to the flight control centre in Kaliningrad, near Moscow, during the final nail-biting minutes, said they were delighted and relieved. John Sharman, aged 51, said: "We have been feeling fairly tense this morning. I always thought the landing would be the most difficult part. It certainly was for us. We are very relieved."

The two cosmonauts who are left on Mir, the Soviet space station, also appeared relieved. Commander Anatoli Artsebarsky, the captain who piloted Miss Sharman and engineer Sergei Krikaliov to the station and who raised feminist eyebrows last week by suggesting that a woman's place was on Mother Earth and not in space, joked to flight control engineers: "Now we can arrange Mir the way we like."

The journey back to Earth started at 4.40am London time as the return crew and Miss Sharman left Mir to take their spring-loaded seats in the Soyuz TM11 docked at one end of the station. After systems checks lasting two-and-a-half hours, the four compressed spring bolts holding the Soyuz to the station were released and the capsule fired into space at about 7.13am.

Impulse engines manoeuvred the Soyuz up over the top of Mir so that the return crew could photograph the ageing space station's exterior for signs of wear and damage. Those will be studied back on Earth.

After orbiting Earth about one-and-a-half times, Soyuz's rockets were fired again at 10.42am to send the craft hurtling through the atmosphere at 8km a second for its final descent. Inside the heavily insulated capsule, Miss Sharman will have seen flames fly past the ship as friction and speed turned the Soyuz's heat shield red hot at 7,000°C.

Eight minutes after re-entry the craft's primary, braking and main parachutes opened successfully at a height of 10km, slowing the capsule to a safe 250-300 metres a second. The four retro rockets fired one metre above the ground, slowing the capsule for a bumpy but safe landing.

The Juno mission may have attracted derision and hostility for its game-style show selection and lack of serious British experiments, but its long-term educational value should not be underestimated in a country where science and technology continue to struggle in schools.

Lyndis Sharman, the astronaut's mother, said that Juno had fired the enthusiasm of schoolchildren in everything from geography and space science to cookery, with infants baking cakes in the shape of Soyuz rockets.

Possibly the most curious disclosure of the mission was the discovery that Soviet scientists have developed a special "health drink" for space made of 53 per cent alcohol and called Senetate, an old Moldavian word for health.

———————◆———————

True to the entrepreneurial spirit beloved of Thatcherism, the programme to put a Briton into space was funded at first not by the state but by private enterprise. Helen Sharman, a research chemist, heard about a competition to select an astronaut in 1989 while driving back from work at Mars, the confectioner. 'No experience necessary' was the tagline, and she was chosen ahead of 13,000 other applicants.

The project was to be run jointly with the Soviet Union, which supplied the Soyuz spacecraft, and Sharman spent 18 months training for it and learning Russian at Star City, near Moscow. When British companies were unable to raise the entire £7 million budget, the cost of the mission was underwritten by the Russians as a goodwill gesture.

After blasting off with two Soviet astronauts and docking at the Mir Space Station, Sharman carried out tests aboard and spoke to schoolchildren listening on the radio in Britain. Several other British-born astronauts subsequently went into space with NASA, before in 2015 Tim Peake became the first Briton to venture there with the European Space Agency.

BLACK WEDNESDAY

17 September 1992

JOHN Major and Norman Lamont abandoned their defence of the pound last night and announced that Britain was suspending its membership of the European exchange-rate mechanism to allow sterling to float.

The decision, which amounts to an effective devaluation, was announced on the steps of the Treasury by the Chancellor of the Exchequer after a tumultuous day in which interest rates were raised in two stages by 5 per cent as the government embarked on a desperate last effort to save the pound's parity with the mark.

It was a defeat for Mr Lamont and a collapse of the main plank of the government's economic policy. The decision to suspend membership of the ERM means that the second rise, an increase from 12 per cent to 15 per cent that would have been effective from today, will not now take effect.

In Brussels late last night Britain was pressing at a meeting of the European Community's monetary committee for the suspension of the whole ERM. German officials predicted that the meeting might be both long and rough.

Parliament is to be recalled next Thursday to discuss the economic crisis, the first time since September 1990, and the cabinet will meet this morning to review its economic policy.

Mr Lamont's future was placed under immediate doubt because of the failure of his policy. Downing Street's first reaction was that there was absolutely no question of him resigning and Sir Norman Fowler, the Tory party chairman, backed him in television interviews. Conservative MPs questioned, however, whether he could stay in office for long after the failure of the strategy on which he had staked his reputation. There was no suggestion that the prime minister's position was under threat, although Tory MPs believed that his credibility will have been damaged by yesterday's developments. In a surprise move last night Downing Street openly blamed the Bundesbank for contributing to sterling's difficulties in recent weeks. Officials presented a summary of comments made by Bundesbank staff over the past two weeks pointing to the need for the devaluation of sterling. It was revealed that the governor of the Bank of England had complained directly to the Bundesbank president on the Chancellor's instructions late on Tuesday night, pressing for a retraction of remarks he made earlier. Helmut Schlesinger had called for a devaluation of currencies other than the lira.

By last night it had become clear that the attempts of the prime minister and Mr Lamont to maintain the parity of the pound had failed, as sterling was quoted below its absolute ERM floor of DM2.7780 at the end of trading in London. After Mr Lamont's announcement the pound fell to DM2.66 in New York, a post-war low.

Looking pale and drawn after a day of unprecedented financial turmoil, the Chancellor told reporters outside the Treasury: "As president of the finance ministers I have called a meeting of the monetary committee in Brussels urgently tonight to consider how stability can be restored to the foreign exchange markets. In the meantime the government has concluded that Britain's best interests are served by suspending our membership of the exchange-rate mechanism.

"As a result, the second of the two interest rate increases which I sanctioned today will not take place tomorrow and the minimum lending rate will be at 12 per cent until conditions become calmer. I will be reporting to cabinet, discussing the situation with colleagues tomorrow and may make further statements then. But until then I have nothing further to say."

◆

With the British economy booming, inflation rose from 3.8% in 1988 to 10.9% in 1990. The Treasury doubled interest rates to 15% as a countermeasure, but this made the economy contract.

An alternative was to try to control inflation by pegging the pound's worth to the most stable currency in Europe, the Deutsche Mark. This was a policy followed by other countries in the EEC through membership of the Exchange Rate Mechanism (ERM), which obliged those currencies that belonged to remain within a narrow margin of a common value.

Margaret Thatcher resisted Britain joining, viewing it as a step to monetary union, but eventually did so as one of the last acts of her premiership. The Chancellor who urged her to sign up was John Major.

In 1992, with the future of the European project uncertain as its citizens contemplated the Maastricht Treaty, speculators targeted weaker currencies including sterling. They sold off their holdings, driving its value down faster than the Bank of England could buy pounds to keep it within the prescribed margin.

Raising interest rates dramatically did not tempt buyers either and Britain was driven out of the ERM, damaging the Tories' reputation for economic competence – although giving them, arguably, the flexibility to subsequently right the economy.

HISTORY IN A HANDSHAKE

14 September 1993

ON A day of passion, drama and soaring hope, Israel and the Palestinians yesterday declared an end to decades of bitter enmity.

In what President Clinton called "an extraordinary act in one of history's defining dramas", Shimon Peres, the Israeli foreign minister, and Mahmoud Abbas, a top PLO official, sat at the table used for signing the Israeli Egyptian Camp David accords 14 years ago and signed an agreement promising Palestinian self-rule.

The agreement had been initialled in Oslo on August 20, after months of secret negotiations led by a small team of Norwegians.

The real drama of yesterday's ceremony on the White House South Lawn came seconds after the actual signing. With hundreds of millions of people watching around the world Yassir Arafat, the PLO chairman, held out his hand to Yitzhak Rabin, the Israeli prime minister. Mr Rabin hesitated. Mr Clinton nudged him. Reluctantly, the unsmiling Israeli lifted his hand, and two men who had dedicated their lives to the other's destruction made their peace to applause from 3,000 American and foreign dignitaries.

Arab ministers and ambassadors not only attended the ceremony, but afterwards shook hands with Mr Rabin and chatted with Mr Peres at a State Department reception. A White House official called these actions "of enormous significance psychologically"; they boded well for the future peace talks.

Reconciliation was the recurring theme. "Let all of us turn from bullets to ballots, from guns to shovels," Mr Peres said. "We shall pray with you. We shall offer you our help in making Gaza prosper and Jericho blossom again ... Let us bid, once and for all, farewell to war."

But for Mr Rabin, the former general who led Israel's lightning conquest of the occupied territories 26 years ago, it was a day of anguish as much as joy as he used his short address to speak directly to the Palestinian people.

"We, the soldiers who have returned from battles stained with blood; we who have seen our relatives and friends killed before our eyes; we who have attended their funerals and cannot look into the eyes of their parents; we who have come from a land where parents bury their children; we who have fought against you, the Palestinians, we say to you today, in a loud and clear voice: 'Enough of blood and tears. Enough'."

The Israelis had no desire for revenge and harboured no hatred towards the Palestinian people, he said. "We wish to open a new chapter in the sad book of our lives together." Quoting from Ecclesiastes, he said: "To everything there is a season. . . A time to be born and a time to die, a time to kill and a time to heal, a time to weep and a time to laugh, a time to love and a time to hate, a time of war and a time of peace. The time for peace has come."

———————◆———————

The handshake between Yitzhak Rabin and Yassir Arafat, captured in a famous photograph, represented the culmination of months of secret negotiations between Israel and the Palestinians.

The Oslo Accords, as they were known, aimed to resolve decades of conflict in the region by giving the Palestinians the right to self-government for the time being while the Israelis undertook to pull their troops out of the West Bank and the Gaza Strip. The two sides would have five years to secure a permanent deal.

Bill Clinton, who presided over the revelation of the agreement to the world, later recalled that the two leaders refused to shake hands before the ceremony, maintaining an awkward reserve. To his surprise, it was Rabin, the hero of the Six-Day War and the capture of the Old City of Jerusalem, who had sounded more passionate than Arafat when speaking to the assembled dignitaries of the need for a new understanding.

Both men, with Israel's Foreign Minister, Shimon Peres, were awarded the Nobel Prize for Peace. Yet, with the two parties doubting each other's commitment to a solution, the accords were never fully implemented, and in 1995 Rabin was assassinated by a religious fundamentalist opposed to them.

THE CHANNEL TUNNEL

7 May 1994

As the first official train glided out of Nicholas Grimshaw's stunning new glass-and-steel Waterloo Station at 9.52am, Mr Major and Lady Thatcher settled into a first-class carriage with the Queen, Michael Howard, the Home Secretary, John MacGregor, the Transport Secretary, John Gummer, the Environment Secretary, and Lord Howe of Aberavon.

While the politicians examined the political landscape, the Queen, dressed in fuchsia pink, spent the historic journey being briefed by Sir Alastair Morton, Eurotunnel's co-chairman, and Sir Bob Reid, BR's chairman, about the new undersea service. Facts, facts, facts, which, at least according to Alan Bennett's depiction of her in his play *A Question of Attribution*, she is keen on digesting. After we had breakfasted from trolleys more like the ones you see in aeroplanes than those that serve teabag tea and toast-style bread on BR's domestic service, our quarter-mile-long train entered the tunnel at 100 mph at about 11am. Nobody seemed quite sure if we had entered the tunnel. It seemed like just another bit of the underground sections that punctuate the journey from London to the South Coast.

Nobody cheered, nobody waved goodbye, nobody got wet, the guard didn't announce a delay because of the wrong kind of seaweed on the line. It was something of an anti-climax, which may be the best compliment Eurotunnel can hope for. It was as straightforward as catching any train, only rather plusher, quieter and more pleasant. Our grandchildren will wonder how we managed without a Channel Tunnel, as we wonder how we did without fax machines and home-delivery pizzas.

At 11.30am, like a mole poking out from its hole to take the pulse of the day, we emerged into France, without any of that frantic preparatory queueing at gangways that accompanies ferry crossings, no last-minute dash to the duty-free: in fact, there isn't one on the passenger train, although there is on the car shuttle. It would take you a good deal longer to travel by Underground from one side of London to the other.

M Mitterrand told the crowds in Calais that it was an emotional and proud moment for all French people. The Queen, speaking in faultless French, hailed the blend of French élan and British pragmatism. After a swift but tasty lunch in Calais that happily owed more to French élan than British pragmatism, we boarded the shuttle, most of us in coaches.

The first to drive on, in the Queen's maroon Phantom VI Rolls-Royce, were the Queen and M Mitterrand. Since car passengers are expected to remain in their cars, it seemed at first that the Queen and M Mitterrand would spend the homeward journey sitting side by side in the Rolls, like one of those couples you see parked on hilltops in Wales drinking tea from a flask and staring at the view through their windscreens.

But after five minutes they emerged warily into a throng of press photographers, the only possible hint of rabid life sighted in the tunnel, and entered a private compartment. Lady Thatcher, dressed in black as if for a funeral, stayed in her 56-seater coach, while Lord Howe took away-day holiday snaps of Mr Gummer and Mr MacGregor. It was at that moment that Mr Major joined us and remarked on the smoothness of his ride.

Will you say just a few words in French? a Parisian television crew asked. "No, no, no," the Prime Minister giggled. "I know my limitations."

Again we weren't quite sure if this was entente cordiale or double entendre. And then we were back on dry land. Most of us, anyway.

———◆———

The Channel Tunnel had a long history. A scheme had first been proposed to Napoleon in 1802, featuring an artificial island at the half-way mark where horses for the carriages could be changed. In 1880, digging had actually started (see Blériot, page 83) before the British press stoked fears of a French invasion, scotching the plan.

An agreement between the two governments was signed in the 1960s, but Labour's lukewarm feelings about the EEC led to Britain pulling out. When the idea was revived in Margaret Thatcher's time, it was for a privately funded project. Her own preference was for a road tunnel. The French wanted trains. She accepted that these were safer – but ensured they would drive on the left.

Construction took seven years. While the British boring machines were given alphanumeric designations, the French gave them female names; the first was Brigitte. The costs were such that Eurotunnel, which ran the project, eventually exchanged shares in the tunnel for the loans it owed the banks. It has first option on any second link, the building of which was originally pencilled in for 2000.

OJ SIMPSON ACQUITTED

4 October 1995

O.J. SIMPSON returned to his home in Los Angeles a free man last night after being cleared of killing his former wife and her friend in a stunning end to the trial that has transfixed America for nearly a year.

Millions of television viewers all over the world had earlier seen the former football star's face break into a triumphant grin as the court clerk read the jury's not-guilty verdicts, reached after less than five hours' deliberation.

But as Mr Simpson patted his heart and hugged his lawyer, relatives of the victims broke into sobs of disbelief. Fred Goldman, whose 25-year-old son Ronald was slashed to death in June last year with Nicole Brown Simpson, was heard shouting "No, no, no. Murderer, murderer, murderer." Later, he told a press conference: "The prosecution did not lose today. I deeply believe this country lost today. Justice was not served."

Mr Goldman is now expected to pursue Mr Simpson in the civil courts. The families of both victims have filed suits alleging that he killed his ex-wife and her friend, and while he remained silent during his criminal trial, he could be forced to give evidence in a civil case.

Mr Simpson meanwhile promised to catch whoever killed his ex-wife and Mr Goldman. "When things are settled a bit, I will pursue as my primary goal in life the killer or killers who slaughtered Nicole and Mr Goldman," he said in a statement read by his son Jason. "They are out there somewhere. Whatever it takes to identify them and bring them in, I'll provide somehow."

He added that he was relieved that "this part of the nightmare" was over and said his first duty was to bring his children up as their mother would have wanted. He is expected to seek custody of Justin, 7, and Sydney, 9, who are being cared for by their mother's parents.

The statement concluded: "I can only hope that someday, despite every prejudicial thing that has been said about me publicly both in and out of the courtroom, people will come to understand and believe that I would not, could not, and did not kill anyone."

The Los Angeles police chief, Willie Williams, nevertheless said he had no plans to reopen the case and Gil Garcetti, the city's District Attorney, said he still believed in the evidence against Mr Simpson.

Mr Garcetti said the jury had allowed emotion to overcome their reason and thought there were "probably more people profoundly disappointed with the result than there were cheering".

President Clinton, who interrupted his work in the Oval Office to watch the verdict, also appeared to acknowledge possible disquiet over the outcome of the trial in a statement saying: "The jury heard the evidence and rendered its verdict. Our system of justice requires respect for their decision. At this moment our thoughts and prayers should be with the families of the victims of this terrible crime."

In the courtroom, there was an air of frenzy as the verdict was announced. Mr Simpson embraced his lawyers and mouthed "thank you" to the jurors, one of whom offered the Black Power salute in return. Mr Simpson's mother, Eunice, sat back in her wheelchair and raised her arms to the ceiling, while the prosecution team sat stony-faced.

Outside, hundreds of Simpson supporters celebrated wildly, dancing on the pavements and waving their hands in triumph.

◆

If O. J. Simpson was not tried by television, his trial was certainly on television. From the moment that 95 million people began watching live coverage of the police pursuit of the star's car, after he had failed to turn himself in for questioning about the murders, America was hooked on the case.

Their impact magnified by the media interest, its twists and turns sharply outlined many of the country's concerns and problems, among them race and the growing obsession with celebrity. Crucial to the verdict given by the predominantly African-American jury was the revelation that a police officer in the investigation, Mark Fuhrman, had used racial slurs, allowing the defence to suggest that he had planted evidence incriminating Simpson.

In the civil trial that followed, Simpson was found liable for the deaths of his former wife and of Ron Goldman, who had been returning sunglasses left in the restaurant where he worked.

Simpson was convicted in 2008 of crimes committed when he retrieved at gunpoint from a Las Vegas hotel items of memorabilia which he claimed had been taken from him. He was released from prison in 2017.

PEACE IN BOSNIA

15 December 1995

THE Presidents of Bosnia, Serbia and Croatia signed the Bosnian peace treaty in Paris yesterday, formally bringing Europe's bloodiest conflict since the Second World War to an end.

John Major, President Chirac of France, Viktor Chernomyrdin, the Russian Prime Minister, and Helmut Kohl, the German Chancellor, added their names to the document, officially to be known as the Bosnia-Herzegovina Peace Accord, as co-sponsors of a Nato-led peace force of about 60,000 soldiers prepared to deploy in Bosnia next week.

M Chirac, the host for the ceremony at the Elysée Palace, said that the memory of 200,000 people killed in 43 months of fighting could not be erased, but added: "We must make ourselves worthy of their memory, worthy of their suffering."

The agreement brokered in Dayton, Ohio, preserves a united Bosnia in name while dividing the region almost equally between the Serbs and a Croat-Muslim alliance and granting recognition to the "ethnically pure" mini-state of the Bosnian Serbs.

The signing took place before mutual recognition pacts between the three leaders of the former Yugoslav republics could be arranged. The three principal signatories, President Milosevic of Serbia, President Tudjman of Croatia and President Izetbegovic of Bosnia shook hands after the ceremony. "I feel like a man swallowing a bitter but useful medicine, but I can assure you we are signing this peace treaty with sincerity," President Izetbegovic said.

President Milosevic said that the treaty "does not solve all the problems between people who have been at war for years, but I am convinced a common language can be found".

President Clinton, who met the three leaders from former Yugoslavia before the signing, said yesterday that, although American casualties were inevitable in Bosnia, the United States would not "cut and run" as long as the Nato mission had a purpose.

However, the most grudging congressional approval of US deployment in Bosnia yesterday gave the President the flimsiest political support for his Balkan peace mission and left him deeply exposed during an election year.

The war formally came to an end amid all the pomp and solemnity France could muster. Paris is 800 miles from Sarajevo and the ornate marbled halls of the Elysée could hardly be further removed from the wreckage of Bosnia, a magnificent setting in which to declare, with cautious optimism, an end to one of the ugliest chapters in modern history.

The Republican Guard, in their red, white and blue uniforms, shivered beneath their epaulettes and then snapped sharply to attention as each political leader rolled through the Elysée's vast gates yesterday morning.

Dwarfed by some of the most magnificent chandeliers in the world and surrounded by gilt, brocade and the leaders of 50 states, just before midday the leaders of Bosnia, Serbia and Croatia signed the peace agreement. The peace is a new and fragile thing; the Elysée, built by Armand-Claude Mollet between 1718 and 1720, is old and solid but, as President Tudjman said yesterday, the enmities that have convulsed Bosnia are older still.

The leaders of the former Yugoslav republics appeared momentarily awed by the solemn weight of protocol and international power arrayed at the Elysée. Presented with the accord documents, President Milosevic seemed uncertain where to sign and began flicking through the agreement, as if he might have to read it all again to make quite sure that nobody was hoodwinking him.

President Tudjman peeked sideways to see if he could get a clue from his Serbian counterpart on where to find the dotted line. French officials rushed forward to find the right page and President Izetbegovic sat back, pleased with himself: he might, as he would later put it, be signing "without any enthusiasm", but at least he had found the right page before the others.

◆

The agreement signed in Paris ended three-and-a-half years of bitter conflict in Bosnia, one of the wider series of wars that resulted from the disintegration of Yugoslavia in the early 1990s.

After Bosnia and Herzegovina broke away from the federation, ethnic Serbs, led by Radovan Karadzic, cleansed swathes of territory of Bosnian Muslims and Croats. The Bosnian Serbs acted in concert with the president of Serbia, Slobodan Milosevic, who had ambitions for a wider Serbian state. The Bosnian Croats, who allied with the Muslims, sought support from Franjo Tudjman of Croatia – itself struggling with Serbia in a war of independence.

More than 100,000 people were killed in the Bosnian conflict, notably in massacres of civilians at Srebrenica and during the siege of Sarajevo. Military reverses for the Serbs in Bosnia and Croatia in 1995, and the threat of Nato air strikes, eventually brought the parties to the negotiating table at the Dayton air base in Ohio.

Although many felt the deal delivered peace at the expense of justice, it has held. Milosevic died in 2006 when being tried for war crimes, while Karadzic was convicted of them and sentenced in 2019 to life imprisonment.

TONY BLAIR LEADS LABOUR TO POWER

2 May 1997

AN EXULTANT Labour Party returned to power today after 18 years in the wilderness.

Tony Blair's party inflicted a rout of catastrophic proportions on the Conservatives, who suffered the worst defeat in their history.

Five Cabinet ministers, including the Right's favourite for the leadership Michael Portillo, were defeated on one of the most sensational nights in British political history as the country decided it was time for a change. Eighteen other ministers lost their seats.

At 3.13 am Mr Blair reached an overall majority which could rise today to close to 190 – easily the largest ever for Labour. Today he will go to Downing Street as the youngest Prime Minister for two centuries.

John Major had privately conceded almost an hour earlier, with a telephone call to Mr Blair congratulating him. He will see the Queen at 11.30 am today to resign and he is also expected to stand down as party leader. But the race for the succession is in turmoil.

Malcolm Rifkind, the Foreign Secretary, William Waldegrave, Michael Forsyth and Ian Lang were the other Cabinet ministers to perish; the Tories looked likely to lose all their seats in Scotland and Wales; and they paid the price for the cash-for-questions controversy when Martin Bell, the former BBC war correspondent standing as an anti-sleaze candidate, took the party's fifth safest seat with an 11,000 majority over the former Trade Minister Neil Hamilton at Tatton.

It was a night of triumph, too, for Paddy Ashdown, who looked set to become the most successful third party leader in British politics for more than 65 years. The Liberal Democrats were on course to win more than 50 seats in the biggest electoral shift of the century.

In an emotional speech after the declaration in his Huntingdon constituency, Mr Major said it was clear that Labour had been successful, and his party had been "comprehensively defeated". He expressed thanks for Tory candidates, both winners and losers, and said he looked to the time – "I hope in the not too distant future" – when the Tories would lead the country again.

Then Mr Major added: "This is a great country he inherits, a country in extremely good economic shape. I wish him every success in sustaining that. Elections always have winners and they always have losers. It is a very great occasion to win an election and a very great occasion to be elected to Parliament."

Mr Major offered his sympathy to the many "old friends" who had lost their seats in the Tory rout and said: "I would like to express to them my thanks for their support to our party and our country. We are a great, historic party, the Conservative party. We have had great victories in our time. We have had great defeats. Tonight we have been comprehensively defeated. We have listened to the voice of the electorate. We will consider what has been told to us. We must reflect upon it." The scale of the massacre left all parties in a state of shock.

◆

Labour – or New Labour as it styled itself – eventually won a majority of 179 seats. The Conservatives plummeted to their worst defeat in 90 years. After almost two decades in government, they were out of power, and it was largely their own fault.

With most of the Thatcherite agenda already ticked off, they had turned on each other over Europe. Besides the exit from the ERM, John Major (who had only a slender majority) had to deal with a rebellion over implementing the Maastricht Treaty and a leadership challenge from John Redwood. There were also a dozen resignations by ministers accused of 'sleaze', or improper behaviour.

By contrast, Labour had been transformed into the modern-looking Party, its candidates impeccably on message and its campaign American in its slickness. Tony Blair had shed the policies that might have frightened voters and targeted the middle ground and the middle classes with the slogan 'Tough on crime and tough on the causes of crime'.

Although the economic outlook was improving, Britain was in the mood for a change and Blair's youthful earnestness undoubtedly had appeal. As he greeted the crowds outside Downing Street that morning, they were about to learn if things really could only get better.

HONG KONG HANDOVER

1 July 1997

THE party is over. The British rule in Hong Kong ended on the dot of midnight last night, in torrential rain but with dignity and panache. The Last Post had been sounded, the retreat beaten.

The weather was awful but the ceremonial superb. The Pacific Empire went out on the completion of a property contract, in a swirl of pipes and a rattle of drums. The massed bands defied the thunderstorms sweeping down from The Peak, and played *The Day Thou Gavest Lord Has Ended*. The flag dipped and a lone piper played the lament. The audience sang *Auld Lang Syne*, the tears mingling with the rain. The Governor admitted he had long run out of handkerchiefs. Tony Blair looked bemused, the Prince of Wales merely wet.

Whoever planned the surrender date to the Hong Kong lease clearly failed to remember monsoons. The outdoor ceremony was supposed to have been cancelled in the event of rain. Yet as the clouds which had hovered all day over the colony duly broke, the organisers went ahead. Never in the history of diplomacy can so much power and money, so many beautiful suits and dresses, have been so thoroughly soaked.

The ceremony was lifted unchanged from every retreat-from-empire textbook. It was middle-brow to the last. Local children danced inside dragons and paraded as three tokens of modern Hong Kong, as world currencies, microchips and academic gowns. Dame Gwyneth Jones acted Vera Lynn, with *I'll See You Again*. Brian Blessed gave a potted history of the place. The orchestra played Elgar. The Prince of Wales made a dull speech, standing in what appeared to be a waterfall. The Governor made a moving speech.

Mr Patten said he was the twenty-eighth and last to hold his office. "Hong Kong people are now to run Hong Kong," he said. "That is the promise and that is the unshakeable destiny." The Patten edge was there to the end. Hong Kong must have political liberty and economic freedom, but for that they must now look to themselves.

Mr Patten was cheered to the skies. He has been a popular Governor and never more so than of late. He offered Hong Kong's democratic leaders a taste of what they should have had long ago. Politicians who once accused the British of kowtowing to Beijing are doing so no longer. The tit-for-tat boycotts of last night's banquet and government inauguration are an ironic measure of Mr Patten's success. He has made politics matter in Hong Kong. The *South China Morning Post's* last poll, conducted this week, has 50 per cent of Hong Kong residents saying they would still prefer to remain British, and shows Mr Patten's stock rising to the end.

Yet China's claim is rightful.

As the guests moved from the sodden parade ground to the huge new convention centre, the Chinese leadership arrived to assert it. They were greeted by a stupendous firework display, punching galaxies of stars into the gloomy clouds and showering firestorms down on Kowloon.

————————◆————————

Hong Kong, acquired in the wake of the Opium Wars with China, had been British for more than 150 years. Having grown into a financial and trading colossus, it was the country's last major colonial possession, and for many observers its handover marked the real end of empire.

The history of the territory, and the changing fortunes of Britain and China in the late-twentieth century, meant negotiations for its return were lengthy and complex. Although sovereignty over Hong Kong had been transferred in perpetuity, most of the land onto which it had expanded was held on a 99-year lease and it was this which was due to end in 1997.

Control of Hong Kong would significantly boost China's economy (then smaller than that of Britain), but its citizens feared communist rule would expunge their liberties and way of life. There had already been agreement that there could be 'one country, two systems', but Chris Patten, the former Conservative politician and the last Governor, controversially introduced new measures that would give the population more say in their future.

These changes infuriated the Chinese leadership, but they were designed to ensure Hong Kong would retain its own laws and constitution, as well as freedom of speech, until 2047 – in theory.

THE DEATH OF DIANA, PRINCESS OF WALES

6 September 1997

THE QUEEN opened her heart to her people last night with a deeply-felt personal tribute to Diana, Princess of Wales, as an "exceptional and gifted human being" who made many, many people happy.

In a live broadcast against a backdrop of crowds of mourners outside Buckingham Palace, she said: "In good times and bad, she never lost her capacity to smile and laugh, nor to inspire others with her warmth and kindness."

The Queen, speaking to the nation "as your Queen and as a grandmother", said of her former daughter-in-law: "I admired and respected her – for her energy and commitment to others, and especially for her devotion to her two boys."

No one who knew Diana would ever forget her, she added, and today's funeral was an opportunity for everyone to join in expressing grief and gratitude for Diana's "all-too-short" life.

Her address was widely acclaimed by those in the crowds in London who heard it on radio, and it combined with a series of walkabouts at three palaces to extinguish most of the criticism of the Royal Family's apparently aloof response to the Princess's death. Prince William and Prince Harry, in particular, captured the hearts of the nation when they returned with their father to their mother's London home of Kensington Palace to confront the scale of public grief.

And in her broadcast the Queen acknowledged the criticisms, saying that there were lessons to be learnt both from Diana's life and the "extraordinary and moving reaction to her death". The remark was an indication that the Queen was prepared to be flexible over the style of the monarchy, with the possibility of greater informality in some areas.

By reminding viewers that she was grandmother as well as monarch, the Queen sought to explain why she had remained at Balmoral in the bosom of her family since Sunday's tragedy. But her family's arrival in the capital was greeted with palpable relief by the massive crowds and the scenes at the palaces were the strongest possible vindication of the Queen's decision – even at a late stage – to change her plans and relax protocol.

The Queen herself was clearly astonished when she caught sight of the masses of flowers outside Buckingham Palace and she let it be known that the extraordinary display would not be moved before next week. A million bouquets have been laid at Buckingham, Kensington and St James's Palaces and a spokesman said: "Careful consideration is being given as to how best to preserve this tremendous expression of sympathy." The three Princes arrived at Kensington Palace from Balmoral at lunchtime to find a crowd of 10,000 waiting to grasp their hands and express sympathy.

The boys were tearful but composed and managed grateful smiles as they spoke to the people.

The Prince of Wales gulped several times before he was able to talk to his sons as they stood together, drawing their attention to various parts of the display. Within moments, people were holding out flowers across the barriers and the sad little family group soon found themselves carrying bouquet after bouquet to add to the mountain.

◆

The Princess had died on 31 August in a Paris hospital from injuries suffered when the car in which she was being driven crashed in a tunnel at twice the speed limit. It was later found that the driver, Henri Paul, had been drinking before setting off from the Ritz hotel, owned by Mohammed Al-Fayed, father of the Princess's companion, Dodi. Like Paul, he too was killed in the accident.

Diana was 36, and she and the Prince of Wales had divorced the previous year. The outpouring of public sympathy that greeted her death was unprecedented in its extent. For all her undeniable glamour, it was her approachability and relative informality that struck people. The spontaneous floral tributes denoted a similar shift in British behaviour, which itself led to pressure on the Royal Family to respond to the nation's mood.

By the time of the Princess's funeral, the flowers piled outside the gates of her home at Kensington Palace lay five feet deep. Three million people gathered in London to see her coffin drawn on a gun carriage to Westminster Abbey, while an estimated 2.5 billion people around the world watched the service on television.

THE GOOD FRIDAY AGREEMENT

11 April 1998

TONY BLAIR declared last night that "courage has triumphed" as two Governments and eight political parties signed up to a new future for Northern Ireland.

He hailed a settlement that would give everyone the chance to live in peace and raise their children free from the shadow of fear.

The accord brings the Unionist and nationalist traditions, including Sinn Fein, together in fresh political structures that offer the hope of ending 30 years of bloodshed that have cost 3,200 lives. There will be a new power-sharing Northern Ireland assembly, institutions linking the North with the Republic, the start of arms decommissioning and the conditional release of all paramilitary prisoners. Dublin has undertaken to end its constitutional claim to Northern Ireland. President Clinton, who made a critical intervention in the last hour of the talks, said that Ulster had chosen "hope over hate, the promise of the future over the poison of the past".

Mr Blair called in the President after an eleventh-hour dispute over the decommissioning of IRA arms threatened to wreck all the progress that had been made. Then, suddenly, 33 hours of non-stop talks ended with the announcement of a deal just after 5pm.

The Queen telephoned Mr Blair to offer her congratulations and George Mitchell, the former US senator who brokered the deal, praised the efforts of the Irish and British leaders and echoed Mr Blair's plea for co-operation.

"This agreement is good for the people of Ireland, north and south. It was made possible by the leadership, commitment and the negotiating skill of Tony Blair and Bertie Ahern," he said.

Earlier in the afternoon there had been doubts over whether David Trimble would be able to deliver on his side of the deal because of opposition within his own Ulster Unionist party. With the agreement ready for approval, Jeffrey Donaldson, one of his negotiators, suddenly raised objections to the idea of Unionists sitting down with Sinn Fein members in the new assembly committees if they had not renounced violence and decommissioning had not begun. Mr Trimble raised the issue in a tense meeting and also asked for an assurance that the agreement's passages on decommissioning meant that the process of giving up arms should be started straightaway. Mr Blair's initial assurances that that was what the deal meant clearly failed to satisfy Mr Trimble's party and word spread that the whole agreement might be scuppered.

The Prime Minister urgently telephoned Mr Clinton at about 4.15pm. The President then spoke to Bertie Ahern, the Irish Prime Minister; Gerry Adams, the Sinn Fein president; Mr Trimble; and John Hume, leader of the nationalist SDLP.

The danger was that if Mr Blair made a fresh concession to Mr Trimble the nationalists might start to unpick the whole deal. In the end Mr Blair wrote formally to Mr Trimble over his concerns that decisions on excluding or removing people from office are to be taken on a cross-community basis. Mr Blair promised that if those proposals proved to be ineffective during the first six months of the assembly, changes would be made to prevent unsuitable people from holding office.

The settlement will be put to referendums north and south of the border on May 22.

———◆———

Since the events of Bloody Sunday in 1972 (see page 278), Northern Ireland's government and security had been run directly from Westminster instead of Stormont. During the years that followed, there were many attempts, often in secret, to find a solution to the Troubles acceptable to loyalists and nationalists alike, but progress only began to be made in the 1990s.

The declaration of a ceasefire by the IRA in 1994 paved the way for Sinn Fein to be included in the discussions, which gathered momentum in 1998. Concessions had to be made by all sides, especially over the sharing of power, which in the 1960s Catholics had felt was used by the

Protestant majority to favour their own community, leading to the first outbreaks of violence.

The language of the Good Friday (or Belfast) Agreement was often ambiguous and lacking in detail to avoid the parties finding reasons not to sign, but devolved government was restored in Northern Ireland, while the Republic renounced its claim to the North. There was also to be a new police force.

Progress thereafter was fitful and disrupted by rogue terrorist attacks, notably the bombing of Omagh four months after the Agreement was signed, when 29 people died, and by concerns over the slow decommissioning of weapons. Yet, the Agreement has allowed a generation to grow up free of the shadow of the gun.

THE MILLENNIUM

1 January 2000

LIKE the shadow of the summer eclipse, midnight rolls across the face of the earth at 775 mph. By the time Big Ben tolled the magic hour in our little grapefruit segment of the globe, the islanders of Kiribati in the Pacific had been partying for 14 hours.

When it came at last to the headquarters of measured time at Greenwich we welcomed it, like our distant ancestors, with goblins and fire. That the celebrations were essentially pagan was appropriate enough; we were marking, not a religious milestone, but a round number.

Eighteen seconds after passing the meridian line, the notional midnight hour was deemed to have reached Tower Bridge, when the Thames blazed to a curtain of fire that followed midnight for a further 10.8 seconds upriver to Big Ben. With 39 tonnes of explosives involved, it formed part of the biggest fireworks display in British history, although the music written by Handel for a previous one has proved more enduring than some of last night's offerings are likely to.

Fire figured last time, too. The sermon in the Vercelli manuscript of 1000 predicting the first millennium warned of resounding flames burning up the blood-mingled earth, destroying all those engaged in great boasting and in the useless sight of gold and silver, fine cloth and ill-gotten property. That preacher would not have liked the £758 million Millennium Dome, which is where the goblins danced last night.

In a 90-minute entertainment to which the Queen, the Duke of Edinburgh and the Princess Royal were welcomed by Tony and Cherie Blair, the only overtly religious element was a two-minute slot allotted to the Archbishop of Canterbury and three Barnardo's children to say prayers.

The Queen wore an apricot coat, Cherie a long purple dress, while between them in the royal box, the Prime Minister sported his usual dark suit, glistening white shirt and red tie. As they took their seats the last stragglers from the chaos of Stratford station were still struggling to their places.

At a quarter to midnight the Queen unhooked a rope on the royal box and released a group of children from the Meridian Primary School in Greenwich who raced across the arena and grabbed eight ribbons, causing a ring of curtains to fall away in a spectacular waterfall effect, exposing the inside of the structure's saucer roof. Martians who gazed down on it from their planet appeared to be right; it will never fly.

The organisers were particularly proud of an elaborate stunt shortly before midnight. As the young choristers began to sing the anthem, Sir John Tavener's *New Beginning*, they approached centre stage where the world's third largest diamond had been positioned to be targeted by laser beams, creating the effect once produced by a rotating glass ball in dance halls. As the delicate first notes sounded, they placed their hands over the diamond to reduce the arena to darkness.

Finally, as the quarter chimes of Big Ben sounded, tradition returned. The entire audience rose to its feet cheering. On the midnight stroke the Queen and Mr Blair toasted each other with champagne and within moments the monarch and her first minister had linked hands with the entire front row of the royal box for *Auld Lang Syne*.

———◆———

The celebrations that greeted the new Millennium perhaps proved, like most New Year's parties, to be more exciting in prospect than in reality, but if so, it was not for want of effort.

Several Pacific nations competed for the prestige of being the first to see the new epoch, employing ruses such as temporarily advancing their clocks or moving the International Date Line – under which a US submarine parked itself in a bid to claim the honour.

In Edinburgh, five tonnes of Hogmanay fireworks were let off in four minutes, while Cardiff staged what was billed as the world's largest indoor music event in the Millennium Stadium. Meanwhile, in London, two million people lined miles of the Thames to watch the stretch between Tower Bridge and Vauxhall turned into a 'River of Fire' by pyrotechnics as Big Ben chimed midnight.

The only damp squib was the non-appearance of the Millennium Bug, which had been predicted to cause computer failures on systems using old software that started all dates with '19'.

The focus of events, the Millennium Dome built close to the Prime Meridian at Greenwich at vast cost, was much derided by the press and attracted only half the 12 million visitors forecast. It now houses the O2 arena.

SEPTEMBER 11

12 September 2001

DOZENS of people – one man said that he had seen at least 40 go "bam, bam, bam" – met their wretched end in a freefall.

The twin towers of the World Trade Centre soared so majestically over the Manhattan skyline that, from the pavement below, it was hard to believe that the writhing shapes falling from the upper storeys were office workers who had jumped to escape the flames. What kind of desperation could drive these people to leap to a certain death when the streets below were lined with ambulances and help was clearly on its way?

From behind a police barricade several blocks north along the Hudson River, I could not see where they were landing. Then, in one almighty rumble, their dreadful reasoning became apparent. In excruciating slow-motion, the southern tower crumbled, its middle billowed out and, before my eyes, one of the world's largest office buildings disappeared in a cloud of smoke that engulfed the rescuers below.

Even before the walls hit the ground, the onlookers around me turned and fled in panic through the canyons of Manhattan, screaming that the unthinkable had happened. A vast and silent dust-ball filled the surrounding streets, billowing inexorably towards me like a morning fog rolling over the normally vital neighbourhoods of Wall Street and Tribeca.

Those unfortunate to be closer to the collapse than I was vanished from view, submerged in the expanding balloon of debris. I felt a sudden pity for the scores, if not hundreds, of ambulance crews and firefighters who had just, I'm sure, lost their lives. Until then, the burning twin towers, holes gaping in their sides, seemed somehow familiar, even inevitable, a staple of our fevered imagination, something that a screenwriter might describe as Towering Inferno times two.

But even the most devilish imagination in all Hollywood had never concocted a scene so awesome in its devastation as the sight, of first one and then another 110-storey skyscraper crashing to extinction.

It was at this point that many of the New Yorkers who had thronged the streets to watch this compelling spectacle – many of them refugees from wars in other parts of the world – decided that it was just safer to go home. Their judgment was soon justified by another terrifying rumble as the northern tower buckled and collapsed. It was impossible to comprehend, but now that the sleek silver symbols of the New York skyline, the embodiment of the city's dominance in the modern world, were no more, New York, the self-proclaimed "capital of the world", had been irrevocably diminished.

We were all wrong, it turns out, to believe all those reassurances after the first bombing in 1993 that the twin towers were built to withstand the full force of a commercial airliner. We are told, only now, that the experts were referring merely to a Boeing 727.

It was said that 50,000 people, enough to populate a small city, worked in those two behemoths. It was immediately and indisputably clear that more people had died than all the Americans had lost in the Gulf War, and probably more than the combined total of all the Allied forces.

◆

The first sign that America was under attack on 11 September 2001 came when a passenger jet flew into one of the Twin Towers of the World Trade Centre, the New York landmark. At first, however, it was taken for an accident, and it was only when a second aircraft hit the other 110-storey tower that it became apparent that these devastating events were acts of terrorism.

Less than two hours later, both burning buildings came cascading down. Two more aeroplanes had also been hijacked. One was flown into the Pentagon, while the other crashed in a field in Pennsylvania as the passengers tried to regain control of it. Almost 3,000 people died in the attacks, shocking America and the world, perhaps as it had not been shocked since President Kennedy's assassination four decades earlier.

Al-Qaeda, the terrorist organisation of Islamic extremists headed by Osama bin Laden, was thought to be responsible. America reacted by invading Afghanistan, where the group was sheltered by the Taliban. The War on Terror would dominate the presidency of George W. Bush and shape much of the history of the next 20 years.

THE DEATH OF THE QUEEN MOTHER

1 April 2002

AS a devastated Royal Family gathered at Windsor yesterday the body of Queen Elizabeth the Queen Mother was borne on the first, short stage of a final journey that will take it through all the pomp and pageantry the nation can muster to a royal ceremonial funeral next Tuesday.

Ten days of national mourning began with a touching, private simplicity as the coffin was carried by six pallbearers from the Royal Lodge in Windsor Great Park to the adjoining Royal Chapel of All Saints. The Queen Mother died peacefully in her sleep aged 101 at 3.15 on Saturday afternoon in a large armchair at the lodge, her daughter holding her hand.

Behind the coffin walked three members of her staff, one carrying a potted jasmine that her favourite grandson, the Prince of Wales, had given her for Easter and which was by her bedside when she died. The coffin was placed on two simple trestles of Windsor oak as Canon John Ovendon, the Queen Mother's personal chaplain, held a brief service and read from Psalm 121: "I will lift up mine eyes to the hills, from whence cometh my help."

Later in the day the Queen, who had missed the regular Easter service in St George's Chapel, was joined by close members of her family for a quiet and intensely personal Evensong in the Victorian chapel where, each year on February 6, the Queen Mother would remember the death of her husband in 1952.

The Prince of Wales, who was particularly close to his grandmother, was said to have taken her death badly. He had to seek the Queen's permission to fly back in the same aircraft as his two sons from their interrupted skiing holiday in Klosters. Security fears would normally rule out such a risk to the first, second and third in line to the throne.

Tributes poured in from around the globe and queues formed to sign condolence books in London, Sandringham and Edinburgh, as Britain and the world marked the passing of a remarkable woman, born in the lifetime of Queen Victoria, the last Empress of India, and the steadfast mother figure of a nation at war.

Tributes are expected to flow from both sides of the House when Parliament is recalled on Wednesday, in the middle of its Easter recess, to acknowledge the death of the former Queen Consort. At St Paul's Cathedral the State Bell, rung only for the passing of the great, tolled for an hour.

At Windsor Castle nearly 100 members of the public kept an all-night vigil. And the Archbishop of Canterbury, in his Easter sermon, spoke of the conflicting emotions between loss and bereavement and the joy of the risen Christ. At Bagram airbase in Afghanistan, British troops held their own service of remembrance for the Colonel-in-Chief of The Black Watch, the regiment in which her brother Fergus, killed at the Battle of Loos in 1915, was proud to serve.

Final farewells will come later this week as the Queen Mother is accorded the same majestic rites as her late husband with what will be a state funeral in all but name. Tomorrow the coffin will be moved to the Queen's Chapel, London, close to her former home at Clarence House, for three days of private mourning by her family and staff.

◆

Few could remember a time when the Queen Mother had not been a fixture in their lives. She was as old, not as the century but as the one before. The First World War had begun on her 14th birthday; she had been much affected by the death during it of her brother, Fergus.

Married in 1923 to the Duke of York, as he was then, she had never expected to become Queen. Instead, she had had to support her husband, who famously suffered with a stammer, through events that became milestones in the nation's history. Among these were the Abdication Crisis and the Second World War, when she and the King had remained in London, sharing the dangers of the Blitz with its other citizens. Then she had seen her daughter in turn ascend the throne.

One of her last public appearances had been some weeks earlier at the funeral of her other daughter, Princess Margaret. The Queen Mother's began with the bell of Westminster Abbey tolling once for each year of her life. Then, with her crown resting atop, her coffin was brought from Westminster Hall. There it had lain in state and there, in the three days before, 200,000 people had gone to bid her farewell.

THE FALL OF SADDAM HUSSEIN

10 April 2003

"YANKEE bastard," yelled the young British peacenik at the first American tank to roll up to the Palestine Hotel. "Go home."

She picked a man who had waited 576 days to give his answer. Marine First Lieutenant Tim McLaughlin leant from the turret of his Abrams tank – nicknamed "Satan's Right Hand" – and screamed back: "I was at the Pentagon September 11. My co-workers died. I don't give a f***."

Lieutenant McLaughlin had with him a Stars and Stripes that he had been given at the Pentagon that fateful day. In Baghdad's Paradise Square, he handed the flag to Corporal Edward Chin, who climbed a giant statue of Saddam and draped it over the deposed dictator's head.

It was there only briefly; the gesture raised hardly a cheer from the gathering crowd and a black, white and red Iraqi flag quickly replaced it as a scarf around the statue's neck. That, too, was removed to make way for the winch that would bring down the hated figure.

Lieutenant McLaughlin's battalion was in the vanguard yesterday when the US 1st Marine Division rolled up to the east bank of the Tigris in central Baghdad, marking the moment when Saddam's regime effectively came to an end.

It was a momentous day, reminiscent of the fall of the Berlin Wall and with it the communist empire in 1989. And no image of it will be more enduring than the toppling of that 20ft Saddam statue by a US tank egged on by a cheering, excited mob which then stamped with undisguised glee on the fallen idol.

Seldom in history has a city almost the size of London fallen. As resistance in Saddam's capital crumbled, and the leaders of a collapsing regime folded their tents and crept away, the US Defence

Secretary condemned Saddam to a place alongside Hitler, Stalin, Lenin and Ceausescu "in the pantheon of failed, brutal dictators."

Celebrating local people said the regime's enforcers – the militias, security apparatus and Baath party loyalists – had quietly melted away. A city that went to sleep under a tottering regime awoke in a power vacuum.

And the people knew it. No one lives under the arbitrary imposition of power for four decades without developing acutely honed antennae for authority, and when it disappears the oppressed need no news bulletin or headline to tell them. The absence of burning oil fires, of checkpoints, of Republican Guard; the field artillery pieces abandoned under flyovers, the empty sandbag positions all told the tale.

Within hours Saddam City, a poor suburb heavily populated by Iraq's downtrodden Shia majority, had exploded into a festival of looting.

As our cars sped east to document the ransacking, delighted Shias waved joyously as they walked, drove and rode in the opposite direction, their vehicles loaded with microwaves, rifles, calculators, car batteries, food, oil and cigarettes. Suddenly shoulders were things to carry booty on, not to look over.

Yesterday *The Times* saw looting by car, looting by pony-trap, looting by bicycle, looting by makeshift sled. One man even pressed an office swivel chair into service to haul away a television. Another youth liberated the barrel of a heavy machinegun from a local police station without even knowing what it was. "I want it for my home," he said, proudly.

The looting was accompanied by the first expression of political opposition in Baghdad for decades. The Baath party headquarters of Saddam City – a prime candidate for the likely rash of renamings over the coming days – had been ransacked and other buildings torched. Posters of Saddam were torn or defaced, one with the name of the Prophet's son-in-law Imam Ali, a symbolic leader for the country's Shia majority.

This in itself is a salutary warning for incoming Americans: a people oppressed for years under Saddam's Sunni Tikrit elite are unlikely to be fobbed off with formulations about a new system comprising "elements of democracy".

Whether the American hierarchy has the sophistication to appreciate this remains to be seen. More at least, one hopes, than the

Marine who arrived in the centre of town yesterday morning with the immortal words: "Which city is this?"

Crucially, the question everyone around him asked was: "Where is Saddam?"

"Have we got rid of the criminal? Tell us. When, when are we going to get rid of him? Help us to find a solution," entreated one elderly man before returning to the criminal business of the day.

With feelings running high, many Iraqi minders – who until yesterday had to accompany foreign journalists everywhere – were too afraid to venture on to the streets. Others read the runes more quickly. "Do we still need a guide?" one colleague asked our driver. "No, khallas (finished)" he grinned.

"Do we take the TV off our car because of the looters, or leave it on top to stop the Americans shooting us?" I asked. "It's s*** both ways," grunted one photographer.

Shrugging, I took out the empty lemon juice carton in which my banned Thuraya satellite phone was hidden, ripped apart the bottom resealed with candle wax, and put it in my flak jacket pocket.

By noon, American soldiers had reached Canal Hotel, the UN headquarters abandoned by the weapon inspectors last month. The Marines simply walked into town, encountering occasional sniper fire, and sat around the huge compound. Most waved. One was strumming his guitar, his feet up.

———◆———

The triggers for the overthrow of Saddam Hussein were said by the United States to be Iraq's backing for terrorists, including Al-Qaeda, and its development of prohibited weapons of mass destruction. Evidence of this had supposedly been supplied by Britain's intelligence service, although it was later found to be flawed.

There had been tensions, however, between Saddam and the West since the Gulf War two decades earlier. The UN had imposed sanctions on Iraq for many years for refusing to comply with inspections for banned chemical and biological weapons. There were also fears it was trying to acquire nuclear weapons.

Entering Iraq from Kuwait, an alliance comprised chiefly of American and British forces quickly overwhelmed Saddam's troops. His fall was symbolized by the toppling of his statue in central Baghdad, and he was eventually captured in late 2003.

Saddam was executed in 2006 by the new Iraqi government. By then, however, the Allied coalition, which had stayed on to oversee reconstruction of the country, had become embroiled in a bloody insurgency sparked by its presence there. The continued involvement of Britain and America became increasingly unpopular at home, too.

JULY 7 ATTACKS

8 July 2005

BRITAIN stood united last night in defiance of the bomb attacks which killed at least 52 people and left 700 injured as the reality of the War on Terror came to London.

Less than 24 hours after the capital had celebrated winning the Olympics, a 56-minute series of explosions blasted the Underground and a bus in what was thought to be an al-Qaeda attack.

Tony Blair stood shoulder to shoulder with world leaders at the G8 summit, opposition politicians and church and Muslim groups, in condemning what he called an act of barbarity.

The first attack came at 8.51am in a tunnel near Aldgate station. Five minutes later, at least 21 people died in a blast in a tunnel between King's Cross and Russell Square. At 9.17am, an explosion smashed through a tunnel wall at Edgware Road station, damaging three trains. Exactly 30 minutes later, a fourth bomb went off on a No 30 bus, packed with commuters forced above ground after the Tube was closed.

The number of confirmed deaths was 37 – 21 at King's Cross, seven at Edgware Road, seven at Aldgate and two on the bus in Tavistock Place. But the full toll will not be known for some time and sources said that at least another 15 had died in the bus bombing.

A leading London doctor, Professor Philip Patsalos, 52, was named among those seriously injured, after losing a leg in the King's Cross blast.

This is the worst terrorist attack in Britain. The previous highest toll was in the 1974 IRA Birmingham pub bombings, which killed 21.

The emergency services were stretched to the limit by a series of bomb alerts and thousands of commuters were stranded after train and Tube services shut down. Transport for London promises a service this morning but there will be restrictions. Body scanners which can see through clothing will be introduced at some Underground stations.

A group calling itself the Secret Organisation Group of al-Qaeda of Jihad Organisation in Europe claimed the attacks on an Islamic website.

Investigators believe that the bomb on the double-decker bus may have been set off by a suicide bomber or may have gone off en-route to its intended target. Tony Blair left the G8 summit at Gleneagles to fly to London for a meeting of the emergency Cobra planning team.

In a televised statement from Downing Street, Mr Blair said that the terrorists were "trying to use the slaughter of innocent people to cow us, to frighten us out of doing the things that we want to do, trying to stop us from going about our business".

He added: "They should not, and they must not succeed. When they try to intimidate us, we will not be intimidated. When they seek to change our country or our way of life, we will not be changed."

George Bush, speaking from Gleneagles, Britain vowed that the terrorists would be brought to justice.

The Queen spoke of her shock at the dreadful events and will visit people caught up in the tragedy today. The Union Jack over Buckingham Palace was lowered to half-mast.

Rudy Giuliani, the Mayor of New York at the time of the destruction of the World Trade Centre, was near Liverpool Street station when the bombs exploded. In a letter to *The Times* today, he says: "Great Britain was there for us on September 11, 2001, and you should know that the United States supports you in your time of need."

◆

Fifty-two people, from 18 different countries, were killed in the blasts, and more than 700 others injured. It was the heaviest loss of life in Britain from a single incident since the Second World War, and the deadliest to have occurred in Britain since the Pan Am bombing. The toll might have been worse had the No. 30 bus not been passing the British Medical Association, where scores of doctors were attending a conference.

The homemade devices, packed into rucksacks, were set off by four suicide bombers. But unlike previous attacks, which had been planned and initiated abroad, these were carried out by British Muslims. Three – Hasib

Hussain, Shezad Tanweer and Germaine Lindsay – were aged between 18 and 22, while the ringleader, Mohammad Sidique Khan, was 30.

Although Al-Qaeda was said to have inspired the bombings, no direct link was established. The quartet had initially been radicalized, however, by contact with Islamic extremists in Britain. The attacks led to major changes in the focus and procedures of the police and security services, who were also given wider anti-terrorist powers.

Reports about the attacks were notable for being some of the first to make use of footage taken by the public on mobile telephones.

THE FINANCIAL CRISIS

16 September 2008

Fears of a global financial meltdown grew yesterday as the world's biggest bankruptcy plunged markets into turmoil.

Investors were left reeling as the abrupt demise of the Lehman Brothers investment bank sparked the biggest shake-up on Wall Street in decades.

Another of US capitalism's biggest institutions, Merrill Lynch, is to be swallowed by Bank of America in a $50 billion takeover to save it from collapse.

Shares fell as fear spread through the financial system. Central banks unveiled urgent measures amid concerns that the world economy was entering a dangerous new phase. The Bank of England injected £5 billion of emergency lending into money markets.

The 5,000 Lehman staff in Britain were clearing their desks yesterday in the country's biggest single loss of jobs since the collapse of Rover in 2005. The majority of the bank's 26,000 staff around the world are expected to lose their jobs

Leading shares on both sides of the Atlantic took a battering. More than £50 billion was wiped off London's bluechip shares as the FTSE 100 index tumbled by 212.5 points, or more than 4 per cent. It was the darkest day for the stock market since January 21, when it fell 5.5 per cent.

Investors were fretting over the financial health of banks that had lent Lehman money – and the fear that more big institutions would be wiped out. "It's clear that we are one step away from a financial meltdown," Nouriel Roubini, a leading international economist, said.

London's losses were stemmed as Bank of America's rescue bid for Merrill Lynch helped to limit yesterday morning's sell-off on Wall

Street. When London closed, the benchmark Dow Jones industrial average was down 300 points, or 2.6 per cent. Sentiment was also bolstered by steep falls in oil prices, which dropped by more than $5 a barrel to $96, closing under $100 for the first time in six months and raising hopes that cheaper fuel would ease economic stresses on Western nations.

However, by close of trading the Dow had fallen by more than 500 points – its biggest one-day drop since the reopening after the September 11 attacks – as concerns mounted over the world's largest insurer. Shares in American International Group (AIG), which sponsors Manchester United, fell by 45 per cent after it made an unprecedented approach to the US Federal Reserve for $40 billion in emergency funding.

Last night the Fed asked Goldman Sachs and J P Morgan Chase, two of Wall Street's remaining big banks, to head a $75 billion emergency package to keep AIG afloat.

As central banks battled to stabilise the system, the Fed eased its rules for emergency lending further. It announced that it would accept company shares in return for crisis loans for the first time. In Frankfurt, the European Central Bank injected €30 billion in emergency funds into eurozone markets.

A group of ten global banks also attempted to foster calm, announcing a $70 billion pool of funds, with any one of them able to tap a third of that should they hit difficulty.

The collapse of Lehman came after the US Treasury refused to bail out the embattled 158-year-old bank, a crucial shift after its support in March for a Wall Street rescue of the failing Bear Stearns. Lehman was felled by the weight of about $60 billion in toxic bad debts. It went under holding assets of $639 billion against debts of $613 billion, making it the biggest corporate bankruptcy since WorldCom collapsed in 2002.

◆

Some observers had believed big banks were so vital to confidence in the economy that they were 'too big to fail', or in other words too big for the governments that had supervised them inadequately to let them fail. Yet, if Lehman's bankruptcy disproved that, at least at first, it also signalled that there were enormous problems throughout America's financial system. These stemmed chiefly from reckless lending.

Some banks had invested heavily in subprime mortgages, loans made to house-buyers with less than perfect credit ratings. As more people failed to make their payments, and as a downturn in the market meant the properties that secured the mortgages were worth less, so the banks' losses mounted.

The web of lending and borrowing between the world's banks had become so complex that in Britain, for instance, the crisis led to Gordon Brown's government, which had already bailed out Northern Rock, having to commit £50 billion in October 2008 to rescue Lloyd's, HBOS – the UK's biggest mortgage lender – and Royal Bank of Scotland.

It provided hundreds of billions more in short-term loans as, with financial institutions less willing to extend credit, especially to each other, central banks pumped huge quantities of money into circulation. Yet, they were unable to prevent the most severe global recession seen for generations.

THE INAUGURATION OF BARACK OBAMA

21 January 2009

Barack Obama promised a new era of American leadership yesterday in which military might would be tempered by humility and restraint.

After being sworn in as the 44th President of the United States in front of an estimated crowd of two million people, Mr Obama reached out to the Muslim world and said that America must earn its greatness once again.

In a clear repudiation of the past eight years, he said that he would not abandon the principles of America's founding fathers for expediency's sake. "We reject as false the choice between our safety and our ideals."

Mr Obama promised to rebuild alliances and said that Americans must recognise their duties "to ourselves, our nation and the world". He said that the military might of America did not entitle the US "to do as we please".

In a sombre speech that had little of the soaring rhetoric with which he is associated, he acknowledged that his nation was in the midst of a crisis and that its challenges would not be easily met. "But know this, America: they will be met. On this day, we gather because we have chosen hope over fear, unity of purpose over conflict and discord," he said. "Starting today, we must pick ourselves up, dust ourselves off, and begin again the work of remaking America."

To underline the challenges that he faces, the US stock market fell 4 per cent, its worst ever Inauguration Day fall, eclipsing the 2.3 per cent decline in 1929 for Herbert Hoover and the advent of the Great Depression.

Amid scenes of euphoria, America's first black president strolled down Pennsylvania Avenue before moving his family into the White

House, which was built more than 200 years ago by slaves. Mr Obama said that the "meaning of our liberty" was demonstrated by people of "every race and every faith" celebrating yesterday in a city where 60 years ago his father "might not have been served at a local restaurant".

To Muslims he offered a "new way forward, based on mutual interest and mutual respect", but warned terrorists that they would be defeated. To those watching, he added, "know that America is a friend of each nation and every man, woman and child who seeks a future of peace and dignity; and that we are ready to lead once more."

———◆———

Barack Obama's electoral victory over John McCain seemed to represent a watershed in American politics in more ways than one. The nation that had fought a civil war over slavery had elected its first Black President, one who was already just the third African-American Senator in 120 years. However, his triumph suggested to some commentators that the country wanted to leave behind its recent past, too.

Obama had surprised many by winning the Democratic nomination ahead of a much better-known figure in the party, Hillary Clinton. His arrival at the White House marked an end to policies that had defined eight years of George Bush's presidency, notably the war in Iraq and the loose policing of Wall Street, viewed as having aggravated the economy's collapse.

While much of Obama's appeal lay in his personal story and in the oratory that echoed Lincoln, what many voters wanted from his administration, therefore, was change – actions and not merely words.

Yet, defeat allowed more partisan voices to be heard more loudly in the Republican camp as well. Obama's would be a presidency which from the beginning risked disappointing its supporters even as opposition from its opponents hardened.

COALITION

12 May 2010

David Cameron will begin today to forge the first peacetime coalition for more than 80 years after becoming Britain's 53rd Prime Minister.

The Conservative leader opened a new political era by cautioning that "hard and difficult work" lay ahead for the new Government that will include five Liberal Democrats in Cabinet and some 15 others in ministerial jobs. Nick Clegg was last night confirmed by the Queen as Deputy Prime Minister.

Mr Cameron struck a businesslike tone devoid of triumphalism as he arrived in Downing Street to end five days of post-election uncertainty and become the first Tory for 31 years to depose a Labour prime minister.

He and Mr Clegg would "put political differences aside" as they moved to tackle the deficit, ease deep social problems, rebuild public trust in politics and bring about a more responsible society. The maxim of his Government would be: "Those who can, should, those who cannot, we will always help." He promised that the elderly, frail and poorest would not be forgotten.

The scale of the political revolution underway – and the extent of the two leaders' collaboration – was underlined with the unprecedented announcement that the next election will take place on the first Thursday in May 2015. Even before taking office, Mr Cameron gave up the Prime Minister's freedom to go to the country when he chooses, with both sides instead committing to a full five-year term.

Last night Mr Clegg won the backing of his party for the deal.

The hiatus since polling closed last Thursday had seemed interminable, and at times fatal, to Tory hopes, but shortly before 9pm the waiting ended as Mr Cameron swept into Downing Street in a silver Jaguar amid deafening cheers and jeers from a crowd of many hundreds gathered in Whitehall.

He went round the car to open the door for his wife, Samantha. Together they walked to the same spot outside No 10 where, 90 minutes earlier, Gordon Brown had bid an emotional farewell to his home of the past 1,048 days. He wished his successor well, said that it had been a privilege to serve, paid a glowing tribute to the Armed Forces – "all that is best in our country" – and, his voice cracking, to his wife, Sarah. In a moment of poignant self-awareness, he said the job had taught him about the best in human nature and about its frailties, "including my own".

Mr Cameron, with his visibly pregnant wife looking on nervously, paid tribute to Mr Brown and promised to "face up to our really big challenges, to confront our problems... so that together we can reach better times".

<hr>

The result of the General Election called by Gordon Brown had been a hung Parliament, the first since 1974. Voters had tired of Labour after 13 years and did not trust it to steer the country through recession. The Conservatives had won the most seats but were 20 shy of a majority. Both parties opened negotiations with the Liberal Democrats, whose leader Nick Clegg had gained wider public approval with his performances during the first election debates to have been televised.

The expectation was that Labour and the Lib Dems were more natural political bedfellows and would find a way to establish a coalition government, though this would still have required the support of the smaller parties for a majority. Yet, although Brown was thought to have acted decisively during the banking crisis, personalities appeared to come into play. Cameron and Clegg, tennis players both, were perhaps more similar in age, background, temperament and outlook.

The last coalition had also been at a time of national emergency – during the Second World War. At 43, Cameron became the youngest Prime Minister since Lord Liverpool, in 1812. Both parties agreed on their main challenge, reducing the budget deficit, but few people expected the government to hold together for the next five years.

THE ROYAL WEDDING

30 April 2011

No royal couple in history have ever enjoyed their own wedding so visibly, or placed their personal stamp on the occasion so firmly. The royal wedding was an extraordinary synthesis of ancient and modern, tradition and invention, soaring solemnity and youthful joy. It began with trumpets and hymns, and ended with pop music and the couple driving away in a vintage car with "JU5T WED" on the number plate.

Every element of the wedding reflected the couple's shared humour and taste, and a determination to remain as anchored as possible in their own normality.

More than two billion people watched the couple exchange vows, as Britain laid on the sort of romantic and patriotic spectacle that takes place only once in a generation. The newly minted Duke and Duchess of Cambridge emerged from Westminster Abbey to be met by deafening cheers, a blizzard of bunting and balloons, and a chorus of tweets.

As the great-great-granddaughter of a Durham miner married the man who will be king, the day offered a remarkable cultural meeting point: between Royal Family and people, between Britain and the world, between blue blood and commoner, and between two very different generations of British royalty, with contrasting approaches to the role.

The Aston Martin in which Prince William drove his bride away from Buckingham Palace, festooned with balloons and ribbons and carrying an L plate, belongs to the Prince of Wales. But whereas in 1981 Charles and Diana made the balcony kiss their motif, for William and Catherine the kiss was perfunctory; the beribboned old car, with two beaming young newlyweds in the front seats and the top rolled down, was their chosen image.

The day contained many such small moments that revealed a new brand of royalty.

As the Prince waited by the altar, Prince Harry, the best man, turned around to catch sight of the bride approaching up the aisle, in a stunning wedding dress designed by Sarah Burton, of Alexander McQueen. He turned to his older brother and muttered in awe: "Wait 'til you see the dress." As the couple waited for the service to begin, they glanced at each other, suppressing grins. William could clearly be seen whispering: "You look beautiful."

The greatest danger was not that they might fluff their lines, but that they might get the giggles when the wedding ring got stuck, and had to be jammed on to the bridal finger.

The 2,000 guests packed into the ancient abbey represented the widest cross-section of British society ever seen at an official royal event: military figures, religious leaders, foreign royalty, diplomats, politicians, but also celebrities, colleagues, charity leaders, sporting figures, pop stars and friends.

The socialite Tara Palmer-Tomkinson arrived in an electric-blue outfit, pointed hat and high heels, making her look like a particularly elegant extra from *Avatar*. The King of Tonga rubbed shoulders with David Beckham, whose neck tattoo peeped out from beneath a stiff collar. Sir Elton John, earring sparkling and his civil partner beside him, belted out *Guide Me, O Thou Great Redeemer* as if he had written it.

Celebration took precedence over precedent and decorum. "We're quite a reserved lot, the British," said David Cameron, as he headed to the abbey. "But when we go for it, we really go for it." That was true of street parties up and down the land.

If William would rather have been married in a country church, as reported, he did not show it. If his bride was nervous, the only trace was a gulp, and a blink, when the Archbishop of Canterbury asked sonorously if there was any impediment to their marriage.

◆

If it was natural to compare this Royal Wedding with previous occasions of the kind, what was striking was how much it marked a break with tradition.

This was in part because it was not an event of State as Prince William was not yet heir apparent, allowing the couple to make it their wedding and not one wholly bound by the dead hand of convention. The guest list and the pop star entertainment reflected their interests and their ages, and the fact that they had lives more like those of most people.

They had known each other for ten years before marrying, they had a maid of honour whose dress threatened to upstage the bride, and instead of accepting wedding presents they did not need, they asked for donations to a good cause. Even Prince Harry's uniform was designed with practicality rather than protocol in mind. The tailor went against the orthodoxy that it should have no pockets by hiding one in a cuff to keep the ring safe.

There was, however, nothing novel about the Cambridges' decision to postpone their honeymoon for 10 days, so that Prince William could return to his duties as a search-and-rescue pilot. That acknowledged the life of service that lay ahead.

THE DEATH OF COLONEL GADDAFI

21 October 2011

Colonel Muammar Gaddafi, the ousted Libyan leader, was killed by forces loyal to the revolutionary Government after being dragged from a storm drain that had become his final refuge in his home town of Sirte.

Badly injured but conscious, the former dictator, 69, was bundled on to the bonnet of a pick-up truck, his shirt stripped from his torso and his body dragged along the ground.

It is not clear exactly when and how he died but his bloody end came at the hands of the angry mob of fighters who recorded his last moments on video.

Pictures of his body taken later after it was driven to the neighbouring city of Misrata appeared to show bullet wounds to his head. Mahmoud Jibril, the acting Libyan Prime Minister, claimed last night that Gaddafi was caught in crossfire and died from a bullet wound to the head.

The militiamen who captured him, after weeks of fighting to take Sirte, brandished a golden pistol taken from the colonel, and may now share the £1 million bounty on his head. France said that one of its Mirage fighter jets had attacked the convoy in which Gaddafi was trying to flee.

Across Libya, the former students, computer technicians or casual labourers who have been the backbone of the eight-month revolution took to the streets in celebration. For them this was the signal that at long last their war is over and their leader of almost 42 years was finally gone.

In the chaotic last stand of the Gaddafi dictatorship, the former leader's son Muatassim was also reportedly killed, while there were conflicting reports about Gaddafi's heir apparent, Saif al-Islam, with a Libyan minister claiming that he had been shot in the legs and captured.

As Libyans celebrated, David Cameron, who was at the forefront of the drive for Nato intervention, said that it was "a day to remember all of Colonel Gaddafi's victims", including those who died in the Lockerbie bombing, WPC Yvonne Fletcher and victims of the IRA who used Libyan Semtex in their bombing campaign.

◆

Colonel Gaddafi had been Libya's dictator since deposing King Idris in a coup in 1969. He espoused what he called 'Islamic socialism', using revenues from the country's oil wealth, which he had nationalized, to raise living standards in what had been a largely unmodernized society. He was also accused by the West of funding terrorism over many years, although latterly he had been attempting to improve his relationship with Europe and America.

The Arab Spring protests in other North African countries encouraged unrest to break out in Libya in February 2011, prompted principally by high levels of unemployment and corruption. Air strikes against the rebels as they advanced towards Tripoli caused casualties among civilians, leading the UN to call for the imposition of a no-fly zone.

This was enforced by Nato and influenced the ultimate defeat of Gaddafi's forces. Moreover, it was a Nato attack on the Colonel's convoy as he was trying to escape from Sirte that forced him to take refuge in the drain where he met his end, his shattered visage captured on video in his last moments. Libya subsequently descended into a civil war.

THE LONDON OLYMPICS

28 July 2012

At the exact centre of the world last night, London turned down the option to celebrate giants and supermen and power and might and chose instead to celebrate people. It was on this fine and not unexpected note that the Olympic Games began – a Games fit for humanity, a Games that might stress joy, rather than triumphalism.

It is also the first Games in which every participating nation has selected female athletes.

The cauldron was lit half an hour after midnight, after the torch had made a journey down the Thames in a speedboat with David Beckham, who passed it on to Sir Steve Redgrave. But after all the speculation about which famous person would do the final bit of lighting – Sir Steve, the Queen, Ian Botham by smiting a flaming cricket ball into the bowl – the job was done by nobody, and by everybody, by seven young athletes who might achieve anything or nothing, not giants but people.

The superpower politics of past Games and their ceremonies of self-aggrandisement were exchanged for one that began with gentle fields, a turning water-wheel – the Opening Ceremony began with a vision of Merrie England, a delicious image of idyll that really should have existed.

There were clouds above, increasingly dark ones, though the real rain mostly held off, and just to stress the point, vast clouds of real cotton wool were carried in procession. Joke, you see. It rains in London, we admit it. And this hint of self-deprecation added something unusual in these ceremonies, when it is more customary to boast. This was a celebration of a pleasant land, still green enough in places, and one that, no matter what else its failings, has always had its being on the right side of the Irony Curtain. And it was the jokes rather than the knock-you-dead special effects that made you feel proud about such things as Britishness.

Humour, above all things, humanises and there were elements of self-mockery that suggested we could make this humorous Games; the Games of humorous humanity in a land in which a joke and a grumble are never far away, and often enough one and the same thing.

There were tricks and all kinds of clever things in this show, but there were still jokes. Britannia doesn't rule the waves any more, but she's always up for a joke; a serious bit about the Industrial Revolution was followed by a platoon of Sgt Peppers and a Yellow Submarine.

Britishness is a vast contradictory concept; well, so it should be. We are old and we contain multitudes.

Perhaps the most remarkable thing about the Opening Ceremony was in the keeping of the secret; the way that nobody felt the urge to spoil the surprise.

———◆———

No other city had hosted the Olympics on three occasions, but the omens for the 2020 Games were at first inauspicious. Less than 24 hours after winning the vote over Paris in 2005, London was struck by the July 7 terror attacks. Then, by the time the Games came around, the onset of the recession meant many expected an austerity Olympics, like those after the war.

Instead, shrugging off the last-minute failure of a security firm to provide enough guards for events, the Games joyfully showed the world a Britain confident in its abilities, proud of its heritage and able to laugh at itself. All three qualities were encapsulated in an opening ceremony, overseen by the film director Danny Boyle, which had the wit and audacity to seemingly send the Queen – escorted by James Bond – skydiving into the stadium.

There were winners everywhere, from Britain's athletes – who won six golds on 'Super Saturday' – to London's mayor, Boris Johnson, greeted by cheers that must have stoked further his ambitions. (George Osborne, the Chancellor, was booed during a notably successful Paralympics.) The Olympics were also the first to feature female competitors in every sport. In the words of the closing address, they were the 'best Games ever'.

ANDY MURRAY WINS WIMBLEDON

8 July 2013

And so he did it. After all that, he bloody well went and did it. In front of us, on Centre Court, in the sunshine, a day so perfect that it would have been a shame to waste it. On the seventh day of the seventh month, in his seventh grand-slam tournament final, 77 years after Fred Perry – remembering that Virginia Wade won in 1977 – Andy Murray won Wimbledon. We can lay the story to rest.

Actually, the story is too good to stop telling. Murray defeated the world No 1, Novak Djokovic, the meanest, fittest, most obstinate player, 6-4, 7-5, 6-4 to win it, and if the last game was not enough to shred every last one of our nerves, imagine what it must have been like trying to serve for this most glorious of events with every last one of us hanging on your shoulders.

The Prime Minister was watching yesterday, the First Minister of Scotland was so agitated one felt he would need a tranquiliser at one stage, former champions such as Rod Laver, Neale Fraser, John McEnroe, Boris Becker, were in the stadium, and if they would not say so publicly, they really wanted Murray to get this done. Not for anyone else, but for him. For the grand old country that gave this form of the game to the world, of course, but for Murray most of all.

And dear old Fred Perry would have loved to see this too. One hopes that he was curled up with a nice glass of something upstairs, looking down with a fond fraternal nod to Murray, the 26-year-old who, at the climax to a day he will rarely better in his life, wandered around the court in a daze.

Indeed, at the end of the final, as Djokovic's backhand landed in the net, Murray turned to the Brits in the press seats, focused on one or two faces and pumped his fists with such fervour that one hoped they would survive the strain. (I'm afraid I shook my fists back and will probably lose my press card as a result.)

The release was only to be expected, the relief palpable. He had carried this burden with him for many moons, a player who could actually win this thing and thus it became something of an intolerable burden, like a ball and chain. When? When? When? Hurry it up! Even winning the US Open last year did not exactly lessen the expectancy, but at least it showed him, showed us, showed the world that he was a grand-slam champion of breadth, depth and brilliance.

It is one thing doing it while half the nation are asleep, but when they are watching, living, breathing your every move as they were in their millions yesterday, it is so much more difficult. Even the entrance of the gladiators was one of the more exceptional ever witnessed, a standing ovation from all those present, royals included. Perhaps it is just as well that the players had their backs to the box, or they might have wobbled a bit.

◆

Andy Murray's victory laid to rest one of the longest and least enviable records in the history of British sport. Not since 1936, when Fred Perry won a third title in a row, had a British man won the championship that has become synonymous with tennis. Indeed, since then no British man had won any of the grand slam singles until Murray claimed the US Open in 2012.

Perhaps it is those decades of disappointment, the hopes invested in the likes of Roger Taylor and Tim Henman, that creates so much fervour at Wimbledon. Fifteen thousand spectators cheered on Murray on Centre Court, giving the lie to those who think the English – let alone the Scots – are undemonstrative.

Murray, who as a boy had been present during the massacre of fellow pupils at Dunblane primary school, had lost the previous year's final to Roger Federer. Yet, since then, he had won the Olympic title and had not been beaten on grass.

Injury had kept him out for a month before the championship began, but he was favoured by the early exits of Federer and Rafael Nadal. The fates had aligned. And as for 1936 – no Scot had won Wimbledon since 1896!

BREXIT

24 June 2016

Britain is heading out of the European Union today after a referendum result that remakes the country's political landscape and shatters the continent's post-war settlement.

Swathes of England and Wales ignored David Cameron's warnings on the economic consequences of Brexit to express their anger over immigration and inequality in a popular revolt that has left the country deeply divided.

The pound plunged to a 31-year low as global markets reacted to the prospect of years of uncertainty, including over the future of the UK itself.

Alex Salmond, the former Scottish first minister, said he was certain that his successor, Nicola Sturgeon, would demand a second independence referendum.

Better than expected results for Leave outside the capital left Mr Cameron clinging to the hope that wins in London and Scotland could spare him from humiliating referendum defeat.

But at 4:39am the BBC called the result for Leave with a projected vote share of 52 against 48 for Remain.

As dawn broke over Westminster, Boris Johnson and Michael Gove, the Conservative leaders of the Brexit campaign, were on the verge of a historic upset — and taking on the responsibility of overseeing an exit from the union Britain joined 43 years ago.

The referendum results exposed a country polarised, with London, Scotland and Northern Ireland the only regions with a majority remain vote.

Nigel Farage, the Ukip leader, called it a "victory for real people, a victory for ordinary people, a victory for decent people".

"We have fought against the multinationals, we have fought against the big merchant banks, we have fought against big politics, we have fought against lies, corruption and deceit," he said. "And we will have done it without having to fight, without a single bullet being fired, we'd have done it by damned hard work on the ground."

Although Brexit Tories called publicly for Mr Cameron to remain prime minister, voters' rejection of his referendum case makes his departure from Downing Street beyond a caretaking period all but inevitable.

If he remains in the short term the prime minister's next decision will be how and when to trigger the Article 50 procedure for leaving the EU. During the campaign Mr Cameron said he would do so immediately after a Brexit vote. Mr Gove has previously suggested that it should be delayed.

With the nature of that exit now set to dominate the agenda in Brussels and Westminster, one Tory MP, Jacob Rees-Mogg, said that there may have to be another general election to mandate the renegotiation.

The insurgency that first registered in northeast England gathered force through the night with hammer blows to Remain's hopes from Swansea, Sheffield and Coventry. The final death knell was sounded shortly after 4.30am when Birmingham voted Leave.

Newcastle upon Tyne, deemed one of the most Remain-leaning of the 382 counting areas, provided the first real indication of the night. Although Remain won, the very narrow margin of below 1 per cent was much less than had been predicted.

In the next significant result Sunderland voted overwhelmingly for Leave, with 61 per cent against 39 per cent for Remain. The pattern was repeated elsewhere, suggesting that Labour had failed to persuade its traditional supporters to reject Brexit.

Although Remain registered bigger-than-expected victories in many London boroughs, some Scottish areas and in Liverpool, they were not large enough to offset thumping wins for Leave elsewhere.

Mr Cameron had relied heavily on warnings of the damaging economic consequences of Brexit from a chorus of experts as he made the case to stay in.

However Stephen Crabb, the work and pensions secretary, said that in many old industrial, white, working-class areas in England and Wales "a large number of voters [were] saying 'sorry, we just don't believe the Labour party or the government in the way they tell us that Europe and the European Union is good for us'."

He added: "I think that's going to be one of the strong themes of tonight, the one that the white working-class in Britain, certainly in England and Wales, just haven't trusted the messages."

◆

Europe had been a divisive issue for so long, at least for politicians, that among the emotions to be felt on the morning after the referendum there was not only shock and triumph but also surprise that the matter had at last been resolved. Or so it seemed.

There might never have been a referendum had the pollsters been correct that the 2015 general election would result in a second consecutive hung Parliament. Instead, David Cameron won a small majority. With Nigel Farage's UKIP having taken just one seat, the Conservative leader made good on his manifesto pledge to hold a vote on continued membership of the European Union. The polls predicted the Remain campaign would win.

But, the Leavers proved better at harnessing discontent with the established order than the Remainers did at showing how far-off countries, of which many people knew little, mattered to their futures. Scotland and Northern Ireland voted to stay in, but England and Wales did not.

Cameron resigned but doubts over the terms of Britain's departure hamstrung his successor, Theresa May. It was left to Boris Johnson to take control and, following his election victory in 2019, Britain finally exited Europe in January 2020.

GRENFELL

15 June 2017

Dozens of people were feared dead in one of Britain's worst fire disasters yesterday after an inferno swept through a London tower block that had been the subject of repeated warnings that it was unsafe.

Firefighters said that the blaze, which began shortly before 1am, was unprecedented in its scale and the speed with which it engulfed Grenfell Tower in Kensington. Witnesses described flames climbing the 24-storey building within 15 minutes.

Trapped parents threw their children from windows in desperate efforts to save them. Others leapt from high floors rather than succumb to the flames. Survivors described having to clamber over charred bodies in corridors and stairways filled with smoke.

Some of those who had heeded official advice from the tower block's management to "stay put" and await rescue perished in the fire. Others defied the advice and made their way down a single, central staircase – the building's only escape route.

The fire is thought to have started when a fridge exploded in a kitchen on the fourth floor. This morning the tower block was still gently smouldering after firefighters worked through the night to dampen down the last of the flames 30 hours after the fire started.

Dany Cotton, London Fire Brigade commissioner, said: "In my 29 years of being a firefighter I have never, ever seen anything of this scale."

This morning she told Sky News that she did not expect to find anyone still alive in the building. She said: "The fire is now out. There are small pockets of smouldering. You will see wisps of smoke coming out all day due to the heat of the building and the remaining contents.

"There are, as we believe, still unknown numbers of people in the building.

"Due to the severity of the fire and the way things are it will take a long time for us to be able to do that search properly to identify anyone who is left in the building but we will do that as soon as we can in conjunction with the police.

"Tragically now we are not expecting to find anyone else alive. The severity and the heat of the fire will mean that it will be an absolute miracle for anyone to be left alive."

Ms Cotton said that parts of the tower were unsafe for firefighters to get to and that the fire service was working with structural surveyors and other specialists to try to make those areas accessible.

Residents of the tower had repeatedly warned local officials that the building was a firetrap and that a "catastrophic event" was inevitable. Survivors said there were no sprinklers in the building. Many were woken by neighbours because no alarms had been activated.

The focus for investigators is external cladding, which appeared to act as an accelerant for the flames that swept up the newly refurbished 1970s tower. London Fire Brigade is reported to have warned councils about the external insulation panels after a fire at a block in Hammersmith last August. Experts warned recently that the use of similar cladding panels was linked to skyscraper blazes in Dubai, and was likely to pose a similar risk in Britain.

Ministers announced a review of fire safety at other blocks with such cladding. The cause of the fridge explosion will also be investigated.

Almost 300 fires a year are caused by faulty fridges or freezers. In London alone seven people have died and more than 70 have been seriously hurt since 2010 because of fridge fires.

Police confirmed 12 deaths among the 600 residents thought to have lived in the tower but expect that toll to rise significantly as the building is searched.

◆

There were 72 victims of what, aside from the Piper Alpha oil platform disaster in 1988, was the deadliest fire seen in Britain since the nineteenth century. The nationalities of those who died reflected the make-up of modern London – not just Britons, but refugees from Syria and Sudan, a young couple from Italy, people born in Egypt, Afghanistan, the Gambia, the Philippines and Nigeria who had sought a better life in Britain. Among the dead there were a dozen children.

From the start, the cause of the fire's severity was identified as the external cladding and the gap between it and the walls of the tower, which had acted as a chimney, drawing the flames higher. Cladding had contributed to the fire at the Summerland leisure centre on the Isle of Man in which 50 people had died, in 1973.

An inquiry found that fire doors in the tower were inadequate, the ventilation system failed to function, pipes did not provide water for hoses as they should have done and there was only one route of escape, the central stairwell. Less flammable cladding had not been fitted to the building during recent renovation, on the grounds that the cost would be too high.

CORONAVIRUS

17 March 2020

Normal life was put on hold for up to a year last night after Boris Johnson was told that it was the only way to save a quarter of a million lives.

In restrictions unprecedented in peacetime, the prime minister urged Britons not to go to pubs and theatres, to work from home if they could, and to stop non-essential travel.

He emphasised that the advice was "particularly important" for the 8.8 million people who are aged 70 or above in Britain. They were urged to avoid other people "as much as you can and significantly limit your face-to-face interaction with friends and family".

Mr Johnson dramatically intensified his response to coronavirus after scientists told him that a quarter of a million people would have died under his previous plans. He was warned that "social distancing" by the whole population was the only way to bring deaths down from 260,000 to at best a few thousand.

Jonathan Van-Tam, the deputy chief medical officer, told BBC *Breakfast*: "What has become clear in the last few days is we're now on the very sharp upward tilt of this epidemic and now is the time to add in additional measures to protect vulnerable people. I can't stress enough that the advice we've given is incredibly important for everybody."

Professor Van-Tam said that Britain was carrying out a "high level" of testing compared to most countries but would "focus on where it's needed most – and we have an absolute ambition to increase testing as much as we possibly can".

Mr Johnson said that powers to enforce the restrictions will be used if needed, but added: "Most people would accept that we are a mature and grown-up and liberal democracy where people understand very clearly the advice that is given to them."

He added that the "very draconian measure" was "overwhelmingly worth it" to save lives and stop the NHS being overwhelmed after the death toll rose to 55 yesterday.

An estimated 1.5 million older people with serious health conditions will soon be asked to "shield" themselves from the virus by staying at home for a possible three months.

Speaking at Downing Street, Mr Johnson acknowledged that he was asking for "a very substantial change in the way that we want people to live their lives, and I can't remember anything like it in my lifetime. I don't think there has really been anything like it in peacetime."

David Nabarro, a special envoy on the coronavirus for the World Health Organisation, welcomed Mr Johnson's decision to advise greater social distancing. "The thinking about the possibility of further more severe outbreaks coming later was perfectly valid, however as it became clear how quickly the virus has been advancing in other countries a shift in position was absolutely right," he told the BBC *Today* programme.

"I'm really pleased this has happened. And I would like to stress that in every other country positions are having to be shifted as we know more about the outbreak. We are just dealing with something that's so new with so many things we don't know that we have to be prepared for a change in tack from time to time even though it's distressing."

Sir Lindsay Hoyle, Speaker of the Commons, announced last night that all non-essential public access to the Houses of Parliament will be suspended from today. He also urged all MPs and peers over the age of 70 "to pay particular attention to the advice of Public Health England".

He said: "All of us recognise the importance of parliament continuing at such a difficult time – the need to ensure proper scrutiny and that our constituents' concerns are addressed." The measures would allow parliament to "continue to fulfil its constitutional duties", he added.

What may in retrospect become the abiding characteristic of the first pandemic of the information age is how little was known for so long about Coronavirus disease 2019, or COVID-19.

It was not certain if it began in a seafood market in China, came from bats or pangolins, or had even escaped from a laboratory. Scientists in different countries worked together as never before but were divided about the best strategy to combat it.

Spain and Italy, among the first to record high levels of deaths, locked down their citizens early. Britain waited to do so until later, then held its breath as oxygen had to be given to a Prime Minister stricken by the virus. In the America of President Trump, meanwhile, it deepened and hardened the fissures in society.

How long would the crisis last? Did wearing masks and 'social distancing' help? Would there be a second wave, or a vaccine? Why did it affect some people more than others? How could those who cared for the sick, at risk to themselves, be so selfless?

There were no apps to provide instant solutions: only newspapers and journalists doing their best to satisfy the eternal human need to keep up with the times.

GEORGE FLOYD

30 May 2020

The white police officer alleged to have killed an unarmed black man in Minneapolis this week by kneeling on his neck — prompting violent protests across the country — was charged with murder yesterday.

Derek Chauvin was arrested on charges of murder and manslaughter, Mike Freeman, the Hennepin county attorney, said. The investigation was continuing regarding the actions of three other officers who were present at the scene. They, like Mr Chauvin, have already been dismissed.

The killing of George Floyd, 46, on Monday was followed by a peaceful protest on Tuesday in Minneapolis, but the gathering quickly turned violent, with thousands of protesters venting their fury against the police in the nights that followed. Protests spread to the neighbouring city of St Paul, where 170 buildings were destroyed or damaged.

Last night, hundreds of people rallied outside the White House chanting "I can't breathe" – George Floyd's last words and those of Eric Garner, a black man who died in 2014 after being held in a police chokehold.

The White House was temporarily placed on lockdown with the US Secret Service closing entrances and exits. Some protesters tried to push through barriers set up along Pennsylvania Avenue by the Secret Service.

One person was killed in downtown Detroit after someone in an SUV fired shots into a crowd of people protesting, said a Detroit police spokeswoman this morning. An officer wasn't involved in the shooting. The victim was a 19-year-old man, who was pronounced dead at the hospital. The suspect pulled up in a Dodge Durango and fired shots into the crowd on Friday, according to the spokeswoman.

In Brooklyn, New York, groups of demonstrators chanted at police officers lined up outside the Barclays Center. The crowd threw water bottles toward the officers and in return police tear gassed the group twice.

New York governor Andrew Cuomo said he stood with the Minnesota protesters.

"Nobody is sanctioning the arson, and the thuggery and the burglaries, but the protesters and the anger and the fear and the frustration? Yes. Yes. And the demand is for justice," said Cuomo.

On Thursday night about 400 people clashed with police in Columbus, Ohio, where windows of the statehouse and nearby shops were smashed. In Denver protesters fought with officers, while scores were arrested in a square in Manhattan. In Los Angeles hundreds of protesters surrounded a police car and smashed its windows. A second car was also attacked.

Hundreds of National Guard troops were on the streets of Minneapolis, where a curfew was ordered by the mayor, Jacob Frey, from 8pm yesterday until 6am. The troops arrived in a city pockmarked by burnt buildings, including a police station that had been captured and set alight.

———◆———

On 25 May 2020, George Floyd, a Black man, was arrested by police in Minneapolis after buying cigarettes with a suspected counterfeit $20 note. While Floyd was handcuffed and prone, Chauvin, who is White, knelt on Floyd's neck for nearly eight minutes. The arrest was recorded on camera by witnesses, who were prevented by other officers from intervening despite Floyd being heard to say repeatedly that he could not breathe. He subsequently died.

His death sparked mass protests and unrest in numerous cities across America, prompting a wider evaluation throughout much of the nation of race relations, discrimination and civil rights, with changes promised and more attention given to the continued legacy of slavery.

Demonstrations were also staged in solidarity in many other countries, including Britain, where the focus became symbols of the historic slave trade. These included the statue in Bristol of the merchant Edward Colston, which was toppled by a crowd and thrown into the city's harbour.

INDEX

Allied victory 196–8
declaration 172–4
September 11th attacks 390–1, 394, 399, 402
Serbia 100, 103, 374–6
Seville 155–6
Seward, Frederick 52
Seward, Major Augustus Henry 53
Seward, William 52–3
Shageya tribe 58
Shanghai 168
Sharman, Helen 360–2
Sheffield 325–6, 360
Shelley, Edmund 64
Sicily 80–2
Silverman, Sydney 255–6
Simpson, Nicole Brown 371, 373
Simpson, O. J. 371–3
Simpson, Wallis 162
Sinclair, Sir Archibald 173
Sinn Fein 105–6, 122, 384–5
slavery, abolition of 16–17
Smith, Ian 304–5
Smith, W. 18
Social Democrats 74–5
Socialism/Socialists 74–5, 114, 267
Sogat 339–41
Somerset, Lord E. 22
Sophie, Duchess of Hohenberg 98–100
Sorbonne 263–4
South Africa 147, 211, 300, 352–3
South Bank 215–17
South Korea 219
Soviet Union 131–3, 157, 194–5, 197–8, 208–9, 211, 214, 219, 227–9, 230–2, 234, 243–5, 265–7, 273, 289, 336–8, 348, 360–2
Soyuz spacecraft 360–2
Spa 114
space exploration 334–5, 360–2
Space Race 273
Spain 425
Spanish Civil War 155–7, 182
Spanish influenza 116–18
Special Air Service (SAS) 306–7
Spender-Clay, Captain 122
Spielberg, Steven 293

445

CERTIFICATES

THE TIMES.

TO CORRESPONDENTS.

Several Poetical Favours are come to hand, and shall soon appear, but it would take up too much room to particularize every signature, as our correspondence is voluminous.

Continuation of the statement of the Finances to-morrow.

LONDON.

Yesterday at noon the three younger PRINCESSES had Divine Service performed before them at their apartments, Windsor Lodge, and in the afternoon walked on the Terrace attended by Lady CHARLOTTE FINCH, and Miss GOLDWORTHY.

Yesterday Mr. DUNDAS, gave a grand dinner to several of the Cabinet Ministers, and a number of Members of both Houses of Parliament.

On Saturday last a messenger arrived at Devonshire-House, Piccadilly, with dispatches from the Duke and Duchess of DEVONSHIRE, at Spa.

On Saturday the three younger PRINCESSES dined with Lady E. HOWARD at Stoke Lodge.

The Earl of CHATHAM, will in the course of a few days visit Spithead, to view such of his Majesty's ships as lay near that Port.

The House of Commons will adjourn on Thursday next for a few days, in order to wait for some business in the House of Peers.

A report is current in town, that the *Caisse d'Escompte*, in Paris, has stopped payment.

The following passages, in Dr. Burnett's h of his own times, wear no very favourable a towards the hero, who has been extolled t skies by his admirers, vol. iii. page 102. had no vice but one sort, in which he was cautious and secret."——Vol. iv. page " About this time the King set up a new fave —Keppel, a Gentleman of Gelder, now from a page unto the highest degree of fa that any person ever attained about the King was made Earl of Albermarle, and soon Knight of the Garter, and by a quick and accountable progress, he seemed to have en sed the Royal favour so entirely that he dis of every thing in the kingdom. He had distinguished himself in any thing, though King did it in every thing." Page 327. " Earl of Portland observed the progress of th vourite, with great uneasiness, they grew not to be incompatible, as all rivals for favour needs be, but to hate and oppose one anoth every thing." Vol. v. page 72. It was not to account for the reasons of the favour whic shewed, in the highest instances, to two pe above all others, the Earls of Portland and A marle."

To prevent deceptions respecting the pr rise of stocks, which may be practised by s lors of all descriptions, the public should a closely to the following *substantial causes* fo rise. Tho' the national debt was nearly do by the war, yet as the interest of the debt i ly provided for, and proportioned to the inc of it, the principal derives as much support the exceeds of the interest, as it did befor war, for when the debt was *130 millions*, th ings of four millions of interest laid out half year, carried the three per cents to n par, and now the debt is 250 millions, the the half yearly savings of nine millions of dend to support that increased quantity; i dition however to this, the annual million out for decreasing the debt, must be conside a new and extraordinary power, which away the brokers and jobbers stock, and h *solutely drained the market*, and that too at riod of the year when more purchases are than at any other. The Christmas divide applied to pay bills, but the Midsummer dend is laid out to increase the principal, this time, on the opening of the books, the cery buys between 3 and 400,000l.—the buy as much more, and in addition to these the Westminster Insurance Company has 100, to lay out in three per cents, which will pu 120,000l.—then there is a speculation tha taken 300,000l. out of the markets, a weekly chase of 40,000l. by Government, and all th mense operation to take place upon *an exh market*, a market that has already *borrowe millions of stock, and is still daily borrowing* When these causes are properly weighed, man and woman who holds stock will lear true value of it, and not be tempted by a